S·U·N D·A·N·C·I·N·G

S·U·N D·A·N·C·I·N·G

A Spiritual Journey
on the Red Road

Michael Hull

Inner Traditions International
Rochester, Vermont

Inner Traditions International
One Park Street
Rochester, Vermont 05767
www.InnerTraditions.com

LIBRARY OF CONGRESS CATALOGING-IN-PUBLICATION DATA

Hull, Michael.
Sun dancing : a spiritual journey on the Red Road / Michael Hull.
p. cm.
Includes bibliographical references.
ISBN 0-89281-850-6 (alk. paper)
1. Hull, Michael. 2. Spiritual biography. 3. Sun dance. 4. Teton
Indians—Religion. 5. Teton Indians—Rites and ceremonies. I. Title.

BL73.H85 A3 2000
299'.7852—dc21
00-061363

Printed and bound in the United States

10   9   8   7   6   5   4   3   2

Grateful acknowledgment to the following:
Jimmy Schulman, for the photograph of the author; Mickey Ford, for the photograph of Chief Fools Crow; Helen West, for the photograph of Mary Thunder; Sandy Bargsley, for the photographs of Dennis Banks and Michael Hull, Chief Fools Crow's bonnet, and Buddy Red Bow blowing the eagle bone whistle; and Michael Hull, for the photographs of Leonard Crow Dog and the tree of life.

Text design and layout by Virginia L. Scott Bowman
This book was typeset in Garamond with Merz Irregular as the display typeface

For Buddy,
a Rainbow Dreamer

CONTENTS

ACKNOWLEDGMENTS

There are many people to thank for this book. Mignon, Michelle, Sarah, and Ronda Sue. James Hull, Mary Sue Tinsley Hull, Kevin Hull, Amy, La Jeune, Doug, Coach C., Mary Thunder, Buddy, Dennis, Leonard, Charles Phillip, Chief Luciano, Phil Crazy Bull, Godfrey, Victoria, Grandpa Wallace, Grandpa Fools Crow, Dik, Bill P., Jo, Burney, Jamie Sams, Jodie, Shari H. and Laurel, Gaboo, Rosalyn, Rudi, Coke, Albert White Hat, Harold, Elva, Ted, Harry Charger, Philip, Roxanne, Cervando, Arvol, Orvil, Stanley, Cecilia, Anne and Jim Scarboro, Ronda, and Nancy.

Sparky, Jackie, Helen, Jimmy, Butch, Bear, Shari V., Wally, Glenda, Paul B., Paul R., Greg, Peggy, Adrian, Alison, Lex, Peggy, Suzanne, Keli Jean, Grace, Suzanne A., Patricia, Don, Beckwith, Steve, Kim, Jo Ann, Aaron, Austin, Horse, Richard, Starr, Wade, Bonnie, Stancy, Don, Jack, Bill, Dirk and Marshall, Bob, Mimi, Carl, Bob L.

Jack Maroney, Joyce, Charlie, Will, Pat, Susan, Andrew, Berry and Mike Crowley.

Jon, Susan, Anna, Peri, Ginny, Crystal, Janet, Molly, and Pam R.

Buddy, I hope this book is what you wanted.

Also Boo, Chira, Nancy, Matt, Ada, Tom Yellow Tail, Tom P., Kim, Norma Gussie, Lloyd, Tina, Maria, Debbie, Dr. Jeter, Dr. Willoughby, Ann, Stephen, KC, Mark, Mary Ann, Bob, Bruce, Bennett, Val, Lynn, Connie, Charles, Mary Trail, Evelyn, Bonnie, Negar, Tricia, Jean Ann, Darryl, Marilyn, Katie W., Red Hawk, Katherine, Delora, Bay, Ralph, Gussie, Beth, Shari P., Jackie, Boots, Ted S. and Jerry C., Johnnie, Chuck Merrill, Frank Hughes, Molly and Magda, Pat M., Mrs. Billingsley, Dr. Turnbough, and Dr. Cook.

ABOUT HOPPING

✤ ✤ ✤

Flying as fast as my understanding permits
unfolding my wings as much as I dare
I mostly hop around.
But sometimes I soar like an eagle—
catching the thermals, working the clouds,
floating through a space that has already found
*   its wings.*

I like to fly with the eagles—
to see from their perspective.
But I also like to hop.
Flying affirms why I learn and that I learn.
Hopping reminds me there is more to learn.
Always more.

I figure God hops every once in a while.
To remember why he flies.
And to stay in practice.
And to learn.
If I hop, and God hops,
you must hop, too.

—Michael Hull

FOREWORD

by Chief Leonard Crow Dog

I HAVE BEEN ASKED to say a few words for the book of my nephew, Mike Hull.

My grandpa and my dad knew about this man for a long time. For many years they would say, "Grandson, there is a man. You will help him. He will come from the South, and you will help him know the sacred way of life." They told me there was a new Indian coming and that I would teach him. I thought they were joking.

My grandson and my dad talked about the sacred sun dance. They said the ancestors were praying for the ceremony to be in the Lone Star State. And then this man, Chief Michael Hull, comes to Paradise, and they tell me this is the man. So he is at Paradise for many years, and he dances here for a long time. He has a dream for a ceremony in Texas to help the children and the future generations. We all talked about the sun dance in Texas for many years, and then, when the time was just right, we gave him the medicine bundle for the sacred sun dance way of life.

That dance has now begun in Texas. We went to Texas and placed the sacred

Chief Leonard Crow Dog

bonnet on his head. We dance there with him and teach the people about this sacred way.

The Red man's way of life is very holy. We hold a key to the sacred way, to the understanding of this way of life. The times are hard for us right now. The old people are taking their journey to the Spirit world. Our young people are tempted by alcohol and drugs. We must hold on to the sacred way of life, the holy tree, the holy breath of life. May all of you be blessed in your life by the reading of this book.

All my relations.

Chief Leonard Crow Dog
Witnessed and endorsed by
Joann Crow Dog
Henry Crow Dog II
Paradise, Rosebud Reserve

FOREWORD

by Mary Thunder

TO ALL WHO MIGHT SEE these words, I say, *"Aho Mitakuye Oyasin."*

Mike has asked me to write some words for his new book. With a smile and tears of remembrance I write these words to you all from a heart that is full of pride for Mike. My memory goes back to a vision quest in Texas, so long ago, where our friend Jimmy Schulman brought his "best friend"—a tall kind of lanky guy who reminded me of Abe Lincoln when I first saw him. I found out he was a lawyer and chuckled to myself about how right on my first impression was. Mike didn't seem to "take" to vision quest procedures like a duck to water right away—or maybe it might be more correct to say he didn't take to me right away. I have the gift of sight and could see he was a most angry young man, and everything I said, did, or suggested would turn his aura into a beautiful shade of flaming red. I heard more than one time on that quest "I hate you; I hate the sight of you" from his mind and eyes. When I checked with Spirit, Spirit said that this was a very special young man who needed to be brought "home to me" for his work on this planet.

I nicknamed him "Tall Guy" and remember yelling "OK, it's time to go" and seeing "Tall Guy" fall out of his tent and promptly drop his vision quest prayer ties into the cactus. Then later on, when I checked on him during his quest, he was in the rain, running through like a river, with about seven ducks flying overhead going "quack, quack, quack." I smiled and told him that perhaps his emotions were running rampant in his life, and his mind needed to clear its chatter. I don't know how, from that start, Mike and I became such close friends. I later found out that Mike had been clear of a major drug for only seven days.

Mike became a member of our group, pulling a strong group of friends from Austin, Texas. He would go on to help Dennis Banks and Buddy Red Bow marry Horse and me; help us come to the land in West Point, Texas, to our Thunder Horse Ranch; be one of our first board members on the board of the Church of Blue Star; help us with the Christmas projects for the elders and children; and help with all our service projects. Mike became very important in my life as an advisor, friend, and supporter.

He called me a teacher, but I called him Mike or Mikey. He was fun. We always loved to share our worst problems with Mike, and by the end of the visit we were all laughing. As a student, Mike was always striving for the best with a good heart that was opening fuller every day. I learned as much from Mike as he says he learned from me. I have only tried to share with others what my elders have shared with me. They helped me to live, and I am grateful.

I have to say that Mike had a competitive side that would show itself sometimes. When I was speaking he would always start a paper ball fight, or when I was sharing some huge principle he would try it out to see if it held the truth. One time I arrived early to find Mike sharing a class on aura readings to all so that they could change their auras and I couldn't tell what was going on. I truly enjoyed it.

Once I officiated at a marriage in Austin to a judge of the court and his wife, who was a doctor. When the couple was in the reception line, I walked over to smoke a cigarette and enjoy the sight of the happy couple. I was deep in thought when a very nice man in a tuxedo tapped me on the arm and asked if he could talk to me. I turned around to find myself surrounded by men in tuxedos. They were mostly judges and attorneys. One man said, "We have found in the past that Mike was one of the most ruthless and cunning men to work with, and then something happened—he just changed. Mike has said that you were responsible for his change. What did you do?" I only answered that Mike himself was very responsible for his own change. He had found God and Spirit, and I was so proud of him!

Sun dance was where Mike "grew up" and left the group to go on his own, I believe, but first let me share with you a small bit of my own thoughts. I had been a part of the lives of the Crow Dog family since 1974, having been adopted into the family by Grandma Mary Gertrude and Grandpa Henry. I was then the adopted niece to Uncle Leonard Crow Dog, a man I had seen healing people, feeding people, and caring about people since the early years. I only went to Crow Dog's Paradise to do the ceremonies and make prayers for a better family life. In 1980 that changed, with a prophecy from Uncle to me about my having a heart attack, dying, returning to the world, and then becoming a spiritual woman. I then had to sun dance. As I am part Indian, the sun dance experience was not so easy for me. Besides the prayers for the people, four days of no food and water, and dancing only to thank the Creator for the return of my life, I also endured much reverse prejudice from full-blooded Indians: being knocked down, kicked, spit on, and called all kinds of names. All I had been told to do was dance for the people so that the people could live, but for a while I didn't think I was going to make it. For many years I would go, knowing my place (nowhere) and keeping to myself. I would go and dance, then after the dance sit on a cooler, eat a bologna sandwich, drink a Pepsi, and help Grandpa Henry Crow Dog pick up trash.

Since I had never sought to be anything, and all that I have done has been told to me to do, the next thing was so mysterious. I had never thought that any-one—oh, maybe my children—would follow me into the dance and become a sun dancer. But then Mike Hull asked my permission to dance. I was aware that Uncle Leonard and Buddy Red Bow had kidded him about dancing, but he asked me if he could dance. Through long prayer, my sights from Spirit of the future, and my own motherlike fear for Mike, I said I was not in favor of it, for I just didn't want to see anyone else go through what I had. But Buddy and I did agree to sponsor him, and when we talked to Uncle Leonard, he asked me if I was willing to support him and dance for him if he did not fulfill his com-mitment. Of course I said, "Yes, Uncle." That was the first year of our camp at Crow Dog's. Then Uncle came to the ranch and invited our whole group to go. I spent that whole year crying, because how would this wonderful group of peo-ple understand service without thanks, being a minority, not being respected, or having any of the things that I had done to me done to them? I prayed and prayed, "Please, Great Mystery, let me have done this for them." The name of the camp went from Thunder's White Camp to Thunder's Angels that year. We survived, and I was so grateful.

That first dance was hard for Mike. Buddy and I saw his red sun-burnt body and the pain he was in, and we came back to our camp and discussed what to do for him. Oh, how Buddy and I loved Mike. So we went to Uncle, and we all talked and decided that Buddy and I would go in and dance to help his energy, and if he got worse we were going to pull him out. I was experiencing some respiratory problems, so I went to the doctor, and he put acupuncture needles in my chest so that I could go out and dance for Mike. Buddy went right into the men's line and danced right beside Mike. I danced behind in a woman's line. It seemed to help, and his energy started to come back up. Then I looked up, and there was Buddy dancing with me and saying, "Hey—you got pneumonia, and you're dancing for Mike, so now I am going to dance with you to help and pray for you!" What a day.

After the dance, Mike was really sick, so Buddy and I decided to take him to the Chipps's for a healing, since Uncle was leaving right away from Crow Dog's Paradise. Pulling into the Chipps's, we were met by Grandma Victoria Chipps, who can't see well. When we told her Mike was sick, she got right next to his nose with her nose and said, "OK, you need a healing, so go chop up those rocks." Now in South Dakota you usually have for a rock pile a slab of the mountain, and then you take a pickax and break the slab into rocks—and that is what she had this dying guy do. I had to laugh. Then she and I went into her little cabin, with a dirt floor, and sat at the table and joked and laughed. I got up and did all her dishes as we talked and laughed. I love Grandma so. Then I went to get some water from the well. I heard Grandma call out to Mike, "Go and carry that pail of water for her—she shouldn't have to be doing that herself." Mike came and carried the water. Then once he was inside, she had him wash the dishes again. When he was through, she picked up a dish, put her nose on it inspecting it, and said, "This is not clean; do them right this time." Yep, I thought, Mike is really going to get a healing. That night in the ceremony house, the Spirits came in through medicine man Godfrey Chipps and did a healing on Mike.

Mike lived and went on to finish his commitment of sun dancing in a good honorable way. I watched as Buddy named Mike. Years later, I have now watched Mike be given a sun dance and watched him receiving a bonnet and being named chief. So, as you read this book, know that Mike is a person, just like Abe Lincoln, who has kept his word and helped feed many, clothe many, and do good things for the people.

Love to my brother today, Mike Hull, and may many read this and find happiness and well-being in their lives.

Aho Mitakuye Oyasin. Amen to all my relations; all things with life.

Mary Elizabeth Thunder
Mother, grandmother
Author of *Thunder's Grace*
Delegate for Women to the Spiritual United Nations formed
by the Dalai Lama
President of Blue Star, Inc.
President of Blue Star Service, Inc.
President of Thunder Horse Ranch

FOREWORD

by Chief Charles Chipps

MY FRIEND, MY BROTHER, Michael Hull, is a tall white guy with curly hair and a "red" heart. On the exterior he lives a white guy kind of life, practicing law, living in the suburbs, and driving a four-wheel-drive Suburban.

On the other hand, I believe Michael is dedicated and devoted to preserving the culture, heritage, spirituality, and ceremonies of the indigenous people, especially the Lakota. I believe Michael did not decide this for himself but rather was chosen by the Great Mystery to build the bridge between the indigenous people and others. As it states in the Bible, many are called, but few are chosen. Through all the years, Michael has shown over and over the willingness, dedication, and devotion to do the ceremonies in the right way, not by the white man's interpretation, but all to help the people live better, grow old, and have health and happiness. This is the essence of the spirituality of the Lakota.

I believe the Great Mystery, the Almighty, the Creator wants all of us to live in peace and harmony despite the wars, hunger, and history of abuse of different peoples. I believe many know this in their hearts, and so they search by religions, drugs, alcohol, tobacco, sex, and whatever else they believe will fill the hole for a relationship with the Great Mystery.

This book will serve as a key for many to open new avenues in completion of the search. In believing there is another way despite all the many ways that have been tried, there is still another way, the way of the Great Mystery. Michael's story is an inspiration to those in search of their truth, to those needing to find another way to live in this world today—the way it is with the troubles that exist, yet live a life of spirituality.

Michael has many names given him by the people he associates with, besides his name by birth. I also have a name for my brother. When we have a blood relation ceremony in June 2001, his name will be revealed. This name will represent who his life spirit is to all the people.

This story tells of a man who walked this earth separated from his heart, found it on the Red Road, and offers it back to the people. My deepest support goes to Michael.

Mitakuye Oyasin.

Charles E. Chipps
Ta Canupa Wakan
Wanbli, Pine Ridge Reserve

FOREWORD

by Jamie Sams

MICHAEL HULL'S JOURNEY into the world of Native American healing and ceremony reminds us of the essence of all native prophecy, which speaks of the end of separation. Michael's piece in the puzzle of wholeness among all people and all races is found in his words. Now is the time that my elders and teachers have spoken of for centuries. Their voices are echoed in this book through Michael's experiences with elders from other nations and tribes. Universal truths remind us time and again that we are the legacy that can bring humanity to wholeness. Michael takes us through that journey by sharing the richness of traditions of his teachers. His personal path of transformation holds a light for each of us to see as we follow the paths the Creator has given us individually. *Sun Dancing* is a bridge that can take the reader into a deeper understanding of life and our human roles as we shape the new way of being that is offered to humankind at the dawn of this century. Well done.

Jamie Sams

1 SACRED QUESTION

*This is the great new problem of mankind. We have inherited
a large house, a great world house in which we have to
live together, black and white, Easterner and Westerner,
Gentile and Jew, Catholic and Protestant, Moslem and Hindu.
A family unduly separated in ideas, cultures, and interest
who, because we can never again live apart, must learn
somehow to live with each other in peace.*
— **Martin Luther King**
Why Can't We Wait

All my life's a circle. . . .
— **Harry Chapin**

Grandpa, thank You for this sacred way and sacred place to pray, and for these sacred people to pray with. Make me a hollow reed so that I can be a channel of Your light and love; help me think with Your mind, see with Your eyes, hear with Your ears, speak with Your mouth, touch with Your hand, feel with Your heart, and give voice to Your words. Help me, Grandpa, so the people who look at me see You and the people who feel me know You. Help me, Grandpa, so that I write the words You would have me say, in the way You would have me say them, for the reasons known best to You. Amen.

IN 1988, I WAS INVITED TO participate in an ancient Lakota ceremony, the sun dance. The Lakota name for the ceremony is *wiwanyag wacipi,* which means "they dance gazing at the sun." The convocation is often brutal because the participants dance barefoot for four days without benefit of food or water while staring at the sun, each blowing on a whistle made from the ulna bone of a golden eagle.

My Lakota friends recognize several major ceremonies, of which the sun dance is the biggest, the granddaddy of all the ceremonies, the one that ensures the life of *oyate,* the people, for another year.

I was invited to dance by Chief Leonard Crow Dog, the leader of the ceremony and the sun dance chief for eighty-nine different tribes. Leonard is in close communion with the Creator, and he has done so many things like pulling live coals out of a fire, healing a diabetic, calling down the rain in Ohio, and whistling for an eagle and watching it land on his arm. He is a larger-than-life character, whom we are all blessed to be around.

Leonard has every reason to distrust white folks and white culture. He has been abused by whites for most of life. His home was raided by the FBI because of his religion. Later, he was imprisoned for practicing ceremony. So when Spirit directed him to share the ceremony with me, a white person, this directive came in spite of what he might otherwise believe. Leonard took a chance by letting me dance in his sun dance. It was a controversial decision because of my skin color, and he had to have known he would be criticized for it.

Leonard moves every year deeper and deeper into his heart. The love he has for his family, his children, and his friends continues to astound me. Recently, Leonard has been distributing the ceremonial way of life to his friends and relations as directed by Spirit, and it is a joy to see.

Leonard is a great example of the transforming power of love. He kept on loving me in spite of what he thought about my race. One day in 1992, at the sun dance, he and I were standing around the fire with about four hundred other dancers. Thousands of supporters were standing around waiting to hear what Leonard would say. The people were mainly Native, and often Lakota. Some of them came pretty close to being militantly antiwhite, and Leonard had been one of their leaders for years.

So they were standing there, waiting to hear what Leonard had to say, and he said, "If *mitakuye oyasin* (Amen to all of my relations) means anything, it means we must love our relations, even the ones we hate." I have never experienced that much quietness among that many people. It was like being at a Cowboys game in Texas Stadium and hearing only the wind.

Leonard is the spiritual leader of the American Indian Movement (AIM), which advocates the separation of the Dakotas from the United States, by force if necessary. It regularly condemns the cultural genocide committed against the *ikce wichasha,* the "common man," or red people, by the *waisichus,* the white man. The American Indian Movement was founded in 1968 in Minneapolis under the leadership of Vernon Bellecourt, Clyde Bellecourt, Dennis Banks, and others. It was originally directed at resurrecting the lives of inner-city Native American youth and helping protect them from, or recover from, alcohol and drug abuse. The organization also intends to provide protection against police and judicial abuse.

Dennis Banks has written that AIM was started "because of the slum housing conditions, the highest unemployment rate in the whole of this country, and police brutality against our elders, women, and children." He wrote, "They were tired of begging for welfare, tired of being scapegoats in America, and decided to start building on the strengths of our own people, decided to build our own schools, our own job training programs, and our own destiny. That was our motivation to begin."

Recognizing a need to combine the secular and the spiritual or, as some would say, recognizing that there could be no distinction between the two, AIM asked Leonard Crow Dog to be the spiritual leader of the movement.

As the plight of the Native American Indian worsened, the call for AIM's resources increased, and it now pledges itself to come to the aid of any Native American anywhere on Turtle Island when asked. The American Indian Movement has created survival schools; held conferences; marched on Washington for the Trail of Broken Treaties; occupied Wounded Knee in 1973; created international Indian Treaty Councils; sponsored the Long Walk, the Sacred Run, and the Run for Survival; and has sponsored conferences to address issues relating to Native American women and numerous other matters.

Deeply committed to preserving the cultural identity of the Native peoples, AIM regularly condemns white participation in ceremony and maintains a "hit list" of people it believes should be eliminated because of their association with ceremony that permits white participation.

The sun dance Leonard leads takes place on his ancestral land on the Little White River just west of Rosebud, South Dakota. His home is called Paradise, and the ceremony is called the Paradise sun dance. If the sun dance is the granddaddy of Lakota ceremony, Leonard's dance reigns supreme among them all. The Paradise sun dance is the largest *wiwanyag wacipi* in the world. Many traditional Lakota chiefs dance there, including Chief Archie Fire, Chief Hollow Horn Bear, Chief Spotted Tail, Chief Iron Shell, Chief Two Strikes, Chief Lightfoot, and others. The ceremony is also attended by chiefs from many other Native American tribes, including the Navajo, the Cherokee, and the Kiowa.

In addition to the chiefs, many dancers participate in the ceremony. It is common to see over three hundred red, black, brown, and yellow dancers among the assembled participants. The dancers come from all over the Americas, Asia, and Africa—indeed, from everywhere except Europe. Thousands of Native Americans come in support of the ceremony. The supporters line the outside of the large circular area called the *hocoka,* or arbor, while the actual participants dance inside the circle, gazing at the sun. Some supporters stand next to sage branches that define the boundaries of the *hocoka,* and other supporters stand under the shade arbor, a structure of cedar posts and pine boughs, dancing and praying for the people. In older times, when the people came together and made camp, they placed their *tipis* in a circle. The open space in the middle was called the *hocoka*, a word that can also refer to the center altar and to one's heart.

Each day of the dance begins early in the morning, before sunrise, after the dancers sit in a purifying *inipi*, or sweat lodge. The dance ends late in the evening after the dancers sit in another purifying *inipi*. Between the morning and evening sweats, the dancers endure several rounds, which often last for several hours, dancing to the accompaniment of the beat of a large drum and the voice of ancient sun dance songs called *wichang wacipi olowans*. Each dance period is called a round and is punctuated by breaks, when the singers drink coffee and eat, and the dancers sit in a place called the rest arbor at the west side of the shade arbor.

The *eyahpi*, the announcer, starts each morning about 3:00 A.M. His voice comes over the loudspeaker, announcing, "Sun dancers, sun dancers, it's time to sweat. The sweat lodges are ready." During the breaks, the announcer talks to the people, tells stories, makes announcements, sings, and offers prayers.

The announcer will occasionally surrender his microphone to other people. At Paradise, the microphone often finds its way to the AIM folks—Russell Means, Clyde Bellecourt, John Trudell, and others—who offer strongly worded pro-Indian and antiwhite cultural speeches. The speeches always begin with the proud history of Native America. A Lakota speaker will often talk about how the *oyate* roamed free across the Great Plains. How the Lakota defeated the white army in battle. How the United States bought peace by promising to secure vast acreage to the Lakota peoples through treaties that it then broke.

The speeches will recount some of the historical horror stories about our white government's treatment of the Indians, including the broken treaties, the policies of starvation and neglect, the intentional exposure to smallpox and other contagious diseases, the theft of ancestral land and ancient culture, the legal banishment of Indian religion until 1972, and the punishment for speaking in the Native tongues. Speakers will call for a renewal of armed resistance similar to that which occurred during the occupation of Wounded Knee in 1973. People will speak out against the FBI and remind the assembled throng that the FBI conducted a paramilitary raid on Paradise itself and imprisoned Leonard Crow Dog and others—a move condemned by the National Council of Churches, the United Nations, the World Court, and other organizations of note. Some of the speakers will remind the crowd of acts of unprovoked violence committed by whites against their Native brothers, and urge retaliation in kind.

The speakers will discuss the prejudice in the court system, where Indians are routinely treated more harshly than their white contemporaries. They will discuss how whites are treated more leniently if they are prosecuted at all. They will discuss the case of political prisoner Leonard Peltier, wrongly convicted by an all-white jury for the death of FBI agents following admitted prosecutorial misconduct.

The speakers will discuss the Hobson's choice whereby Native Americans must either leave their ancestral home, move to a big-city slum, and work at a minimum-wage job if one can be found, or survive harsh Dakota winters with no job and no money, huddled around kerosene stoves and living in railroad-tie houses. Do they expose their children to a foreign, hostile, white culture, or do they risk raising their children in two of the poorest counties in the United States, places with high rates of alcoholism, joblessness, and alcohol-related crime? Do they freeze in their homes with their families and friends, or do they starve in the city, friendless and alone? Do they take another handout from the government that has abused and horribly mistreated and invaded a people that actually defeated the United States Army, or do they eat food polluted by uranium tailings, and drink water contaminated by unregulated mining? The speakers always conclude that the cause of their suffering—the evil, the devil, the Satan in their midst—is the white man.

I'm a white man. A tall, pale-skinned, big-nosed, curly-headed white guy.

The invitation to dance occurred in the summer of 1988, five months after I received a vision in which I was told to "tell the people I AM." I call that experience the Mayan vision because I received it on the ninth and last day of a spiritual pilgrimage through the Mayan jungle—the place Mary Thunder, my teacher, calls the heart of the world—on the Yucatan peninsula. Our trip was scheduled to end in Mexico City at the Aztec pyramids, but Thunder decided at the last moment that we would spend our last day six hundred miles east of Mexico City in the town of Chichén Itzá. Our last day was March 20, the spring equinox.

The spring equinox in Chichén Itzá is notable because of El Castillo, a pyramid the Mayans built there. The pyramid has a seven-tiered staircase with banisters made of stone. The banisters begin at ground level with a massive carved snake head, and each level of the staircase looks like another section of a snake, making each banister look like a snake with seven parts. On the equinox, the setting sun lights, exactly, first the top section of the banister (the tail of the snake), then the second section, and so forth until the entire body and head of the snake are illuminated. This event occurs only during the spring and fall equinoxes. The Mayans say that it represents the grounding of the energy from the male sun and the female moon to the earth.

Mary Thunder and I went on this pilgrimage to discover our purpose. Thunder promised me that my purpose would be revealed on this trip.

We were there waiting for the earth to receive energy from the sun and moon and looking at the ruins. I passed a spot in front of the stairs, midway between the banisters, and was thrown to the ground. I clearly heard these words in a very strong male voice, with strong male energy:

> *"I Am the answer to your problem. I Am all there is.*
> *I Am the life, light, and truth. Tell them I Am the*
> > *answer.*
> *Then your purpose will be complete.*
> *That is all there is."*

I started to rise up, dazed, and was again thrown to the ground. I clearly heard these words in a very strong female voice, with strong female energy:

> *"My child, sitting on the ground, do not fear, doubt,*
> > *and worry.*
> *I Am all there is and all there is Good.*
> *What is not of me is not.*
> *Tell the people I Am all there is.*
> *Share your faith. That is your fate. That is your*
> > *purpose.*
> *Follow this road and you cannot stray from your path*
> > *and your purpose.*

Follow your heart, for it is me and knows the way.
This communication is all there is to say.
It is the simplest and most complete of statements.
I Am all there is.
What else can be said.
Your purpose is fulfilled in the speaking.
Go, walk your path. You now know your purpose.
Shalom."

Ever since, I have worked to respond to the Mayan vision. I have prayed about it, meditated on it, sat with it, talked around it, fought it, believed it, doubted it, and staked my life to it. "Telling the people" is tricky. What am I supposed to do—walk around saying "I AM"? How does one created being convey to other finite humans the nature of the Creator? Especially when the one doing the talking is twice divorced, a drunk, and a drug addict? I am not exactly a poster child for the Vatican.

It is very tough for most of us to know or talk much about God. How, after all, can a tree describe the forest? What most of us can do is talk about what it is like to be a tree in the forest. So it is with this story: what I can do is describe God as I understand God based upon my relationship to God.

The abridged version of the tale is that I have acted like a jerk for much of my life and God has loved me anyway. My conduct through the years was so sick that I eventually died from a lack of love. And when I was raised from the dead, I came back because God loved me—directly when I could take it, indirectly when I couldn't, through many wonderful people who were compassionate enough with their love to help me become a human being and experience through their love the reflected light of God's own.

Since the Mayan vision, most of my life has been learning about, and helping others learn, living and loving through the heart. And I have learned most of those life lessons with my Lakota friends, with a few alcoholics struggling to stay sober, and with other family and friends kind enough to put up with me.

All of my life, my new life, my second life, is a gift of grace, something freely extended by the Creator to a lovingly created being. Yet, the gift of grace, while free, has a cost. My sober friends tell me that the price of my sobriety, freely given, is the maintenance of my spiritual condition. So I struggle with how to maintain my spiritual condition. How to learn about loving my Creator, loving my neighbor as myself. How to live a Spirit-filled life and do no harm. I cannot declare my road as the only path to God, but I can acknowledge it as one path. Looking back over my own road leads me to believe that God is both compassionate and forgiving.

One problem with abridged versions of life stories is their tendency to declare rather then tell. And it is the tale—the sitting around the fire, seeing our faces reflected in the soft light, feeling our opening hearts relate to one another—that helps God love us. The tale is the show that keeps us interested while God heals us, while God reveals the I AM to us.

And so it will be here. My job is to tell a few stories sufficiently interesting to keep you hooked while God reveals God's self to you. My tale will cover lots of ground, including being a drunk, my Lakota friends, sweats, sun dances, vision quests, channeling, energy work, getting sober and staying that way, and various assorted "-isms." What all the topics share is a description of relationship. My longest relationship has been with God. I have loved God, been in love with God, hated God, been apathetic toward God, been agnostic about God and about everything in between—but I have always been *something* in relation to God. I started out loving God, thought I was going to be a preacher, became an agnostic and a drunk, died, and was loved back to life by the people who looked past all the sickness that was my life to the child of God I am.

Today, my eyes are wide open and my life is filled with love, gratitude, and happiness. The gift of love and life I share with a wonderful wife, an angelic child, family and friends, and work I enjoy. All this love, everything, is attributable to God's love for me—unwarranted, unmerited, and sometimes unwanted.

My story is neither exceptional nor important. In fact, you might be like the elder brother of the Prodigal Son and wonder why anyone should care that I finally started acting right when you have been acting right all along. But if you are one of those folks who is a little lost, who might be searching, then you might see a little of yourself in these pages. And if you do, then hopefully you will find in my story of God loving me the comfort of knowing that God loves you.

Today I know that since God can love someone like me, God can love just about anyone. It is my prayer for you that you find that love for yourself as I tell my story around this campfire. Not because my story matters, but because yours does, because you do. What is abundantly clear to me today is that God loves all of us, that God will take us just as we are, that God aches to hold us and comfort us and be known by us, and that all of this and more is ours just for the asking by the miracle of divine grace.

Throughout this book, I refer to myself as white. I do this mainly out of respect for my enrolled Native friends who were raised in the Native world. I am told that I have white, Cherokee, and Kiowa blood. Leonard Crow Dog says I am related to Frank Clearwater, a Cherokee killed by the FBI at Wounded Knee. My great-grandfather was a Spoon from Arkansas and Oklahoma—places where one finds many Kiowa Spoons. I have not traced any of this very far and acknowledge that I was raised in the white world. Consequently, I simply refer to myself as white.

One other language note. I use the phrase "my Lakota friends" in referring to my own Lakota friends and their general views. It does not imply a statement about what the Lakota believe as a group. For a white to speak on behalf of the Lakota makes no more sense than for me to speak on behalf of all women or all whites. In fact, as in all groups of two or more, there are often widely varying views on a wide variety of topics among the Lakotas I know. So, I relate only my imperfect understanding gleaned from the teachings of my Lakota friends coupled with my own experience.

Beginning in the late 1980s, it was not uncommon for me to receive phone calls from traveling healers of all persuasions who would stop by for a visit and would end up staying at my house in Austin, Texas, for several days. My Lakota friends would follow a similar pattern, although for them the idea of stopping by for a visit might extend to weeks or even months. One such visitor was sun dance Chief Buddy Red Bow, a noted Lakota singer. Buddy was famous in Indian circles. He was a great singer and was the first person inducted into the Native American Music Hall of Fame. Buddy sun danced when he was seven, when the dance was still illegal in the United States, and was a sun dance chief for the remainder of his life. He lived with me off and on for several years until his death. I always knew some exciting times were in order when Buddy called to say he wanted to stop by for a visit. For you and me, a visit might mean an hour or two. For Buddy it might mean two or three months. During those two or three months my house would be filled with musicians and artists and poets and all kinds of creative people. Buddy loved to be around those people, and he took his experiences and turned them into song.

Buddy produced several albums and was a recognized figure on the reservations. It was always fun to walk around Pine Ridge or Rosebud with him and see all the young kids come up to touch him and shake his hands or want to touch the big ten-gallon hat he always wore. Buddy always carried a feather or two, and he would give those to the elders he met and talked with.

Buddy was a big believer in the way of the heart. He didn't take much to external rules about right or wrong. To be sure, he would listen to what you or I or someone else thought was right. But then Buddy always decided for himself. And he always told me the place to decide was from the heart. Whether the discussion was about doing ceremony or going to work or what we should do in the evening, Buddy's touchstone was always what his heart told him to do.

One fun thing we did was buy a buffalo for Mary Thunder. Mary Thunder hosted a gathering at her Texas ranch, and several of us sang. We all took the money Thunder gave us and went to see a rancher in west Texas who raised buffalo. We bought one and brought it back to Thunder. She named it Star Keeper, and she still has it. The buffalo now has a mate and has produced offspring, and when I see him I always think of Buddy.

Another time, Buddy officiated at Mary Thunder's wedding to Horse. Thunder is of Irish and Cheyenne descent, and originally from Indiana. She is about five feet tall, and at that time she wore jeans and boots and a big cowboy hat. She has sparkling eyes and a bright laugh. She's good with a story and has a great heart. Horse is white as snow, with a great laugh and a heart to match.

Mary Thunder is one teacher who loved me when I wasn't very lovable. She taught me about the life of faith in Spirit. Her teachers told her to give up her home and travel around the United States in a van, being of service to the people. She lived like that for years in a kind of continuing meditation that required her active commitment to the voice and life of Spirit. By seeing the example of that in her life, I was able to risk following that voice in my own.

Thunder is a Spirit interpreter and the author of a book, *Thunder's Grace,* which I recommend. I traveled all over the United States with Thunder, doing ceremony for the people, and I saw her do many wonderful things. I saw blind people see, AIDs victims heal, the lame walk, and people receive all sorts of physical healings. But beyond that, I saw broken hearts mended by and through Thunder.

Buddy led the marriage and brought Dennis Banks, a cofounder of AIM, with him. I was the coordinator for the wedding, so I spent a good amount of time with Buddy and Dennis. Buddy performed the wedding wearing Grandpa Fools Crow's headdress with eagle feathers from head to toe, an eagle staff, and an eagle bone whistle. While we were there, Dennis Banks taught me my first sun dance song, a vocable to be sung when people are piercing. I was pleased to be able to sing that song for Dennis while he took flesh offerings from the people for the wedding.

Buddy was always kind enough to give me medicine for ceremonies. If I needed a rock, a stone, or some other piece of medicine for a lodge or a healing, I could always count on Buddy to provide it. One piece of medicine I will always be grateful for was the opportunity Buddy gave me to meet Grandpa Fools Crow, who is one of the most revered of all the medicine men. Buddy had asked me to go with him to Rapid City, where he was playing in a concert with Jackson Brown, Willie Nelson, John Denver, and others. Grandpa Fools Crow came to the concert. Buddy told Grandpa about the ceremonies I was leading, including the sweats and vision quests. I was afraid Grandpa Fools Crow would say something negative about a white guy doing ceremony. He didn't, though, and the next time I saw Buddy, he had medicine for me from Grandpa Fools Crow that I was to use in the ceremonies. I still keep those things and use them when they are called for, and I will always be grateful to Buddy for that introduction.

Buddy always talked about having rainbow eyes. He said that he saw people with rainbow eyes, and before he died he gave me the gift of seeing with those same eyes. Through working with gay men, federal prison inmates, and other groups, I have been able to see past external differences, to see peoples' hearts first and the people second. Buddy told me that when I was doing piercing in the sun dance, if I paid attention to their heart and not to their skin color or anything else about them, I would be fine. Today, when I go into lodges or run ceremonies, it's the heart of people that I see with Buddy's gift of rainbow eyes.

Buddy is largely responsible for bringing this book to life. In 1991, leaving my house after one of his extended visits, he suggested that I write or record the stories about my experiences with my Lakota friends on the Red Road, as well as my stories about walking the road of sobriety and recovering from the worship of the wrathful God of my youth. After much grumbling, I committed those stories to paper and shared them with a few friends, but I stored them in a box in my closet for the next several years.

In July 1998, I felt directed to review those stories, make some modifications to them, and edit them into a book. The process of doing this has been very illuminating for me. I've had to dig deeper and harder into stories and memories than I had thought possible and at times further than I wished to go. I have gained a deeper understanding of how all the various stories over time have tended to link together and demonstrate how the Spirit through my friends has been teaching me about this life and how to live it, how to be a good man among our common men. To the extent I have succeeded, the credit is theirs, and to the extent I have more work to do, I have them to thank for giving me the tools.

Not long before Buddy died, he asked me whether I had recorded the stories as he had requested. He told me that he felt his Lakota people were at a crossroads. He feared that many of their tools and sacred ways of living, necessary for the people as a whole to survive, were being lost because the old people were dying and too few younger people had shown enough interest in them. He believed that each race of people had a different piece of the puzzle necessary for all of us to survive. The Spirit had given each of us possession of and responsibility for a single important piece of the entire puzzle, but holding these different pieces of the puzzle made all of us look different to one another. Buddy thought that we had been fighting one another for a long time because we could see only those differences. Buddy thought that the injuries and the damage we had all done to one another over the years were probably not fixable themselves and that we had to look past those hurts, whatever their cause, and begin to share our own puzzle pieces with all other people if we were to survive.

Today, I believe we live in a sacred community. Each of us is responsible for a unique piece of the puzzle, a particular part of the engine of happiness and health. Unless we all contribute our parts, the engine won't work, and the world and all its inhabitants will slowly grind to a halt and die away. I think we have to share these pieces with one another, not because we trust each other, or like each other, or have a historical basis to have faith in one another, but rather because if we don't do this we will not survive. We have to realize that no one's piece is more important or less important than any other but that all pieces are required for the engine of the world to continue to run. If we value one piece over another, we value ignorance over truth, and we value death over life.

The simple fact of the matter is that we are all in this life together, whether we like it or not. Leonard Peltier has recently written about this and says:

> Out of death comes life. Out of pain comes hope. This I have learned these long years of loss. Loss, but never despair. I have never lost hope or an absolute belief in the rightness of my cause, which is my People's survival.
>
> I don't know how to save the world. I don't have the answers or The Answer. I hold no secret knowledge as to how to fix the mistakes of generations past and present. I only know that without compassion and respect for all of Earth's inhabitants, none of us will survive—nor will we deserve to.
>
> The future, our mutual future, the future of all the peoples of humanity must be founded on respect. Let respect be both the catchword and the watchword of the new millennium we are now all entering together. Just as we want others to respect us, so we need to show respect to others. We are in this together—the rich, the poor, the red, the white, the black, the brown, the yellow. We are all one family of humankind. We share responsibility for our Mother the Earth and for all those who live and breathe upon her.
>
> I believe our work will be unfinished until not one human being is hungry or battered, not a single person is forced to die in war, not one innocent languishes imprisoned, and no one is persecuted for his or her beliefs.
>
> I believe in the good in humankind. I believe that the good can prevail, but only with great effort. And that effort is ours, each of ours, yours and mine.
>
> We must be prepared for the danger that will surely come our way. Critics will attack us, try to distance us from each other and mock our sincerity. But if we are strong in our beliefs, we can reverse their assaults and grow even stronger in our commitments to Mother Earth, our struggles, and our future generations of children.
>
> Never cease in the fight for peace, justice, and equality for all people. Be persistent in all that you do and don't allow anyone to sway you from your conscience.

Sitting Bull said, "As individual fingers we can easily be broken, but all together we make a mighty fist."

The struggle is ours to win or lose.

Buddy and my other Lakota friends, and many others before them, have sacrificed their lives to preserve a sacred way so that all the people have a chance to live. As a consequence of their sacrifice, on the third day of the Paradise sun dance, I sat in the rest arbor hoping to discover from somewhere enough strength to step back into the *hocoka* when the drum resumed its incessant pounding. My throat was parched. My skin was burned so badly it was blistered and starting to peel. My bare feet were cut and bruised and bleeding.

I held in my hands two pins, two pieces of wood each about the size and shape of my little finger. One hour earlier, I was lying on a buffalo robe next to the sacred cottonwood tree that defined the middle of the arbor. I was biting down hard on a bundle of sage because Leonard Crow Dog had just cut holes in the flesh of my breast and stuck skewers through the holes. I tried to avoid wincing when I was led from the buffalo robe to a spot about eighty feet from the tree. A $^1/_8$-inch-diameter sisal rope was tied to the top of the tree, and the other end was attached to a harness, which in turn was tied to my pins. I tried to pray while three thousand Lakota people watched me pull against that harness until my skin ripped as the skewers pulled through my flesh, while I was led back to the tree, and while the skin flaps were cut from my chest, wrapped in red fabric, and tied to the tree in a offering to the Great Spirit.

As I sat there exhausted, burned, and bleeding, hearing my race vilified by speaker after angry speaker, John, a fellow dancer, looked over at me and through his own dry, parched, chapped lips said, "What in the fuck are you doing here?" I said, "Just trying to stay alive." I thought, "That is a very good question."

John's question certainly wasn't a new one. It's a question I often asked myself and heard from my family and friends. "Why do you do that?" It's a question I heard at work and heard from my Lakota friends. I address John's question in the pages that follow. I examine why I chose to jump headlong into a foreign, often hostile and very strange religion of another culture. This book is also my effort to examine why my Lakota friends caught me, whereas other Lakota people think I am stealing their culture, call me a "wanna-be" and a "plastic medicine man," and think I should leave them, their land, and their culture as soon as possible.

For to be sure, my Lakota friends did catch me. A decade later, I stood in the Lone Star sun dance arbor, on land our community owns in Texas, at the conclusion of a sun dance I ran. There, in the presence of Mary Thunder, chiefs, dancers, singers, drummers, and supporters and members of AIM, I received from that same Leonard Crow Dog the sun dance *wahpa* eagle bonnet, a sun dance bundle, sun dance medicine, and lineage-based traditional authority to lead the *wichang wacipi*.

My Lakota friends gifted me with this responsibility as an expression of their heart. I accepted it in response to the Mayan vision directive: "Follow your heart, for it is me and knows the way." When I get lost, it is because I quit listening to my heart. My friends showed me how to find my heart and pay attention to what it has to say.

In the lodge last night, You showed me Your beautiful creations. Seven souls sitting together praying, each with their own struggles and hurts and disappointments. Their wonderfulness was so staggering that words like *beautiful* demean what I saw. I felt complete awe for You and what You have made. I prayed that they could see themselves as You allowed me to see them. I know that when I do not see Your creations in that light, I have more work to do. I saw that what they are doing, the messes they are in, does not in any way diminish the beauty they are. Thank you.

2 SACRED DREAM

*If we are looking for God's peace, we must begin with the
storms, the dark sea of our own soul. The good news
of the gospel is that God's grace is in the storms. We cannot
save ourselves. Most of the ways we try end up doing
violence to somebody, some place, or someone.*
           —**Chuck Merrill,**
           Methodist pastor

*A crisis is exactly what is required to shock people out of
unaware dependence upon external dogma and to force them
to unravel layers of pretense to reveal naked truth about
themselves which, however unpleasant, will at least be solid.*
           —**Rollo May,** *Existence*

I WAS SITTING IN TOTAL darkness with twelve sweating, steaming, naked gay guys. We were gathered inside a sweat lodge just west of Waco, Texas—the home of Baylor University, the largest Baptist university in the world, and also the former head-quarters of the Branch Davidians. The men asked me here to lead them through a sweat lodge and pray for one of their friends, a recovering alcoholic with AIDS. While pouring the water to make steam, I thought, "Here I am—a straight, white, sober lawyer leading a Lakota-style sweat lodge for gay men on the outskirts of Baptist heaven. Most of my life is represented in this lodge."

✦ ✦ ✦

I am a native Texan. My dad was a fourth-generation Texan. I grew up in small towns in west and north Texas, went to college and law school in Texas, married a Texan, and now live and work in Texas. I come from a family of farmers: my mom's family farmed in Oklahoma and Arkansas, and my dad's family were sharecroppers. My parents met at an Air Force dance and were married six months later. They settled in west Texas, with my dad the proud possessor of one of the first college degrees in our family: a Bachelor of Science in agriculture.

I was one of the lucky ones, growing up. I had a good home, loving parents, three meals a day when I chose to eat them, a place to sleep, a car to drive, friends to hang out with, girls to date, sports to play, music to listen to and play, a little money in my pocket, summer jobs, good books to read, coaches to follow, churches to attend.

✦ ✦ ✦

In November 1981, I drove to the airport in Midland, Texas, to pick up my fiancée, Stancy, a lawyer. I had already been married and divorced, and had fooled around. Now Stancy and I were on the way to her house to talk to her family about marriage. I had gotten divorced, I thought, because I had "picked" wrong, although I now wonder how anyone could have lived with me for even one day, as miserable as I was. Despite all the goodness in my life, all the advantages I had been born into, I had utterly failed to take advantage of them. I was an agnostic and a practicing alcoholic. I was about to be in a car wreck that would accelerate a process already begun. Much later, by the time I found my friends—or they found me—I was a zombie, a specter on the Ghost Road. By then I was a drunk and a drug addict. I was broke, twice divorced, almost job-less, unhappy, dishonest, fearful, sexually promiscuous, cut off from God, sepa-rated from family and friends, lonely, and alone. An absence of love was the culprit. I had made a series of decisions, all of which seemed perfectly logical at the time, that gradually but inexorably separated me from the love of God.

I tend to hurry through this part of my tale. There is no magic here, nothing fun or exciting about a self-imposed disease process that hurt my family and friends. Nor do I want to dramatize or publicize what was a godless life. Yet, for me to convey a sense of the miracle of God's love that is my life, a brief stay here is necessary. I follow the example of my Lakota friends, who are great story-tellers. They tell a piece today, another piece tomorrow, and still another next year. The parts of the tale come in no particular order and with no warning that the teller has returned to that particular story. My own tale is like that, in a way. I must weave together several decisions I made, which in combination led to my death. Bear with me.

✦ ✦ ✦

I was born with an innate sense of the divine. I don't think I am special in that regard—I believe that most of us are also born with that knowing and with a child-like reverence for the divine. My Lakota friends have since taught me to honor the children and the elders because both are closest to God: the elders, who are just about to go home, and the children, who have just come from there.

My earliest memories are related to God. As a child, I aspired to be Jesus. I always figured that if the choice came down to being a lawyer or a plumber, or feeding the five thousand, raising the dead, and healing the sick, then the choice was an obvious one. My heart resided in a simple acceptance of the divine. There was no question about the existence of God. There was a kind of joy and peace about God.

Growing up, I had plenty of chances to feel that peace: going to church twice on Sunday and on Wednesday nights, attending Vacation Bible School and Sun-day School, reading the Bible every day, praying before every meal and at night before going to bed. God and religion were everywhere.

Along with a sense of the divine, I was born with an innate sense of selfish-ness: an unquenchable desire to be the center of attention, the center of your world, indeed the center of everyone's universe. I call it the "I want" disease—I want what I want, when I want it, in the quantity I desire, on the timetable I set. I also want you to share my wants, and I think you are not acting right if you voice the slightest disagreement. I also came here with a grand desire for your approval. I wanted, needed, craved your approval. I would go to great lengths to get it and would gladly sell myself down the river for a little of your approval. My Lakota friends said I erred by seeing the world through the lens of a self-centered me, and judging you (and myself) by whether you were focused on me or on someone or something else. "You" could be the person in front of me, the crowd in my mind, or just about any person other then myself against whom I measured my value.

My innate sense of the divine developed at church. In fact, in some way the original face of God was modified into approval by you. What I learned was that when I did the right thing or when you approved of me, then God approved of me. But when I did what I wanted to do, or when you did not approve of me, then God did not approve of me. And disapproval was bad. I fused "doing the right thing" with godly conduct and "doing what I wanted to do" with sinning.

At church I learned what Satan liked and God hated. Satan, I learned, liked the things I wanted to do, the fun things. God, though, did not like very much— including, regretfully, little boys from west Texas. I soon learned that God kept track of my transgressions in a big black leather-bound book made especially for this purpose. Apparently God had a big library full of these books, and every time I sinned, down would come my book, and God would put another check mark into the book next to my name. Over time I collected a lot of marks.

Just as my heart was with God as a presence, my mind was busy trying to figure out the nature of God. This proved to be a little more tricky. I asked my family, the pastor, and the Sunday School teachers questions about God. "Why do folks suffer?" "Why do they die?" "Why do some folks have lots of stuff and other folks next to nothing?" "What does it mean that He died for me?" "Why doesn't anybody heal the sick today like Jesus did then?" "What happens when little kids die?" "What happens when people die in the jungle who have never heard of the Protestant God or Jesus of Calvary?" "Was Mary really a virgin?" "How did that work exactly?" "And what is a virgin, after all?" "Did Jesus really have a brother James?" And on and on. I have spent a lot of time with many different people trying to get answers to these questions. God used them to keep me hooked until I was beat up enough to let God love me.

A lot of good things came from church: a love and reverence for God, an awareness of right conduct, a belief in setting examples, an abiding love of faith communities, wonderful songs, a wonder about the power of the pulpit. For all of these things and more, I am grateful to the church. Yet, I heard one message as a child that overshadowed all the good: God punishes sin. God keeps track of sinners and sends them to hell. It is beyond me today how I missed the aspect of God's grace that the church surely taught. Yet, miss it I did.

And the consequence of missing this lesson became important as the "I want" part of me led me to act in ways that were inconsistent with doing what I thought God wanted or what I thought was right. Or when I decided that what I thought I had to do to get your approval was neither right nor what God wanted.

Doing right and doing what I wanted to do were on a collision course. In an internal contest between doing the right thing and doing what I wanted to do, I almost always chose the latter.

Picking my wants, or your approval over God's wants, or what I thought was right, eroded my self-esteem. As my own self-image fell apart, I lost that child-like innate sense of the divine and began to remake God into my own self-image. As I became fearful, God became something to fear. As I judged myself, God became judgmental. As I kept score of my bad acts, God became an accountant walking around with a black book. As I became incapable of being with God, God became less interested in keeping me safe.

This process of remaking God was not a conscious one. I thought the Baptist God was the problem. Several years ago when I was asked to describe the God of my youth, I wrote, "God is all powerful, all knowing, fierce, fearsome, punishing, and he score keeps; he keeps a black book full of check marks by my name, does not take care of me or of the people I love and does not help keep me safe in the world."

I pushed away from God. I did not want God to see me, to know how bad I was. As I hid from God, I also hid from you and feared you. I thought you might know how bad I was, and to prevent that I attempted to act right on the outside. I looked good. I sounded happy. But inside, my disease was eating away at me like a cancer. I believed I was a bad person because I could not help doing what I wanted to do regardless of the consequences. I was sure I was doomed. I was ashamed of myself, afraid of you, terrified of God.

This kind of circular process continued until I was almost ten. At that time, the battle between my wants and God reached an apex. And God lost.

The battleground was prophetic. It was an area that ultimately would save me: my interest in healing. I cannot recall a time when I did not aspire to be a healer. I always wanted to be a healer, just as Jesus was a healer. My motivations were mixed, though. Along with the "good" ones, I was also looking for your approval, for a way to feel OK about myself. I figured that if I could heal, I would be famous. You would think well of me; you would like me; you would not look past the healer and see the miserable person I was. I thought that if I could heal, I could perhaps work my way into God's good graces.

And part of me was trying to figure out how bad I was, how much trouble I was in. I saw healing as a kind of metaphysically magical test of faith. It worked this way. I thought the Bible said that if one had faith as small as a mustard seed, one went to heaven, and if one lacked the faith of a mustard seed, one went to hell. An empirical way to measure one's faith had to do with mountains. That is, if one had the faith of a mustard seed, one could move mountains.

So, to figure out how much trouble I was in, when my family took road trips through west Texas, I would try to move mountains. I would look at them, see them moving, tell God I had the faith of a mustard seed, tell God I would be good if the mountains would move. Nothing happened.

The Bible also says the faith of a mustard seed will heal the sick. When I was nine, my grandfather had terminal lung cancer. I was determined to heal my grandfather and picked his health as my battleground. I decided I had picked my wants in the past from poor motivation. So, since I so much wanted my grandfather to live, I knew I would be motivated to act right. I tried my very best to do good and act right. I didn't want to move a mountain, just heal a couple of lungs. So I prayed and prayed and acted the best I could for as long as I could. I woke up every morning with a vow to be perfect. And then I would forget and do some little something that my hypersensitive self was sure was a sin. Then I would redouble my efforts, only to fail again and again. I would pray and pray, asking for omnipotent God to give me strength over my sinning self.

One day I stood at the porch screen inside the house looking outside, wanting to be outside. I was grounded, stuck in the house over some infraction. The phone rang. My grandfather was dying. We rushed to the hospital, where he died a few days later. I knew then, at the age of ten, that my wants were stronger than I was, stronger than my prayers. I knew God would not help me refrain from sinning. I knew I had failed to heal my grandfather. I knew I lacked the faith of a mustard seed.

Now, I know that lacking the faith of a mustard seed was not good—that lacking even this small quantity of faith, I was doomed. Doomed by a lack of faith and doomed by black marks. Doomed to eternal hell and damnation. Doomed to hiding my miserable self from all the other people who were saved. Doomed to hiding myself from God. Doomed to hoping that God did not exist so that I would just die, not die and go to hell.

These conclusions—that I didn't fit, wasn't right somehow, was doomed—produced enormous grief and pain. The pain in my heart was so intense that I was constantly looking for an escape, for relief. I took steps to cover up, hide, and anesthesize the tremendous grief, guilt, and fear I felt.

The help came in the form of beer, scotch, bourbon, tequila, pot, speed, cocaine, painkillers, tranquilizers, morphine, and just about anything else that would produce a high or a low or a feeling—any feeling—that was different from the terrible way I felt.

I drank to excess the first time I drank, at age fourteen. When I drank, I became more handsome, better endowed, more witty and charming, a better pool player, a better driver, a better everything. By age fifteen, I drank a fifth of scotch every weekend and beer from whatever keg was available at whatever party was going on that weekend.

To cover up how inadequate I felt around you, I chased women relentlessly, because if they approved of me, I felt better. I took extravagant risks so others would comment on my courage. I gave to a fault so people would say I was generous. To mask my fear of you, I became angry and resentful of you so I could justify hiding. To mask my insecurity, I became boastful and proud. To mask my inadequacies, I became possessive and a braggart. To cover up my pain, I found I could hide myself and my feelings in work. To assuage my guilt, I spent money and acquired possessions. And to cover up my fear of God, I became an agnostic. I could not easily deny the existence of God, but I could hope. I thought that God, if even existing, was remote, distant, cold, unavailable—a tyrannical dictator of unkind proportions. To get relief from the constant barrage of thoughts that I was doomed, I concluded that God might not exist. To me, this was both good and bad news: bad in the sense that life might end at death, but good in that I wouldn't go to hell even though I might not get to heaven.

With time, my promiscuity and drinking increased. The sex part was easy. The drinking part was also very easy. Lawyers drink, you know, and law students being recruited by law firms have a lot of chances to drink with them. I was doing pretty well in school, so I was invited to lots of parties. Drinking produced a kind of altered state in me, and that altered state tended to show me that God did exist, that my basic agnostic pose was false. That feeling aroused my feelings of doom all over again, leading to more drinking, more sex, more work.

Some weird part of me, the grace part, knew that only God could save me from a hell defined by no God. Accordingly, I had been doing a kind of experiment that involved saying that if there was a God, I might know that in a way that would be irrefutable. I have been told to be careful about this prayer, since the answer to it might take the form of a shocking experience.

I first heard the phrase "shocking experience" from my friend LaJeune, a counselor I started seeing while I was still in college. LaJeune was the first teacher to appear from outside of my paradigm of life experience. She was like a coach who kept encouraging me when I hit one stumbling block after another. She reminded me there was another reality than the one I know, and she urged me to maintain my effort until I found it. She repeated, like some kind of mantra, "There is more. There is a piece you are missing. You can do this. Whatever the question, the answer is love. Love is the Reason. The Reason is Love. Whatever the problem or concern, the response is love, to be in love, to be loved, to be loving."

LaJeune concluded that my points of view about God, the world of faith, church, healing, and myself were so imbedded that I could not see anything else, that I could not see the forest for the trees, and that the trees I saw were false, but real enough to me. She believed that I would require a shocking experience, or perhaps a series of them, to even begin to heal.

A shocking experience, as LaJeune defined it, produces an experience that we cannot rationally explain. As we develop our points of view they become so imbedded that we forget we have them, but they operate as filters through which we view our world, and our filters tend to interpret our experiences in ways that confirm our points of view. We come to believe that the world works a certain way, and that we are right about how it works. A shocking experience is something big enough for us to notice and so unusual that it does not fit inside our filtered points of view. It forces us to realize that we have points of view and that they might be wrong.

I had my shocking experience in November 1981 on the road from Midland to San Angelo, Texas. Stancy and I were driving to her family's house. My finals started in a week, and then I was off to a real job at a law firm. We planned to be married in a few months. The moon was darting among the clouds, and Alabama was singing on the eight-track. I am so in love with her, I was thinking, so glad we have work and each other in common. We stopped for a cup of coffee, discussing some fine point in the law. I pulled out of the convenience store parking lot, onto the highway, and into the path of an oncoming Buick.

The middle of the hood of the Buick hit the middle of my door. The Buick's motor was pushed back into the driver's body, breaking both his legs. He would later be released from the hospital. I never met him. I do wonder about him: How did he do? How is he now? Does he know that he helped save my life? Did he know he was sacrificing part of himself so that I might live?

I lay on the asphalt, hearing Stancy scream from the back seat of my car. Someone pulled me from the car. I had, I would later learn, a broken jaw, broken ribs, a broken pelvis and hips, a punctured lung, a punctured spleen, and a lacerated liver. My liver, in fact, was so badly damaged that I was bleeding to death on the asphalt highway.

Stancy was still in my car. The force of the collision had driven her into the backseat, where she was trapped with a broken cheekbone, broken legs, broken hips, a broken pelvis, and, I later learned, a broken heart. As I lay on the highway in the warmth of my blood, I heard her beg the paramedics to get her out of the car before it caught fire and exploded. I wanted to help her but could not move. I just lay there, listening to her beg and scream, feeling totally and completely helpless.

How many of you have ever really hurt someone you love, or hurt someone and then been unable to help? The aloneness of it, the strange quietness of it, the godlessness of it. As in a dream, I wanted to yell, "Stancy," and thought that no sound was coming from my lips. I wanted to struggle to get up and help her, but I couldn't move. God, I thought, was nowhere to be found, could not or would not help, and did not care one more time about me or those I loved. God was going to let my whole sorry life dribble away on a highway in west Texas, listening to the cries of someone I loved who was moaning in pain that I had caused.

And then the ambulance people picked me up and put me inside an ambulance with space enough for only one of us. I wanted to say, "Take her—let me die—please—take her." And then the door of the ambulance closed, and only in my mind could I hear Stancy screaming, crying, begging, because of hurt that I had caused.

The paramedics carried me from the ambulance into the hospital. I watched them do this from across the street. They pushed my body on the little cart into the emergency room, and I walked beside them, watching myself die, watching them talk about watching me die. And then someone took me into an operating room.

Nurses bustled around. One surgeon split me open from pubis to sternum and started poking around inside of me. Another surgeon found that broken jaw and peeled the skin away from my face as if he were giving me a face-lift. I watched them from a corner of the ceiling as the surgeon sewed and prayed.

Floating in my corner of the ceiling, I felt the presence of a force, a presence, an undefinable something. I did not head down a tunnel; no loved ones sang the Hallelujah Chorus; no white light enveloped me. I was just aware of this presence that was there, really there, in a total sort of way. And I was there in some strange way with the presence. Not praying, not singing, not rejoicing, not even especially caring. Just being with the presence, as if I were sitting on a fence with someone, hanging out, waiting while a decision was made about whether I would live or die.

I was transfered to intensive care, with one punctured lung, when the second lung began to fill with liquid. My grandfather died because his lungs quit working. My God died when I could not save my grandfather's lungs. And now my own lungs began to quit working.

The doctor was not the only person praying for me. Family and friends came to visit and comfort and pray. LaJeune convened a prayer group each evening to pray for my full recovery. Three separate church bodies prayed for my recovery.

One day, hanging out with the presence, I began to be aware of the prayers being offered on my behalf. I could feel those people and their prayers pulling me back into my body and into this life. I am convinced that I would not be here today but for the active, prayerful intervention of those family members and friends. The prayers were like an energy, a siren's voice whispering firmly, "Wake up, wake up." And I did. One day I woke up in the intensive care unit. The liver was healing. The broken bones were mending. And the lungs were clearing.

I learned three things from the wreck and my recovery from it, with help from all my friends. God exists, love matters, and prayers are answered. I know that I am here because people asked in prayer for me to be here, and that I get to stay only so long as they want me here. I am on borrowed time, so to speak. I have an obligation to use this chance to help others know what those kind folks gave to me.

The wreck erased any doubt in my mind about whether there is a God, which was not especially good or welcome news, because if God exists, I was doomed to face an eternity in hell.

I tell friends who ask that the distance between hell and hope can be one of the longest journeys, considering the space between them is nothing at all. Most of us reach a point in spiritual space where we gain exceptional clarity about the truth of the problem while also seeing old half-truths about the solution. I think of this place as the Place of No Hope. I have been there several times. Knowing God existed was one, since that knowing represented a problem whose only solution, that I could see, was damnation. Another was admitting I was powerless over my drinking and drugging, yet not knowing any solution about being sober. Still another, later, was learning that leading a God-centered sober life meant experiencing the emotions I had run from and drunk over without having the tools to feel. Or knowing that my father was dying and seeing no end to the grief. Each time I returned to the Place of No Hope. Each of these experiences, and more, produced in me a kind of claustrophobic feeling of doom: I knew the train was coming but I was locked inside the tunnel and tied to the track.

From this vantage point, things seemed hopeless. At the tender age of twenty-three, what I saw before me was a highway to hell with no detours, no rest stops, and no exit signs. And in that arena of despair I did what I knew how to do—I anesthetized myself. I drank and drugged to the point of numbness. I hid from those who loved me so they would not see the failure I was. I hid from God; I could not bear the pain of absence. And I hid from my heart. Hiding from my heart cost me you, cost me people. Stancy recovered, but our relationship did not, in part because I could not be found in it.

Eventually, I hit bottom because I found myself alone: separated from others, irredeemable, cut off from myself, and without hope, or separate from God. In other words, I became teachable. And when I finally became teachable, God began to restore my hope by revealing God's self to me through direct revelation. God began to help me see who I was and gave me a purpose, a way to relate to others.

My Lakota friends often speak in relational terms. For them, everyone is related to everyone else. We are related to our Creator, who gave us energy, life, and form. We are related to other families, and we are related to one another. We all share a common Creator, a common life, a certain death. My Lakota friends who hear my story have little difficulty understanding it. For them, my story reflects a cutting of relations: relations with God, with my people, with myself. This, they say, cannot be. It is an out-of-balance way to be; it is against nature and will be corrected. They say that we relate through the common language of our heart and that I could not relate to others because I was not relating to my own heart.

It was plain that my ideas were not working. All of my scheming and planning were for naught. I needed some new ideas. I was ready to give away my definition of God and the pain I caused others and myself. I was ready to ask for help.

The solution was not terribly complex. The problem was my definition of God. I had made God into something profane and then bemoaned my fate. Yet, the step between hell and hope was so simple. Since I was the one responsible for my misdefinition of God, hope lay in the direction of recognizing my false beliefs and asking God to help me understand God.

3 SACREDNESS

*It is precisely anguish and inner crisis that compel us to
seek Truth, because it is these things that make clear to us
that we are sunk in the hell of our own untruth.*
—**Merton,** *Confessions*

*Errors made about creation will result in
errors about God as well.*
—**Thomas Aquinas**

MY LAKOTA FRIENDS CALL God *Wakan Tanka*. The name means something like "the Great Mysterious." It describes a kind of vast, life-giving, moving energy. It is a picture phrase, designed to create the image of a something too big, wondrous, powerful, and mysterious to be defined or described or understood. *Wakan Tanka* is different from the fearful God of my youth. When my Lakota friends describe *Wakan Tanka*, I hear them talking about the presence I felt after the wreck.

It was this sense of presence that kept me hooked, that held out some promise of hope in the midst of my misery. It was the presence I had heard described by healers. My interest in healing had not died with my grandfather. For every step I took away from God, I stepped forward with my pursuit of alternative healing.

I spent substantial time with people who were indigenous healers. Almost all indigenous cultures have a healing tradition. Among white people, traditional healing takes the form of folk medicine or remedies.

Traditional healing generally comes through two different kinds of people: the pharmacist, the herb person, the one who knows how to set bones, deliver babies, lance boils, tend wounds, and the like; and the spiritual healer, the one who treats the untreatable, the one who goes to the Spirit for a remedy. I found that spiritual healing was what captured my interest. As my own work began to focus on people who did spiritual healing I began to bump up against my own sense of presence and my beliefs about God, and the healers' own beliefs about God.

God used a woman named Jo Todd to help me change my understanding of God. La Jeune had insisted that I find a God who would help me heal. My friend Jo Todd helped me find that God. Jo taught me that God is bigger and more wonderful than I can ever imagine. She also taught me that God lives in my heart. Jo taught me to be true to my feelings even when they are unpopular or when I don't like them very much. This teaching is very important as we learn to sort through the emotions of our heart. Especially on the spiritual path, it seems to me, many people will tell us not to feel a certain way because we shouldn't. But a statement such as that is likely to produce only guilt and shame.

Jo has become like a sister to me. She sings for me in lodges. She is a marvelous singer, who can really carry the energy of a lodge. Songs have the capacity to move energy, and Jo is a master at the movement of energy. She can move and flow with the energetic consequences of choice better than any person I have ever seen.

She began that help after the wreck following a meeting we had both attended. I asked her whether there had been anything wrong with the lights in the meeting room. She said "No," and wondered out loud why I had asked. I replied that I thought I had seen flashes of red around a particularly angry speaker and wondered if someone had been playing with the lights. After Jo assured me that nothing was wrong with the lights, I shrugged and said I had probably just been tired.

I had been seeing lights around people for years. At church, I would notice a whitish glow around the preacher's head. Later, I began to see the glow around the heads of other people. Over time I practiced seeing these lights until I could see not only white but other colors as well. My hope and belief was that I could use the ability to see these lights as an entree into the world of healing.

I don't know why I asked Jo about the lights that night—grace, perhaps. She cautiously mentioned that perhaps nothing was wrong with the lighting and that I had indeed seen flashes of red. A few more minutes of talking led to the discovery that Jo also saw lights—and that she taught classes in what they are, how to see them, and how to use them to heal.

But there was a catch. To heal, I needed God's help. So I explained to Jo that although I knew God existed, I thought God was a jerk. She suggested that I write down my description of God. I then described God as an all-powerful, all-knowing, fierce, fearsome, punishing scorekeeper who kept a black book full of check marks by my name, who did not take care of me or of the people I loved, and who did not help keep me safe in the world.

Jo said I had to quit running from God. To do that I had to find a God I didn't fear. I asked Jo how to find a God I wasn't afraid of. She told me to make it up. She said that after I wrote down a description of my "old" God (the jerk), I should write down a description of God as I would like God to be, a God I could believe in, whom I thought I could love with all my heart. Jo said that whatever description of God I wrote down would be infinitely less wonderful than what God was really like, since I was much too narrow, limited, and sick (therefore human) to really perceive God.

How did I know what God was supposed to look like? My picture of God was based on what other people—family, the church, religious friends—had told me they thought about God. My picture was not based on God revealing God's self to me. So I agreed to write a description of a new God: a God I could love, not fear, and one whom I didn't have to run from.

I wanted a gentle, loving, gracious, kind, compassionate, forgiving God. I wanted a God who would love me, help me, and keep me safe in my world. I also asked for a God big enough to let me be angry with God. (My friend Glenda, one of my helpers at the sun dance and a great teacher in her own right, once said, "If your God isn't big enough to get mad at, you're in trouble.") I also asked that my new God be based on revelation from God.

I named my God Walter, after the fish Henry Fonda chased in the film *On Golden Pond*. In the film, after Henry Fonda has been pursuing the fish for years, he nearly hooks him, but Walter gets away. Henry looks at the water, shakes his fist, and says, "Walter, you're a crafty old son of a bitch." An example of God's craftiness is his use of my interest in healing. My desire to heal like Jesus was stronger than my fear of God the jerk. So Walter used my desire to heal to help me find a God I could trust.

I wanted God to have a sense of humor. Walter teaches with humor and doesn't seem to mind if I kid back. In fact, when something in my life seems a little screwy, a friend says that Walter must be getting bored.

An example of God's rather odd sense of humor occurred at a recent sun dance. It was the last round of the last day in my fourth year at Paradise. I was one of the first white people to dance there, and I was so proud that I was finally going to be a sun dancer. To get the proper effect, you should see me as I saw myself then, with cherubs dancing around me, a heavenly symphony playing, and angelic choirs singing "sun dancer, sun dancer." As I was about to walk out of the dance I had an attack of diarrhea. My first actual act as a sun dancer was to shake hands with my Lakota friends with soiled shorts.

I wanted a God I could approach, a God I could talk to, listen to, try to follow. I wanted a God I could be with all the time. Jo helped me understand that the divine is indwelling, not out there somewhere. This essence of God in me is like a glowing cloud that expands with prayer and meditation. Ceremonies, participation in spiritual discipline, and church all help me identity the divine in me and create space so there is less of me and more of God in me.

I wanted a God who could help me have less fear of you. Jo helped me understand that you have a piece of God in you. When my piece of God relates to yours, magic things can happen. When my piece of God sees your stuff that hides God, I am in compassion. When my stuff sees your God, I am with a teacher. And when my stuff starts relating to your stuff, disaster is on the way.

I put the new God description on my refrigerator and prayed to the new God. In this process, I began to find a God that was approachable. I began to find a God I could talk to, try to listen to, try to follow. I don't even pretend to suggest that my list describes God. In fact, my list has changed over time so that I am now more willing to let myself see God as infinite and indescribable. But back then, I could not start there.

As I fell more deeply into God's grace I also began to reacquaint myself with my heart. And what a disaster zone it was—hurt, broken, despairing, angry, fearful, full of the refuse from all the hurt I had caused. Living in my heart was incompatible with my alcoholic lifestyle. I had to get sober.

My Lakota friends made a similar decision to turn toward God and away from alcohol in the early 1970s, in a process that was parallel to mine. The vehicle for change was AIM, which began as a program to help inner-city Native American youth battle their addictions to alcohol and drugs. It did this in part by seeking to restore in those youth a sense of pride in being Native American.

With its successes, AIM grew. Its militant, pro-Indian tone found an especially responsive chord among the Lakota, many of whom live on the Pine Ridge Reserve in South Dakota, where alcoholism is prevalent. Pine Ridge was originally the reserve allocated to Chief Red Cloud and his followers in 1868. It is also home to one of the most infamous acts in our white history, the 1890 massacre at Wounded Knee.

In 1972, AIM retook Wounded Knee and started an armed standoff of the U.S. Army that lasted more than five months. The story of Wounded Knee has been told by others, so I won't repeat it here. But while my Lakota friends occupied Wounded Knee they made the decision to stage traditional ceremonies, including the sun dance, sweat lodges, and the ghost dance. My Lakota friends say this focus on ceremony, on finding and being with God, marked a turning point in their life. As this small band of brave people renewed their ceremonial life, under the auspices of AIM, with its emphasis on sobriety, the health and happiness of the people began to improve.

Shortly after I made the decision to get sober, I met Mary Thunder, and before I asked her to be my teacher, she gave me medicine. *Medicine* is one of the loaded words that has been horribly abused by the New Age. Medicine is a quality, a power, a grace to do something. Medicine is something like a charism, or a gift of the Spirit. Medicine is gifted by one who has access to a power to one in need of it.

I had spent just about a day with Thunder when she gifted me medicine, something to wear around my neck. When I asked her what it was for, she said, "For your broken heart." Thunder taught me that we live when we follow our heart vision, and we die when we live without dreams. My journal at the time said this: "You have lived much of your life as a jilted lover. One whose love for God was somehow abused or mistreated. God did not jilt you. But you could not find a place for God in the world of no dreams. So you went without dreams and God."

Not long ago, I dreamed that Buddy Red Bow asked me to stop in for a visit. After coffee and a little gossip, Buddy said, "What have you learned?"

"It is just this," I replied. "That we are love because God made us that way, and nothing we can do, or undo, can alter that, make it less or worse, or reduce it. We cannot change what God made; the love that we are is bigger than all that would threaten it; the light of our love reveals what is untruth hidden in shadow; with this love we can re-dream a world. We are the wave and love is the shore; love is the wave and we are the shore; we are both wave and shore; love is the wave and love is the shore."

"Hoss, you learned all of this from drinking and whoring and hating and hurting yourself and others?"

"No, I learned this because God loved me while I was doing these things."

My life was a mess when I quit drinking and using. But God did not see the mess of my life, or perhaps God saw past it to the love that I am because I was made that way.

So God, in an expression of infinite grace and compassion, loved me to health and used the most unlikely group of people to do it—Jo, the short Yankee who heard voices and saw colors; those "savage" folks known as Lakota Indians whom my kind had almost killed and had certainly abused, and who had plenty of reasons to hate me; and a fellow named Burney and a whole bunch of his alcoholic friends. Patient—meet thy doctors!

4 SACRED PLACE

A man may still be able at the last instant to concentrate his whole soul in a single glance toward that heaven from which cometh every good gift, and his glance will be intelligible to himself and also to Him whom it seeks as a sign that he nevertheless remained true to his love.

—**Kierkegaard,**
The Living Thoughts

You hang around those people, and you're going to evolve like a son of a bitch.

—**Frank Hughes**

I WAS SITTING IN A ROOM filled with people who were living a sober life. The year was 1986. I had been sober for two days. I hated everyone in the room. They were all discussing the joys and benefits of sobriety. One particularly sadistic, lying son of a bitch claimed he had been sober for ten years. I knew he was lying. No one could have been sober for ten years—not even God. And when a woman mentioned that she was grateful to be sober, I thought these people were crazy liars. My only question was why these particular folks had decided to come to this particular meeting to lie to me.

I had been sober for two days, and I was neither joyful nor grateful. Two nights earlier, I had just finished a sixty-three-day binge that culminated in a long weekend in a cabin with a friend, doing every drug I ever wanted to do but had never done, and supplementing those drugs with alcohol, mainly beer and tequila.

As my new God began to replace the old one I also realized that new behavior would have to replace old behavior if having a new God was going to mean anything at all. Changing behavior in part required cleaning out my God hole.

I believe we are born with a God hole, which is our heart. It is the center of everything, the *hocoka*, the point around which all else revolves. We are born with an almost insatiable desire, an ache, a longing, the symptoms of a midlife crisis, to fill the God hole. Our God hole makes indifference to God a difficult state to achieve. The presence I began to feel after the car wreck was God in the God hole. The pain I covered up with drinking was my agnostic refusal to experience God in that hole.

But who wants to fill the God hole with God if God is a jerk? I certainly didn't. It would have been like asking me to turn my will and life over to the care of a jerk. So, like most of us, I tried to satisfy my heart with all sorts of things related to my desire for ease and comfort: alcohol, drugs, sex, money, and work.

Although finite things may quiet the ache of the God hole for a while, ultimately the God hole is not satisfied because they are not the real thing. It is impossible to satisfy the infinite with the finite. Ultimately, we must fill the God hole with God.

This principle protects us when we make up our God list, like the list Jo Todd had me make. It is my experience that God must be at the center of my life. This special infinite, this hole without boundaries, is as jealous as the prophets said it was: it is of its nature that it can be satisfied only with itself. If I place anything else at the center of my life besides God, including a wrong understanding of God, God will systematically remove it so that God can be there. It has to be removed so that the God hole can be filled with the correct stuff, which is God. The God hole will be filled with people who support God being at the center of our life.

To fill my God hole, I must first clean out from it the things that don't belong there. The same people who spoke of the joys of sobriety talked about the importance of cleaning the God hole. They said my God hole was cluttered with my wrong reliance on substances, sex, money, and work. They said I also had to surrender the emotional devices I had used to keep myself safe—fear, resentment, dishonesty, selfishness, and being the center of attention. I had to become reliant on God and end my reliance on myself. I had to ask God for help (what we call prayer), and listen to God (meditation).

My sober friends said I would have to develop an active prayer life if I wanted to stay sober. I went to Burney for help—to the older brother I had never had. Burney loved me as completely as he could, and he held my hand while I learned how to love. He gave me the example of loving past the risk of the heart pain because there was no other choice of value.

As I learned about the divine combination of God, Spirit, and me that lived in my heart, Burney helped me understand that this divine trinity must be exercised. He showed me that we exercise by loving, past the risks of pain and loss that prompt us to want to protect our hearts. Burney told me that we must extend our hearts through risk by loving because it is our nature. Burney and others also taught me to remove the obstacles to loving with my heart, including dependence on external things and dependence on internal garbage. I used those personal filters to cover up my heart, protect it, and reflect the false belief that I could die and that you could be the instrument of my death.

Burney had grown up not far from my home in the Texas panhandle. He had been sober for years when I first met him. We would sit around drinking coffee, lying about this and that, and Burney would slip in a drinking story. Well, I would think, I have a better story than that, so I would tell him one that I thought was better. And we would laugh at his story and mine, and then after a while he would tell me another. I would generally let Burney tell the last story because he was older and I thought it was the respectful thing to do. But in my mind, I always had another story and thought the ones I had told were better. After this had been going on for a couple of years, it occurred to me that if Burney's inferior stories had convinced him he was alcoholic, what did that say about my stories and me?

After I started leading sweat lodges, Burney became my fireman. The fireman is the most important person at a sweat. At the end of a round when it is really hot and the people inside are ready to have the door opened, we all say *"Aho Mitakuye Oyasin."* And the fireman is supposed to open the door. But it is the fireman's prerogative to move a little slowly to open that door. I always tell people at the lodge to be nice to that fireman or else we might cook a little longer than we had hoped.

Burney went with me to those sweat lodges for gay men just outside of Waco. One of the funniest things I ever saw with Burney happened there. We would all drive up to Waco together in my van and park it not far from the lodges. On this particular night, unbeknownst to us, the guys had built an outdoor shower right next to where I normally parked the van. After this sweat lodge was over, Burney discovered the shower, and since he was very hot from having worked around the fire, he decided to take a quick shower before the ride home.

Now, for a man, one of our most awkward times comes after the shower when we have our shorts around our ankles and have to bend over to pull them up. Well, just as Burney, buck-naked Burney, had those shorts around his ankles, one of those naked gay guys came running up to him and gave him a big bear hug. You should have heard us howling in the van. Burney got into the van cussing up a blue streak, and the more he cussed the louder and longer we laughed. I later held Burney's hand and cried with him when we learned that one of the men at the sweats, who later became a good friend, had died of AIDS.

Burney has a heart as big as Texas, and he has healed a lot of people over a cup of coffee. Those of us who know him well think of him as the "redneck with the healing hands." When Burney first responded to my plea for help, he told me to make a list of everyone I was mad at, find out why I was mad, and then discover my part in the situation: what I had done to place myself in a position to be hurt. I had to identify what I was afraid of and why. I had to identify my sexual misconduct. And I had to tell someone else all of my nasty secrets. This process was like opening that lead box I had made and hid in so many years before. When I was through, I stood in my bedroom crying, sobbing, and pulling things out of the box one by one, hurling them at God and waiting to be deserted by this loving God. "I did this [pause] and then I did this [sob]." But the more honest I became, the more conscious of God's love I became.

And then one day I told another human being all my secrets, and he just kept right on loving me. And this kind man Bob taught me that maybe I did not have to hide so much from my fellow humans. Bob helped me give my flaws to God, including my desire for perfection, which had grown out of my need for your approval, my fear of your withholding approval, and my fear of God. I turned me, my growth, my place on the path, my sex life, my money, and my job all over to God. Then I made a list of all the people I had wronged, and I told them I was wrong, for my part, in whatever situation it was that troubled my heart. And somewhere along the way, my faith deepened in God and you and me.

To stay sober, my sober friends told me, I had to keep my house clean, keep my emotional resentments and fears minimized, acknowledged, and amended. They told me to pray and meditate. And they told me to be of service to others as directed by God.

One day, Burney said, "Let's sit down and pray." And we did. I was expecting a conventional prayer full of thees and thous as if we were talking to King James, or stiff and formal prayer as if we were talking to our date's parents. I was getting all ready for the "Dear God" introduction when Burney opened his mouth and said, "Hello God." I looked at Burney a little funny, and he said, "C'mon Bud, just talk to God like you were talking to me." It is rare to find people like Burney who pray as if they were talking to their best friend (if God isn't your best friend, you might consider revising your list).

Many of us were brought up to think of prayer as a series of isolated events. We start with "Dear God," we end with "Amen," and everything in between is the prayer. But my Lakota friends say that everything we do is a prayer. Every thought, act, smile, laugh, cry, sigh, frown, and word is a prayer. Everything is an offering to the Great Spirit in an expression of our creation.

I pray to accept each moment joyfully as it comes. To see past the pain and fear to the beautiful and perfect children of God that we are. To be that reflection for others and to see that in myself.

Prayers are answered. Not always in the way I would like, or at the time I would like, or with the answer I would like, but answered nonetheless. Or, to quote Burney, "Pray and duck."

At one sun dance, I prayed for help around the issues of pride, power, and lust. God answered those prayers in a typically unique fashion.

The first prayer to be answered concerned pride. I had been asked to be the chief piercer, to do the piercing at the sun dance, and my ego had grown to a considerable level. Everything went smoothly until the sun dance chief lay down to be pierced. Both his first and second piercings broke through, so now he carries two extra scars by my hand.

While I was praying about power, a rain cloud appeared from the west and stopped at the edge of the arbor. It stayed there for some time and then moved into the arbor, and the rain began. Within minutes I went from hot and dry to cold and wet; I was absolutely powerless over both conditions.

As for my prayer about lust, at the same dance a woman began to dance right in front of me, in a very erotic manner. Wherever I moved, I would see her when I looked up. Four days of swishing and swaying—it was very seductive. Whenever I noticed her, my attention would focus on her and I would quit praying. At that point I would feel very weak.

At that sun dance I learned that pride injures people, real power comes from God, and lust can deflect me from focusing on God.

Recently, I received two additional teachings on prayer and praying. The first came from my friend Shari Valentine, who is the adopted daughter of a Lakota elder. We share adopted ties to this family. The teaching was a simple quote from the matriarch of the family into which we are both adopted, Grandma Victoria Chipps. It is simply this: "Prayer changes things."

The second teaching came when I was continuing my prayers about prayer, and a rather strange instruction popped into my mind. Prayer for me today is like communing or eating; something happens in the process of prayer that somehow allows me to experience the divine. I can't explain it and sometimes don't even want to try for fear I might mess it up. But in the midst of doubts and communing, I received the rather clear instruction to refrain from praying for something unless I was willing to do it: for example, not to pray for another's relief from blindness unless I was willing to sacrifice my own sight, not to pray for the life of another unless I was willing to give my own. This kind of praying produces an intensity and purposefulness about prayer that aids the communion I crave.

My sober friends also told me I needed to develop a meditative life—that it wasn't enough to talk to God; I also needed to sit quietly and listen to God.

To many, the word *meditation* conjures up an image of the Buddha sitting in a funny position, humming, and burning some funny-smelling sticks. That may be one type of meditation, but I believe that meditation includes just about anything we do that quiets our mind and lets us hear God speak to us. Some of us write, some read, some sit quietly, some chant, some run. Others drive, swim, ride a horse, do carpentry work, paint, work, or play music. Many of us have worked on a project, become completely absorbed in it, and "snapped to" later as we were finishing. That's meditation. Looking back, I think I began meditating at age twelve when I left the church to silence my Baptist tapes. In my case, I had to meditate a very long time to get quiet enough to hear God in the shocking voice of a car wreck and in the quiet voice of my God hole.

When we have a God we are willing to place our faith in, and we start praying to fill our God hole, and there is space in our God hole, God begins exercising us. Sometimes we call that testing our faith. We step out on faith that this God is the one that will be there to answer our prayers. As we do that, our faith is confirmed. We step out, and we have an experience that confirms our faith. Trust is faith plus experience.

As we develop trust in this picture of a new God, it gives us a degree of comfort in stepping out again the next time on faith. Each time we do this, we increase our reservoir of trust. It is my belief that we must continually step out on faith to increase our reservoir of trust, which lets us start with the little things and move to the big things.

I used the fears, resentments, and character defects in my heart to protect me from you. As I released those defects while entering into a prayerful and meditative state I also accepted that God's love, rather than my fear or resentment, would keep me safe in the world.

The great gamble of our work on the path is that love will win in the end. Force is so immediate that the use of it seems to overpower anything in its way, including, and perhaps especially, love. And yet if there is a First Cause, can any effect ever surpass it in the end?

I choose the loving way. And the loving way is more real, yet well-nigh impossible without an active prayer life. But with a conscious contact with God, with a heart filled with God's love, I am willing to take the risk. My life is an example of the rightness of the great gamble. For through today, at least, love is winning. It is a force that continues to transform me.

Recently I woke up chanting. I don't really know whether the chant was in my mind or out loud in my voice. The chant was this:

> *My love is bigger than your conduct*
> *My love is bigger than what you do to me*
> *My love is bigger than what you say to me*
> *My love is bigger than what you say about me*
> *My love is bigger than what you think about me*
> *My love is bigger than my idea of right and wrong*
> *My love is bigger than my hurts*
> *My love is bigger than my wounds and angers and*
> *   resentments*
> *My love is bigger than my selfishness and self-*
> *   centeredness*
> *My love is bigger than the hurt I feel when you don't*
> *   act right*
> *My love is bigger than anything else in me or outside*
> *   of me*

What seems true to me is that I want to come from a place of love. And when I respond from this loving place, it is bigger and more powerful than any of the other places. But at other times, when I am very angry or very scared, for example, then it is as if I am in a universe or colored ball of fear, and my thoughts and conduct relate to the fear inside the ball. At those times, my fear is bigger and more powerful than my love. In fact, sometimes the fear is so big that I forget that I want to come from a place of love. And then something will happen, and I will remember, and then there are tools to help me move from the fear place to the loving place.

What all of this says to me is that sometimes my fear or my anger is bigger than my love, or seems to be. Yet, when my love is the biggest, everything else seems small by comparison. Coming from a place of love does not dictate conduct. It does suggest that I choose my conduct while existing in a place of love, and not from where my fear is in charge.

Amy, my sixteen-year-old niece, just died from a tumor that infiltrated one lung, consumed a second, covered her heart, and invaded other parts of her body. I struggle with the dual experiences of a loving God and the death of a child active in church and doing all the right things. I appreciate the concept that God does not punish, and I also acknowledge that sometimes life sure feels like punishment. At these times I am reminded that all I know, or think I know, amounts to nothing, because in the end we do not have the power of life. We are created beings. The trappings of ceremony, the drama of sun dance, the gossip of my life, the petty disturbances to my serenity, the phrase "having a hard day" all become uniquely poignant thoughts.

I believe there are times when we decide for a God-filled life for no reason except that we decide. No hope of health or happiness or sobriety or healing, no gift in return, no surety, no promise, no understanding, no experience, and perhaps substantial reasons to doubt the sanity of our choice. For me, Amy's death is one of those times. It is hard for me to remember that my love is bigger than her pain, or the family grief, or my belief that a just God would not let this happen, or my pain and the pain of those around me. I remind myself that I can be in love and feel the pain, and the pain won't carry me away and swallow me up and deposit me on some distant shore.

Most of my life I have run from pain to get where I am today, when recovery and spiritual growth mean being in love and hurting all at the same time. I have followed the direction of those crazy lying sober people for many years, and now I am one of them, talking about my gratitude for being sober. Of course, I am not grateful for the harm I caused while drinking. Yet, I lived long enough to find a loving God, a prayerful meditative life, new sober family and friends, a passion for life, and a clarity about life I had only imagined. And the clutter in my God hole is much cleaner. Certainly it is fresher rubble: more current fears, more recent resentments. I now have experienced-based trust growing out of my extended faith and confirming experience that helps keep me sober, and I have room in that heart for love to grow through inventory, personal prayer, meditation, and service to others.

5 SACRED FAITH

The Sacred Pipe wasn't put on this Earth to serve one man or his personal agendas. It was put here for all of its children.
—**Frank John King III,**
***Lakota Times* columnist**

I'm from the government and I'm here to help you.
—**Ronald Reagan**

WHEN I BECOME DISCOURAGED or full of self-pity about my own challenges with losing and finding my heart, I think of my Lakota friends. Although my loss was individual and self-imposed, I believe an entire generation of people have lost sight of their heart and are now struggling to find it. The loss was one we did to ourselves in our pursuit of the good life as we understood it.

My Lakota friends have struggled to hang on to their heart in the face of systematic efforts by our government to eradicate their lifestyle and their culture, which for them is very much a heart-based system. Before we whites appeared, my Lakota friends lived a nomadic, free-ranging existence as hunters and gatherers. The *oyate,* the people, roamed across the vast plains of Middle America, from Canada to Texas and from Missouri to the Rockies, eating healthy seasonal fruits, nuts, berries, and grains, and pursuing wild game, principally the *wakan tatanka,* the big, mysterious, sacred buffalo. The *oyate* had a rhythm of life whose high point was an annual gathering in the foothills of the Black Hills in what is now known as South Dakota. There, families would reunite, medicine would be exchanged, news would be traded, names would be given, games would be played, chiefs would be recognized, contests would be held, and weddings would occur, all culminating in the great sun dance. And then the *oyate* would slowly disperse across the plains to again chase the *tatanka* across the rolling hills until they met again in the moon when the chokecherries are black: July and August.

Over time, my Lakota friends became imprisoned on large reservations through a series of treaties with the U.S. government. The passage of time, the madness for gold, and the surge of people moving westward put greater and greater pressure on the reservation system. The U.S. government responded to that pressure by breaking treaty after treaty and incrementally reducing the size of the reservation lands. Today, my Lakota friends live on land a hundred times smaller than their original roaming area and only about a tenth of the area our white government first promised them.

As a white man brought up in a white culture, I was astonished to hear, while sitting inside an *inipi,* a sweat lodge, that the practice itself was a crime in 1970. I thought the statement was a joke. Yet, it is true. In 1884, the U.S. government made the practice of any Indian religion illegal. This regulation was not formally abolished until 1978 with the passage of the Indian Religious Freedom Act.

45

Even today, I find it beyond rational belief that a government founded on freedom of religion could have even contemplated banishing the religious life of a people. In addition to the prohibition against ceremonies, participants were punished with jail time and a loss of commodities.

We took the sacred Black Hills and desecrated them, creating Mount Rushmore, a monument to white leaders responsible for the decimation of Native peoples. The *Paha Sapa*, the Black Hills, are sacred to the *oyate*. The *Paha Sapa* are the place of creation, the door out of which the people walked into this world. This sacred place is the home of the *wakinyan*, the great winged beasts who guard the west; it is the location of the Crystal Cave, where sacred dreams and visions occur. We took other sacred sites, including *Mato Tipila*, the Devil's Tower, in Wyoming, and *Mato Paha*, Bear Butte, where the *oyate* have from time immemorial come to pray for the people, to *hanbleceya*, or cry through the night for a vision (what we call vision quest). We big-city dwellers who have little or no ties to land often fail to appreciate the loss of these sacred sites to a people whose heritage is so closely interwoven with place. The closest approximation I can give is the holy city of Jerusalem, the sacred place recognized by Jews, Muslims, and Christians alike.

We turned these warriors and hunters into farmers and planters. We told them they could not work the job they had always held. We took their *shunka wakans*, their sacred horses, and saddled them to plows, made them beasts of burden, and forced them to plow: to make cuts into the deity known by the people as *Unchi Makata*, the sacred Grandmother Earth, the source of life and health. We replaced natural, seasonal, healthy food with spoiled, sugar-rich, saturated-fat–soaked commodities that ruined the health of a nation of people and produced generations of diabetics. We distributed this food out of boxcars, so that the people were forced to gather together like cattle during feeding time to receive rotten, stinking commodities from the same people who had taken their religion, their Jerusalem, their way of life, and their language. And still more was to come.

After we slaughtered the buffalo to wear their robes and gorge on buffalo tongue, we left the stinking rotten carcasses in great piles spread across the plains, further promoting pestilence and disease, and always reminding the *oyate* of what we had taken from them. And we gave them cow meat, an animal called stupid buffalo by a people who believe that we are what we eat.

And we replaced their religion with one of our own. The Roman Catholics and Episcopalians divided the reservations among themselves and imposed their religion, tenets, and beliefs on the people. We took their language and jammed English down their throats. We took their round, warm houses and put them in square, cold ones. We took their source of warm clothing and gave them inadequate, cheap clothing that did not protect them from the environment. We brought new, foreign diseases to the people, who had not developed the immunity we had, and withheld medicine that would treat them. With the imposition of the reservation system, we withheld access to traditional medicines found in other places.

We took their children—literally grabbed them up and took them far away. We cut their hair, put them in English-speaking schools, gave them foreign clothes, physically and sexually abused those children, covered up the abuse, and prohibited the use of their language. We created a situation where it was very difficult for them to learn their own culture and force-fed them our own, which taught these children to hate everything they stood for and everything their family and their entire culture had ever stood for.

We took an independent people and made them dependent on our language, our medicine, our food, and our clothing. We took their form of government, their system of controlling crime, their system of punishment, and gave them our system. We took their leaders and recognized leaders whom we wanted, who would be compliant and obedient. If we couldn't trick the people into selecting the leader we wanted, we killed the leaders the people revered, such as Crazy Horse.

We took their sense of safety and replaced it with victimhood. In 1890, in the dead of winter, Chief Big Foot and his band were camped in the snow at Wounded Knee. Tensions were high at the time between the Lakotas and the U.S. Army. The army was still smarting from Custer's defeat at the Battle of Greasy Grass, and many believe they were looking for a fight. The army took the weapons of Chief Big Foot and his band, and with the white flag of truce flying in the air, shot and killed the band: 193 men, women, and children. The massacre victims were buried in a mass grave, and the soldiers hid their shame by pretending this was a great victory. But this "victory" was more like someone sitting in a deer blind taking pot shots from thirty yards at deer gathered around a feeder.

And then, we did one further thing, one more cruel injustice that has slowed the people's efforts to recover from all that we have done to them. We took their story. We retold their story in our way, and in our language, and we lied. We created a mythic, romantic picture of a stoic, storybook Indian who could live off root dirt and like it, who could endure all forms of physical torture, who had the endurance to run from here to there and back without breaking a sweat. We created a romantic, mythic caricature of a nonexistent people and put this caricature up on a pedestal. We covered up the reality of the people and the horrible atrocities and abuse and neglect we committed. We covered up the shame of our sin with a lie that further prolonged the disease of a people. That disease has raged on for so long that many of the people are now old, ill, separated from the traditional way of life, diabetic, alcoholic, broken in spirit, cut off from their language, their history, their heritage and their religion, all the ways of recovery a people need to survive.

This is the proud story of our dealing with the noble red man. This is the reason for the hate and mistrust in the eyes of the Indian people when they see the white man. This is the systematic destruction they see when they see me sitting in a rest arbor in a place dedicated to the recovery of the Native people. All of this distrust, fear, anger, and resentment come rolling together in a single turbulent point of energy inside the question "What in the fuck are you doing here?"

To experientially feel something of the impact of our treatment of our indigenous relations, imagine that you are a Baptist who has been going to church every Wednesday and twice on Sunday ever since infancy. Imagine that all of your friends and their families have also gone to the Baptist church for as long as they and you can remember. Now, imagine that you and your friends one day discuss your heritage and realize that the Baptist church was given to your people in a time beyond anyone's memory. Imagine that you keep the original Ten Commandments in your home, carved on their sacred stones. One day, Nazis appear at your door, telling you that you may not ever go to church, or even pray in your native tongue, ever again, for as long as you draw breath, and that doing so will result in fines, imprisonment, starvation, and death. You may not speak your language, eat your food, tell your stories, travel as you have traditionally done, or visit your sacred sites. You must move, and you must give up your children to be trained by the Nazis. And then imagine that the Nazis want to exhume your grandparents and put their remains on public display in museums. Furthermore, they want to take those sacred Ten Commandment stones and put them on public display.

All of this is what we whites did to my Lakota friends.

Your old people decide to protect the sacred stones, the way of life of the people. And so they hide the stones; they keep the way alive; they conduct communion in secret in the hills. They perform secret baptisms and weddings and funerals—all in the hope that one day the Nazis will let you resume your life.

Now reverse your thinking and imagine that your ancestors were Nazis. And then imagine that after hundreds of years, the Baptist elders come to you and say, "Please, come see our baptisms, come sit in our services. Please, let me give you the sacred stones to take care of for a while." That, in effect, is what those elders did to me when they let me into their ceremonies and when they gave me a pipe, authority to lead ceremonies, sun dance bundles, and a chief's bonnet. In effect, the elders said to a white drunk, "Here, hold our heart." I wonder why?

6 SACRED CONNECTION

---

*Whenever there is a form devoid of spiritual power,
law will take over because law always carries with it
a sense of security and manipulative power.*
—**Source unknown**

Young preacher: *It is blasphemous to smoke while you pray.*
Old man: *Can I pray while I smoke?*

THE FOUNDATION OF LAKOTA ceremony is the *chanupa wakan,* the sacred pipe, which was brought to the *oyate* long ago by White Buffalo Calf Woman. She is a figure most revered by my Lakota friends; some say she is the Morning Star. She said that the *oyate* were to use the *chanupa* as an instrument of connection with the Creator and that when the *oyate* smoked the *chanupa,* she would be there to carry their prayers to the Creator. Long, long ago the *chanupa* was given to Standing Hollow Horn to be its keeper. The *chanupa* and the job of keeper have been passed down to Arvol Looking Horse, the present keeper of the pipe, who lives in Green Grass, South Dakota. The *chanupa* lives in a small, well-built home. I have been blessed to sit on the hill next to the pipe house, and I always come away with a feeling of awe and peace. Arvol fulfills the difficult requirements of his job with grace and ease and has the respect of many people for his good work. His job is a tough one, and a prayer for his continued good health is appreciated.

The *chanupa* was given to the *oyate* at a perilous time in their history so they could pray when disease and starvation threatened to eliminate them. The pipe is a solution to dangerous times. Now, all of the people, not just the *oyate* live at a perilous time. We all face extinction as a species for many of the same reasons: disease, war, and famine. How fitting it is, then, that my Lakota friends have given us the pipe to pray with—a way to meet the challenge we surely face.

The pipe comes in two pieces: a bowl and a stem. The *pahu,* or bowl, generally used by my Lakota friends is made from a deep red stone called *inyan sha,* or pipestone, by them and catlinite by whites. Pipestone is found in only one place in the world: Pipestone, Minnesota. Although Native Americans had always known of the place, the stone was "discovered" by the nineteenth-century artist and author George Catlin during one of his forays through the West, and it bears his name. The *oyate* say that pipestone comes from the blood of those who gave their life so the people could pray. They say that long ago all the people died in a flood except one woman who was saved by an eagle. The blood of the people who died became the pipestone. The woman gave birth to twins, who were the ancestors of the Lakota. Some of my Lakota friends use black pipestone, although that kind of pipe is more generally found in the Southeast.

Red pipestone comes from the ground in sheets like shale. When it is fresh from the earth it is moist and soft, like clay, and easy to work with. The longer it is away from Mother Earth, the drier and harder it becomes.

The bowl is considered the female part of the pipe. Pipe bowls are generally one of two shapes: a T-shaped bowl for men and an L-shaped bowl for women. Some of my Lakota friends say the T-shaped bowl is for ceremony and the L-shaped bowl is for personal use. This understanding is consistent with the word itself: *cha nu pa, cha,* meaning "wood"; *nu,* meaning "two"; and *pa,* meaning "head," or one wood and two heads. Some pipe bowls are more fancy, being carved to resemble bears, buffalo, or eagles, for example. One pipe bowl carved by a Native American was made to resemble the USS *Enterprise.* People also make fetishes from the smaller pieces—turtles, rabbits, and the like. The dust of pipestone is also valuable and is saved for paint and for protection from sunburn.

The *sinte* (tail or stem of the pipe) is considered the male part of the pipe. It is often made from ash or sumac, although here in Texas we make a nice stem from red cedar. The mouthpiece is the *oyape.* The pipe bowl and the stem are generally wrapped in sage and cloth and carried inside a *cante juha.* This word provides a fine example of meaning lost in translation. *Cante juha* is translated "pipe bag." The literal translation is "container of the heart."

The bowl and stem are joined together at the *joinin oagle,* or holding place. The pipe represents completion and all creation. The pipe is filled with prayers and *cansasa,* which is the inner bark of the redwood willow tree. The prayers invoke the powers of the universe, whom we ask to hear and grant our prayers. Some say that the *cansasa* holds all the prayers of the ceremony and that when the pipe is smoked, the white smoke is the Spirit carrying our prayers to the Grandfather.

Hatred and jealousy (some say anger and greed) lie on either side of the hole that runs through the stem. The hole is the path we must walk, the eye of the needle. When one picks up the pipe, one makes a vow to the four steps of pipe knowledge: knowledge, wisdom, power, and gifting (love). One also faces four tests: power, money, ego, and sex.

My Lakota friends recognize several major ceremonies. Some of them say the ceremonies were also brought to the people by White Buffalo Calf Woman. Other people insist just as strongly that some of the major ceremonies came with the pipe and some came after the pipe. All generally agree that the *inipi,* the sweat lodge, was here from the beginning.

The major ceremonies include the *inipi* (sweat lodge), the *hunka* (making relatives), the *hanbleceya* (vision quest), the *wiwanyag wacipi* (sun dance), and the *nagi gluhapi* (ghost-keeping and -releasing ceremony). Some of my Lakota friends speak of the seven ways of the Lakota, but others think that is an effort to Christianize Lakota ritual. The Lakota have many other ceremonies, including star ceremonies, healing ceremonies, adoptions, naming ceremonies, house ceremonies, burial ceremonies, pipe ceremonies, repentance ceremonies, marriage ceremonies, ceremonies involving the use of sacred sites, and countless others. All of them rest on the foundation of the *chanupa wakan.*

The *chanupa* is an instrument of prayer. The Lakota word for *prayer* is *cekiye,* a verb that translates into what we do, how we are, and that seeks or defines or enlarges our relationship to the Creator. *Cekiye* is a relational verb and implies activity. For example, the people say that walking is a prayer and one must therefore walk in a sacred manner. The meaning of *cekiye* helps me understand what my Lakota friends mean when they say "let's pray." The *kiye* part is a request to create. It is the creation principle in the world. The *ce* part is an acknowledgment of something that is done. So, when my Lakota friends *cekiye,* they are asking something, but before they even ask, they express their gratitude for what has already been done.

I have a very distinct method of filling my *chanupa.* I was taught to use seven pinches of *cansasa,* or red willow, to fill my pipe over time. As I purify myself and clean my pipe before filling it, I become aware of the God hole, my heart space. I check to see whether it has any refuse that needs cleaning. I ask for permission to enter ceremony. When the Spirit gives its blessing, while the song is sung, I prayerfully fill the pipe with *cansasa.* As I do, recognizing Grandfather, Grandmother, the four winds, and the Great Spirit, I feel or sense their loving presence in my heart space. And then I know I am in ceremony. Mary Thunder, Leonard Crow Dog, and Buddy Red Bow all gave me specific instructions on filling my pipe. Additionally, I was given specific instructions about that process at a vision quest, and it has resulted in the creation of a ceremonial space that opens in my heart when the pipe is filled. I know to hold on to a pinch of the red willow and continue to pray until that prong of the space has opened, and that's how I know that this space has been created.

Nicholas Black Elk says that when the pipe is filled, all space is contracted to and represented within the bowl of the pipe, so that the pipe contains the entire universe. But since the pipe is the universe, it is also the people, and the one who fills the pipe should identify oneself with it by establishing not only the center of the universe but also one's own center. That person so expands that the six directions of space are actually brought within. By this expansion, one ceases to be a fragment and becomes whole, holy. This person shatters the illusion of separateness.

On a later vision quest, toward the end, the Spirit asked me whether I was committed to living a God-filled life, to prayer and mediation, to personal inventory, to being of service to others, and to being a truth speaker. In the darkness, I experienced all of my "nos," all of my fears and doubts, all of my withholds. And the Spirit again asked whether I was willing. I saw different fears about control of my life, about having a family, about falling headlong into the pool of grief that lay just beyond my defiance. Four times I was asked.

In the sun dance, at the end of each round, some of the dancers will present pipes to supporters in the sacred manner: the pipe is offered three times and refused, and is then accepted on the fourth effort. In the same way, in my dream at the end of that vision quest, I was offered a filled pipe on four occasions. The first three times I refused, but on the fourth, I said yes. I prepared to receive the pipe as we do in the sun dance, but instead of handing me the pipe, the Spirit grabbed me, opened my mouth, and forced the pipe stem-first into my chest. And then I woke up. The Spirit inserted a filled pipe into my body, so I believe that I walk and speak at all times through my heart with a filled pipe in ceremony.

My Lakota friends share my father's passion to do the right thing. The Lakota term *Original Instructions* reflects that desire. It refers to the right way of doing things, which is a deeply ingrained spiritual value. When White Buffalo Calf Woman brought the sacred ceremonies to the people, she directed that the ceremonies be conducted according to the Original Instructions. She also brought songs to use in the ceremonies.

The pipe-filling song, for example, is an instruction about Original Instructions. It is sung from the standpoint of the Spirit, who guides the ceremony, and it says, in part:

> *Friend, do it this way.*
> *Friend, do it this way.*

If you do it this way,
then all that you ask will come to pass.

Over time, disputes have developed about the Original Instructions. These disputes bear remarkable similarities to those of other religious groups. Some people believe that the right way refers to conduct—that there is a form, a right method, a correct series of steps to follow in ceremony. This group is splintered among various factions, who all claim to have the right instructions even though they all have different instructions. Conduct people generally espouse the view we should do things exactly as they were taught by White Buffalo Calf Woman many years ago.

Another group recognizes that ceremony is driven by vision. Vision people believe that within the context of a given ceremony, the Original Instructions may be altered by a dream or vision.

A third group, the heart people, believes that the "right way" only generally refers to conduct, but refers specifically to the condition—the heart space—of the ceremonial participant. These people give least heed to the ritualistic aspects of ceremony.

My Lakota friends recognize that it is difficult to follow the right way when that way is inconsistent with what I want to do. In fact, many Lakotas will say, "The Indian way is the hardest way." In other words, it is very difficult to do things the right way, yet they must be done that way. You could put ten of my Lakota friends in one room and ask whether they agree one should follow the Original Instructions. They all would say, "Yes. Very important. Must be done for the people." But if you went a step further and asked them to describe the Original Instructions, they would all disagree.

✧ ✧ ✧

I once asked a Lakota friend, Harry Charger, about the Original Instructions. Harry is from Green Grass, South Dakota, where he is part of a society responsible for providing physical protection for the original White Buffalo Calf Pipe and other sacred objects. Harry showed up at a vision quest one day and came in with a pretty strong opinion that white people probably shouldn't do ceremony. However, Harry exemplified what I have often found among my Lakota friends. They never let their point of view get in the way of what their heart tells them. No matter what they may say or think, including whether whites should participate in ceremony, once they are touched by their heart, they generally let that, rather than their opinions, guide and control their thoughts and conduct. This has been one of the most profound lessons my Lakota friends have taught me, and I have tried to share it with others.

In any event, Harry reported being impressed with our sincerity and our desire to pray and be of service, and he stayed around for quite a while. He taught some of us how to make a *chanupa,* and even went so far as to present one to my stepson Austin. Harry made several of us honorary members of his society before he left. I have a gift from Harry representing this honor. The recognition is nice, of course, but I really like it because when I see it I am reminded of Harry and of the importance of the Original Instruction, "Follow your heart."

Harry is from the right conduct school of thought. I asked him what one should do about following the Original Instructions and resolving the conflict between the various points of view. He said that when he was a young man, one of his uncles asked him to sing for him. Harry learned the ceremonies and the songs, and got them just right according to the Original Instructions, when Uncle One said that Uncle Two needed a singer. So Harry went to Uncle Two, got ready to sing, and was bopped on the head by Uncle Two, who asked why he was singing the songs incorrectly. Uncle Two then taught him the correct way to sing the songs according to the Original Instructions—which of course differed from the correct way of Uncle One. Harry went through ten uncles in this fashion, and each of the ten used similar songs but sang them in different ways. They used similar altars but set them up differently. They sang the songs in similar but slightly different orders. All of their interpretations of the Original Instructions were different. When I asked Harry how one should go about resolving this conflict, he told me, "Do the right thing." When I asked for clarification, he told me, "Follow the Original Instructions, and do what's right."

✿ ✿ ✿

Many people are touchy on the subject of the right thing where their pipes are concerned. Most of us have been taught specific ways of taking care of and using our pipes. But in all of those ways, people approach their pipes with a clear sense of the sacred, with the same reverence others have when they come to Mass or enter a cathedral. People will create a sacred space, clean it a little, and make sure their hands are clean before even opening the pipe bundle. Then they comb the layers of wrapping, do more cleaning, and sing and pray as the pipe is joined and filled. I wish we treated our neighbors as well as we treat our pipes. I wish we entered into interactions with our own kind with the same reverence and awe we have when we come to communion. I wish we treated our homes with the same respect we do our cathedrals.

It's odd, really, that we label something God created and we shaped, such as a pipe bowl and stem, as holy and sacred and then act nice around it. We will even caution people, "Be careful what you say! The pipe is out." Yet, here we are, at least as sacred and as God-made as any rock or wood, at least as shaped by human hands as a bowl or stem, but we do not treat ourselves or each other with the same respect and the same sense of awe we extend to a pipe bag. The divine mystery of a loving God is probably the lesson I see and learn over and over. But a close second, a very close second, must be the value of seeing each of us as living creations of the sacred Creator. If we were to start out just being nice to one another, that would do a lot to help our current situation. When asked, I offer three "rules" about walking the path: Don't mess it up, be nice to each other, and have fun. Be grateful for this fabulous gift of life.

We are like a pipe in so many ways: a pipe bag and a skin bag of bones, a heart in a pipe bag and a human bag, a wooden stem and a skeleton—both instruments of prayers, both creations of the divine. The pipe is filled, as are we when we sit in ceremony. We are both cleaned and clothed. We both get nicked and banged around, we are cherished and ignored, revered and reviled. We both come from a woman; to dust shall we both return.

Charles Chipps describes our bones as sacred stones. He says our bones are a sacred, rare stone. This, he says, is our way of knowing that we are related to the *inyan,* the stones. He also says our lungs have the same properties as the red willow and are our genetic relation to the plant world.

✦ ✦ ✦

There is a distinct ceremony for the pipe—the pipe ceremony—and I have had the privilege of sitting in and sitting through many of them. I learned a fair amount about the creation of sacred space from my friends Bear and Butch when they set up Mary Thunder's altar for her pipe ceremonies. Bear and Butch were some of Thunder's first road students—they left their homes, jobs, and families and actually lived with Thunder, traveling in her van for a year or more. This gave their sacrifice and learning a different character from that of people such as myself who kept their jobs in life but would only travel to be with Thunder from time to time. Bear and Butch were incredibly hard workers and had a painstakingly careful approach to creating Thunder's altars.

When I was with them, we would roll into some place where a pipe ceremony would be held on a Friday or Saturday night, often a Unity church or a bookstore. Someone would start sage burning in an abalone shell to purify the room, then would carry in Thunder's Pendleton blanket and lay it out in the spot Thunder was going to use for her altar.

Then onto the blanket would go her buffalo skull; a shiva lingam, which was a large crystalline rock from India; a huge seventy-pound triangular rock from the Catskills; Thunder's pipe; a candle; a glass of water; her healing feather; and whatever other objects Thunder wanted on the altar at that time. After everything was situated just so, Thunder would come in. She was always bright and bubbly, laughing and talking to all the people. We would eventually all get together in a big circle, with Thunder sitting directly behind the altar. She would make a few brief comments about how nice it was to be there, and then we would conduct the pipe-filling ceremony. Thunder would then ask everyone in the room to talk. For a long time I wondered why she spent the time to have a conversation with each person. Sometimes there were fifty or more people in the room, so it could take two hours or even more for everyone to have a chance to talk with her.

Once, at a pipe ceremony in Chicago, I had been in ceremony with Thunder for about nine days straight, so I was in a really centered place. I saw then that Thunder created a connection from her heart to each person in the circle as conversation occurred. By the time the conversation was over, there was a direct linkage between her and everyone else in the room. After everyone had had a chance to talk, we might take a small break to let people go to the restroom, but more often Thunder then would begin to talk. She would relate to something someone had said, or begin to talk about a current tragedy that someone had mentioned to her, and there would come a time when it was clear that the Spirit was speaking through Thunder. In a long conversation, she would give a teaching, a kind of extemporaneous talk on some such topic as sacred conversation, creating sacred space, or being in sacred relations one to another. Then, just as suddenly as the Spirit had been there, the ceremony was over. Thunder would quickly move to have the pipe smoked, releasing the prayers of all the people, and she would then shake hands with everyone in the room. She would leave, and we would undo the altar and take everything apart after the candle had been extinguished and the water drunk by the people who were there.

Eventually I saw other people do pipe ceremonies, including Buddy Red Bow, Charles Chipps, and Leonard Crow Dog. Although the contents of their altars changed, the basic setup for doing the ceremony was consistent from person to person. What varied was the process each of them used to create a connection with the participants in the ceremony.

My Baptist upbringing still stumbles over the pipe. I was brought up with the idea that a priest need not mediate between me and the Creator and that religious objects should be kept to a minimum lest the injunction against idolatry be broken. I have now come to believe that the ritual of connection with a pipe creates a kind of unspoken language in my body and heart that helps me make or become aware of my connection with the Creator. The process of coming to the ceremony, taking up the bag, removing the bowl and stem, and cleaning them serves as a reminder that I am about to enter into a sacred space, a sacred ceremony, and a sacred conversation, much like stretching and warmup prior to a game somehow serves to remind my body that it's basketball I am about to play. I don't think I need the pipe to maintain sacred space, but its presence nonetheless reminds me of the sacredness of the moment, of the solemnity of our responsibility to pray for the life of the people. Completing ceremony in a good way reminds me to complete my own life in a good way. It reminds me to pay attention to my heart and keep that space clean and clear. It reminds me of the fragility of life, of the food we need to take those next steps. I am reminded of our dependence on the Creator for the life that we have, the privilege of communication in sound and silence with our Creator, and of the gift of any communion at all. I am reminded that we stand in relation to all our brothers and sisters of all persuasions through the place in our heart where we were all made and where our Creator resides in an indwelling, invited peace.

My use of the pipe as an instrument of connection to the Creator has not been without cost. I have already mentioned that some of my Lakota friends wonder why I use the pipe and wish I would do something else. Some of my white family and friends voice a similar wish. The Lakota path can be scary to people whose spiritual experience has been confined to a four-walled clapboard church that meets on Sunday morning and Wednesday night. The Lakota services are louder, longer, dustier, and dirtier. They occur at irregular times, at odd hours, and with strange-looking structures. The language is different, the songs are different, the method of worship is different. I freely tell my white friends that if I could achieve or experience the same connection with my Creator in some easier way, I would. I don't know why it takes this way for me to trust my relationship with the Creator. I only know that it does.

Looking at the people around me, I believe I am not alone in needing something more in my communion with the Creator. I find myself with many people—most white, and most in recovery—who yearn for God and cannot find what they seek in church. Should they be denied what is holy because they find it on the Red Road? Surely no thinking person can answer in the affirmative. And so, in my and our odd way, we pray and ask for understanding and guidance and love from the Creator. We ask for relationship with the Creator and the people. We ask to be of one heart.

7 SACRED SPACE

*The more you walk on a path, the more defined it is
and the easier the footing becomes. Gradually, it becomes
an effortless path on the level of feeling; one doesn't have
to think about it, one you can rely on. It allows you
to be totally confident when you hit the ball.*
—**Kjell Enhager,**
Quantum Golf

The Road Goes on Forever and the Party Never Ends.
—**Robert Earl Keen Jr.**

THE SACRED CONNECTION occurs through the pipe. The sacred connection occurs in sacred space. When you walk in sacred space, you walk on the path. People interested in alternative religions often use the phrase "on the path."

I believe that the path is my heart and the phrase "being on the path" refers to honoring the call of my heart. When I follow my heart, I am on the path. Following one's heart can be a difficult and daunting task. One must learn to listen for the heart song, learn to hear and understand the language of the heart, become aware of and help clear away the filters that interfere with our ability to learn. Then, once we have heard and understood, we must respond with commitment, compassion, passion, tenacity, and willingness. And we must develop a capacity to stay in our heart when challenges come our way.

The phrase has acquired additional meanings. For example, one tenet of many religions is that judging is bad. Now, setting aside the more obvious truth that the maxim itself is a judgment, it can become fairly tricky to convey disapproval without being disapproved of or disapproving. To avoid this, some people have developed roundabout statements; for example, "being on the path" (which is good) or "being off the path" (which is bad). So, if someone isn't acting right, you might hear "What happened to John? He has really fallen off the path." Or, if someone is acting right, you might hear, "John is really walking the path today." People who are relatively new to alternative religions will discuss "trying to find their path." Others assure us that all paths lead to the same destination, so we can just pick the one we like (a particular favorite of mine, since it implies that the speaker has personal knowledge of all paths and knows the end point of each, and is often spoken by a smoking, drinking, overweight, out-of-shape, oily-haired person who does not, at first glance, seem transformed by his or her experience). Then there are the cynics who claim "that path is a dead end" and the victims who were "led down a garden path."

My Lakota friends also talk about a path. They call it a *cangleska wakan,* or sacred hoop; whites tend to call it the medicine wheel. The *cangleska* is the heart. The path of the heart describes ways the heart learns and lives. The *cangleska* is also a teaching tool, a way to explain things. The *cangleska* is our circle of life. It is the experience about which we teach. The *cangleska* itself is fairly simple: a circle, with some identification of the cardinal points and an identification of the center point. The cardinal points, also called the Four Directions, are *Wiohpeyata,* where the sun goes down (West); *Waziya Takiya,* where *wazi* lives (North); *Wioheyanpata,* toward the light of the sun (East); and *Itokagata,* the place that makes the face (South). These terms can be confusing. One might ask how directions can exist in a circle, or what is sacred and holy about a compass point. My Lakota friends might tell you that the "directions" are a mistranslation of a power that sits in a particular relation to the middle of the hoop. Thus, *Wiopehyata,* the place where the sun rests, or *Waziya Takiya,* the place where the wise old pine trees grow, are somehow translated into West and North and lose the beauty of their full meaning.

The East is the place of ideas, the place where we get new ideas and modify old ones. In the East we are taught through direct revelation the exact Original Instructions. The East is the place of spiritual maxims such as "Everybody gets to heaven but nobody wants to die." Or, as a Lakota friend once said, "One of the hardest things in the world to do is to become a human being." Or, as another teacher said: "It is damn hard to grow up and quit being a jerk."

The South is the place where we live out our ideas from the East, try them on for size, get a little experience with them, see how they work out and see how we like how they work out. The South is also the place where we learn about faith and gain trust, where we learn about our commitment to God and a spiritual life. It is the place of works, the place where practice makes perfect.

Faith is a verb. Faith is a decision of the mind and an action of the heart. There's a story about a tightrope artist who walked across Niagara Falls while the crowd said, "Ooh" and "Ahh." The tightrope walker then got a wheelbarrow and asked, "How many of you have faith that I can push this across Niagara Falls?" Everyone said, "I do; I do; I believe it." Then the tightrope walker asked, "Well, how many of you who have faith will get into the wheelbarrow and let me push you across?" The South is the place where, as one teacher said, "You learn the difference between talking and walking."

The West is the place of introspection, the place where the bear goes to hibernate, the place where we go to lick our wounds and think about what we have learned while living our ideas. It is the place of silence and meditation. In the West we began to understand the Original Instructions. It can also be the place of depression. In the West we decide what's what, or, as one teacher said, "Shut your mouth and open your ears, and you might learn something."

The North is the place of realized, experiential wisdom. The North is the place where we have had an idea, lived it, reflected on the experience, and come to some wisdom about it. In the North we further that understanding by beginning to teach others about the Original Instructions. In the North we may elect to pursue new ideas or modify old ones. The North is also the place of the children and the elders, the place of their childlike faith and battle-earned trust.

In *Black Elk Speaks,* Nicholas Black Elk describes a dream or vision he had as a young man. Because the dream was published it is probably the best-known dream concerning Lakota culture. In that dream, Black Elk saw the gradual but steady destruction and death of the *cangleska wakan,* the sacred hoop. He wept as he came to believe that the sacred hoop would die and that all the Lakotas would be lost. But at the bottom of his despair, he noticed a small, fine nation growing on the *cangleska,* and he rejoiced because he believed that the dream meant the Native people would survive.

The *cangleska* is sacred space, an important teaching of my Lakota friends. After Mary Thunder accepted me as a student, I vowed to spend a weekend a month with her. Being with her would create many occasions for John's question to come to mind. What *was* I doing there? For instance, we would find ourselves on the side of the road cleaning Thunder's van. I would leave work on a Thursday for wherever she was and return to my office on Monday. We often went to odd places. If the van broke down, all of us—often ten or more—would pile out of the van while someone set about trying to fix it. Thunder would take this opportunity to have the rest of us take everything out of the van, clean it, discard the refuse, and repack the van. The van would often be repaired just about the time we completed our task. Thunder's road students, Bear and Butch, reminded me that the cleaning out and repacking also occurred with each ceremonial and overnight stop. Thunder treated her van as sacred space.

My Lakota friends say that when we enter into sacred space we walk in a different world. They taught me that we carry our heart as a sacred space. For some, our home or office is also sacred space. Others see the great outdoors as sacred.

My older Lakota friends are often approached by younger people seeking spiritual advice, hoping for a message from the universe that will solve their life. What they often get is, "Did you make your bed this morning? Did you take out the garbage? Why is your car so dirty? Why are you so dirty?" The young people often walk away downcast, thinking they have missed a great spiritual teaching. God is inside of us, right in our hearts, and yet we let God live in mess and filth. We let ourselves live in mess and filth. When we create sacred space and keep it clean, then God has some walking-around room.

My Lakota friends deliberately create sacred space. Creation is done slowly and painstakingly to get everything just right. The creation of sacred space begins with the *hocoka,* the altar. Vision quest spots have an altar—a center place representing all of creation. The same center is in the pipe bowl, the rock hole of the lodge, the sacred tree of the arbor, and our God hole—our heart. The *hanbleceya* space is defined by four chokecherry sticks. The sticks are connected by prayer ties on all four sides, 101 per side. A prayer tie is a small piece of fabric filled with a tobacco prayer offering; each prayer fabric is tied on a string until there are 405 ties on a single continuous string. It is said that the 405th tie reflects our personal hope for a ceremony: yellow for new ideas or purple for a spirit connection, for example. The tie will go any place in the string, although the person leading the *hanbleceya* may direct placement in a particular location. My Lakota friends say there are 405 nations of people, each represented by one tie. In the created space one will find the quester, his or her pipe, perhaps a blanket or two, and whatever God puts there. The space is created and defined by prayers, and our quester is defined, surrounded, and protected by his or her prayers.

A sun dance arbor is built to precise measurements. At the center of the arbor stands the tree of life. The tree is decorated with thousands of bouquets and prayer banners. It is very beautiful. In a circle around the tree, perhaps eighty feet in diameter, is the mystery circle: the place where Spirit and human dancers meet and converse. The mystery circle's outer boundaries are defined with sage and have gates at the cardinal points. Many people spend many days building the arbor to these precise instructions.

Our homes should have a center, an altar, where people gather together to pray. The center of most homes used to be the kitchen, but that is changing now. Our homes should be surrounded and defined by our prayers, not our walls. We need to have a sacred space at work; we need to create a sacred space in our relations with others. So, if you don't have a sacred place in your home or office, make one. Decide where the space will be. Start simply. Work at the space when your heart is clear and prayerful. Define the parameters of your sacred space, then place an altar in it. It is important that you place things in your sacred space in the knowledge that you purposefully include or exclude them. Over time the things you place there may change, so be flexible, but remember that the objects and the altar represent what you value. They represent what you want ceremony to respond to or for. The space is a huge metaphor for life. Keep the space clean and simple. Thunder taught me that our life reflects our space. I am working on the similar proposition that my space can influence my life. What is there is placed purposefully. If your space is messy, your life may be in a mess. If your space is cluttered with unnecessary objects, then your life may be cluttered.

My Lakota friends emphasize avoiding clutter inside sacred space. Everything there is placed by act of God or by a conscious, fully informed human decision. Inside the space of uncluttered prayer, we pray to God. If we are to hear and understand the language of the heart, our heart space must be clean. Because we are trying to hear inspiration from God through our heart, the words of God pass through our God hole, and whatever clutter is in there flows into our mind. The more clutter we have in our space, or the more of our stuff and the less of God's stuff we have in our space, the less clear the message will be. I think of the clutter in our space as filters that exclude or obscure pieces of the message. Clutter can be substances, work, emotional safety devices, anger, resentment, selfishness, dishonesty, or fear.

Shortly after the wreck, Walter (my name for God at the time) told me about the need to clean out my space in what I have come to call my cornucopia vision. I began praying to see the face of God. My meditation centered on visiting a small church to which I had the only key, sitting on a bench, and praying to see the face of God. During one of these meditations I was sitting in the corner of the church, watching myself sit in the front row. Suddenly my perception shifted such that I moved into the church and saw myself become the person on the bench. In front of me was a cornucopia, out of which poured all sorts of people dressed in garments consistent with their walks in life; for example, I might see someone dressed as a painter, then another dressed as an electrician, then another as a nurse. A strong, clear male voice said: "Forgive all of these people; then you will see the face of God." The process of forgiveness clears clutter from sacred space. And once there is space, then God can begin to fill it with what God wants there.

LaJeune, my counselor in college, once told me to visualize each person I wanted to forgive and say the following prayers until I had done so:

1. Thank you, Lord, for *loving me* just as I am. Therefore I love myself as I am.
2. Thank you, Lord, for *caring for me* just as I am. Therefore I care for myself just as I am.

3. Thank you, Lord, for *accepting me* just as I am. Therefore I accept myself as I am.

4. Thank you, Lord, for *forgiving me* just as I am. Therefore I forgive myself as I am.

My Lakota friends would say that clutter-free, clean, sacred space is important because the clutter can act as filters to distort an image or a message from the spirit. So, the more clarity we have in our space, the clearer and more free of distortion the Spirit message is. One example of this principle occurs in the prayer of St. Francis, who asked the Creator to make him a clear channel. A clear channel is one without obstructions, through which the moving energy can flow free and clear of obstruction without becoming muddy or distorted.

Grandpa Fools Crow taught us to ask to become a hollow bone—that is, a bone without calcium structures, marrow, or other hindrances to the flow of energy, the message of Spirit. All of these concepts express sacred space because they refer to a space that is free of obstruction, clutter-free and clear so that the Spirit in the message and the energy of this Creator can flow through us cleanly and reach the recipient without being diminished or altered or changed.

Thunder tells a story about wearing a red dress and going to see Grandma Grace, the wife of Grandpa Wallace, who was one of Thunder's first teachers. Thunder was very proud of her red dress and eagerly showed it to Grandma, but Grandma took an instant dislike to the dress and told Thunder that she looked like a whore. Grace said Thunder should take off that dress, hang it up, and never wear it again. Thunder did so. She admitted to being very hurt by Grandma's comments. Some time later, Thunder received a recall notice from the manufacturer of the dress. The red dye in the dress had been found to cause skin cancer.

As I interpret the story, Spirit sent Grandma a message that the dress posed a danger and should not be worn. As the message worked its way through her filters, the "danger" posed by the dress was that Thunder looked like a whore—but in either event, the dress should not be worn. Instructions from the heart are like that—they go through my filters before I hear them. We don't receive the instructions perfectly because of our filters. Rosalyn Bruyere, the renowned healer and author of *Wheels of Light,* says that on our best day we receive only 65 percent of what is sent; we don't do it perfectly because we are human.

One way to maintain sacred space in that clutter-free way is to be careful about what is placed inside the space in the first instance, to recognize that we are completely responsible for what goes into our space and to be aware of that when presented with the choice of whether or not to place something there. We can be careful about what goes into this space so that it does not become cluttered at all.

A second way to maintain that space is through the inventory method I was taught by my sober friends. They told me to make sure I don't clutter up my space with my resentments, fears, angers, self-centeredness, selfishness, or out of balance sexual drives. They taught me a process of identifying those problems and releasing them by identifying and recognizing my part, talking to others about those problems, and making amends where my clutter has caused harm to others. So, in addition to watching what goes into this space in the first instance, there is a second process of cleaning up the negative things that might otherwise clutter up the space.

Walking the hoop, being on the path, all of this movement of the heart occurs around the middle, the God hole, the place of Spirit. Since all we know is less than Spirit, we constantly give away our learning to walk with gratitude for our life.

As one walks from North to East, there is a place called giveaway: an emptying of the fullness of wisdom to enable one to receive new inspiration, to wake up refreshed. Just as the sun gives away all his light and wakes up renewed, so too does the *cangleska* call for us to give up our hard-earned wisdom to support our looking at the world with fresh eyes—or rainbow eyes, as Buddy Red Bow called them.

The *cangleska* often recognizes conduct "off the path" as conduct actually on the path. In fact, the *cangleska* recognizes all conduct as occurring somewhere within its boundaries. This compassionate view of life holds that if what we learn in the North is that something doesn't work out well, we can give away this understanding as we awaken in the East in search of a new and fresh idea.

I like the giveaway place. Here, to my Lakota friends, what looks like a failed life is in reality a life filled with the wisdom of what does not work. And when I was discovered on the path, I was wise in the ways of what does not work. Because I was not burdened with the illusion that some things might have worked, it became much easier for me to walk into the East unburdened with the thought that I knew very much about anything. When White Buffalo Calf Woman brought the pipe to the people, she walked in a sacred manner, according to the song. This means that she walked in truth, with her heart, openly, in faith. This means she was walking her talk, walking the wheel.

An example of walking the wheel is my picture of God. My early idea of God produced unhappy experiences, periods of darkness, the loss of innocence, and the absence of wisdom. So I modified that idea. My new understanding of God produces happier relationships, a willingness to hear the joyful silence of God, experiential wisdom, and a desire to reclaim lost innocence.

The wheel requires movement. A failure to move is a cause of sickness. For example, we all know someone with lots of ideas that never go anywhere, someone who is a great starter before the ideas drift away: say "hello" to someone stuck in the East. Do you know anyone who is always in the same bad relationship with different people? You know someone who stays in the South. The person who is quiet and depressed, with no new ideas and no dynamic relations, is someone locked in the West. And the person who is always spouting wisdom while his or her life falls apart is a person locked in the North.

Movement creates experience. Our most lasting, permanent learning occurs through experience. The *cangleska* is the path of the heart because it is based on experience. My Lakota friends teach through experience. One cannot read a fire; one cannot read a sweat lodge. So we learn through experience. What we learn through experience is how to follow our heart, or, the meaning of the Original Instructions.

The wheel is the path of honesty in movement. I learned this when Thunder invited me to accompany her to Big Indian, New York, a small town in the Catskills near Woodstock. Big Indian is the home of the Rudi Ashram.

Swami Rudivananda was a Brooklyn Jew who ran an antiques store in Manhattan and taught meditation classes. He taught that everything is energy and that it is our job to digest it and use it. The kind of meditation he taught involved receiving energy in the heart and then releasing it. As Rudi's message grew, so did the number of his followers, and they eventually built several ashrams, including one in Texas. Once, Rudi left the Texas ashram and flew by private plane back to New York with several of his students and friends. The plane crashed, and everyone walked away from the wreck unharmed except Rudi, who died without a mark on his body. An autopsy revealed that his heart had exploded. Rudi's students believe that Rudi took in the energy of the plane crash as a service to his students—a kind of teaching.

Rudi's first ashram at Big Indian served as a base for Thunder for many years. She conducted many vision quests there, and I was fortunate enough to get to vision there. Thunder also taught me how to put people out on the hill during a vision quest while at Big Indian. In typical elder fashion, she gave me very few direct teachings. She just had me run the lodges, put people out on the hill, check up on them at night, and pray for them. One evening, Thunder had to leave Big Indian and drive into Manhattan. She had put several people on the hill at the time and took the occasion to transfer the vision quest medicine to me so I could look out for them while she was away.

Thunder helped me obtain and strengthen a kind of spiritual connection to Rudi, so that he often appears to me and comments on the questions of the day. His answers are direct and to the point, and they generally involve my failure to perceive and use energy. Rudi was a big believer in the necessity of doing spiritual work to grow and develop, and I am grateful to him for that teaching.

I used to wonder whether I was making up the connection to Rudi until I led my first vision quest. Someone had asked me to lead the ceremony, and after securing Thunder's permission, a group of us went to New Mexico to serve the people. One of those who came had been Rudi's student and had led the Texas ashram. We were several days into the ceremony before I knew about the connection, and then recognized that the fellow had come to let me know that Rudi was there at the ceremony.

Out on my blanket in the Catskills, I had a vision of the *cangleska*. To be candid, I first saw snow—big falling flakes of snow. When I finally came down from my spot, frozen and cold, I learned that we were snowed in without electricity or phone service. That was when I had another experience of John's question: What was I doing there? I had missed several court dates because of the snow. When I finally got through on the phone, I was trying to explain to a west Texas judge that I was in upstate New York at an ashram founded by a gay Brooklyn Jew, participating in a Lakota ceremony in a blizzard. The judge said, "Son, you are white—what are you doing there?"

In the vision, I saw that if I walk around the wheel with someone else's truth, my walk is not useful to me. One purpose of walking around the wheel is to start with the truth that is then modified through the walk. If I walk with something that is not my truth but someone else's truth, then their truth is modified through the walk, but not my own. Only by walking with my truth can it be modified through the walk on the wheel; otherwise the walk is a lie.

The medicine wheel is both the reality of and the metaphor for my walk with God. The hoop is the circle without boundaries, the hole without sides, the center that has no edges. The God hole is at the center of the hoop. The hoop itself is the path of inspiration. It is the road of learning right relations between God, myself, and others. I live my life walking the hoop—one foot in this world, one foot in the God hole. The tree is the middle, its branches the path. The middle is the divine; the wheel the path of the divine. I live in love in this world by hearing the Original Instructions emanating from the God hole and following those instructions on my walk.

We hear the Original Instructions with our heart. Once when Buddy Red Bow was staying at my house, I told him about Harry Charger and the Original Instructions. I asked Buddy whether he agreed that we should follow the Original Instructions and he said that he did. So I asked him whether he was aware of the conflicts and disputes among the elders as to what those Original Instructions were and he said that he was. I asked him, "How should I know what to do?" He said that I should do the right thing. I asked how to do that. He said, "You must always follow your heart. If you follow your heart, you will do the right thing and correctly discern the Original Instructions."

When I asked Buddy whether I as a white man could do ceremony, he said that I should do the right thing and follow my heart. If following my heart meant doing ceremony, then I should do it and just ignore the criticism that would be leveled at me for following my heart. He said that if you follow your heart, you will inevitably be criticized by those who do not follow their own. Those are the people who most need prayer, because they are not following their own heart, and a symptom of that is criticizing one who does.

Following the heart is risky. Following the heart creates intimacy and vulnerability, which creates the risk of feeling pain—wracking emotional pain. I have heard people say that emotional pain is not real. It is real; that is why we fear it. Many of us, in our desire for ease and comfort, and in our desire to avoid loss of place, face, and life, actively avoid creating the risk of emotional pain and close ourselves off from the lessons of the heart. Moreover, we lose control when we live with God in our heart. We use so many devices to stay in control. Fear protects by letting us avoid what we do not understand or cannot control. Resentment lets us protect ourselves from what can hurt us. Following the heart requires honesty, and honesty is risky. Being honest, truthful, and straightforward invites comparison and promotes growth.

The heart takes us out of the comfort of self-imposed restrictions. Heart time is nonlinear. Heart restrictions are false. Heart deeds are unlimited. In our circle, anything is possible that comes from the heart. Nothing will be denied that is needed to do a deed of the heart. Anything the heart needs is available.

Thinking is one of my favorite ways to avoid my heart. For example, on my first *hanbleceya* (vision quest), Thunder would periodically come up in the rain and ask me how I was doing. I would lie and say, "Fine." Finally, she said I might be having a little problem because I might be thinking a little bit too much. Right after she left, a big flock of geese flew in a straight line over the top of the blanket, formed a circle, and flew in a circle over the top of the blanket, round and round and round, making geese noises: "wack, wack, wack." I had a caffeine absence headache, and I was hungry and tired and irritable from being wet and cold. I finally yelled out at them, "Please shut up; I can't hear myself think."

Today, my mind may help me follow the instructions emanating from my heart, but it is my heart I must follow. And regardless of the risk of pain, regardless of the painful memories or the many times I have hurt in the past, if I am to live and heal I must follow a heart-filled path. Emotional needs are like physical needs: a failure to satisfy either will result in the death of both. I was taught that by my friend Burney, who helped me learn to pray when I was getting sober. After a particularly painful loss, I asked Burney how I could ever love again. He said that I would pull my heart in because it had been trampled on; I would pull it in and hold it close to myself and nurture myself. With love I would heal. Then, when I was healed, I would hold my heart out to risk having it trampled on again, because otherwise I would die.

We risk loving, we seek out love, because it is our nature to create loving relations. What love looks like to each of us may vary. Our expressions of love may appear to be significantly different, but regardless of the form or the expression, it is our nature to love and it is our need to love. When we live from our heart in love, we can learn the Original Instructions because they are taught in the language of the heart.

To learn the Original Instructions from our heart, we must develop an understanding of the language of the heart. At my first sun dance, Grandpa Wallace talked at length about different languages. Grandpa Wallace is a great example of someone living his truth even when the consequences can be less than pleasant. He had a vision years ago of sharing the Lakota way with people even if some of them were white. He has been roundly criticized for this decision, but he has stuck to his vision, and many people have been healed as a result of his integrity. Grandpa Wallace taught me that God speaks in the language of the heart. He pointed out that lawyers talk in their own language, doctors in theirs, engineers and secretaries and cowboys in theirs, and so forth. Grandpa Wallace said that because of our various languages we could not talk with one another. We were still living in the Tower of Babel. He said there could be no meetings of the mind or of the heart because we all spoke a different language. Wallace advocated that we should all speak in one language—the language of the heart—so we could communicate with one another and thereby avoid many of the problems of our relations.

To walk the path, one also needs to keep a sense of perspective. Laughter is important. Sometimes Spirit will put humor into a ceremony that is too serious. For example, one year at Grandpa Wallace's sun dance, we worked very hard to create a sacred arbor space. This job involved a lot of hard work with some very serious guys who never laughed. The night before the dance, Grandpa Wallace and Charles Chipps agreed to answer any questions the dancers might have. The Chipps family is a traditional *yuwipi* family on the Pine Ridge reservation in South Dakota. Woptura is considered the first Chipps. He and Crazy Horse were both orphans and grew up together. Woptura became the mentor to Crazy Horse and was his medicine man. He gave Crazy Horse the power of invisibility to help him in battle and gave him the magic stones that protected him from Custer's bullets. *Woptura* means "a part of everything," and when that phrase was translated into English, the phrase was thought to be too long for a name and was shortened to Chipps. The Woptura lineage was carried forward through Horn Chipps and the Moves Camp family. Horn Chipps's son Ellis was the father of Godfrey, Phillip, and Charles Chipps and the husband of Victoria. Godfrey Chipps and Charles Chipps and their mother, Victoria, still live in service to the people in the old way, offering ceremonies for the health and healing of the people. Charles taught me to love with my heart. He also gave me the gift of seeing with my heart, of seeing past the internal obstacles we have in our heart to guard us from the risks of loving.

In addition to leading sun dances, Charles also runs sweats and vision quests. He is a little older than I am but not quite as tall. After he decided to adopt me, I started calling him "little brother." It's fun to see people treat Charles and other medicine people with such respect and then observe the look on their faces when I call him "little brother." Charles is a big fellow with a large face and a grin that covers up everything except his sparkling eyes. When I see my Charles, he always says, "There is who my heart has been praying for."

I first met Charles at a sun dance in Oregon. A group of the dancers decided they wanted to have a meeting where Charles and Grandpa Wallace would respond to questions. But as a rule, my Lakota friends do not teach in the manner we are taught in school. Philosophical discussions are rare. The teaching is experiential, and one might receive a few comments to aid in understanding the experience, but generally after the ceremony is complete. So, the thought of getting two medicine men together to answer questions was novel, to say the least.

Well, all of us were gathered around the fire, and one fellow asked whether we could go to the tree and pray. I looked at Thunder, she looked at me, and we both rolled our eyes. I was thinking that in six hours I would have to walk into the mystery circle, and I wanted some sleep instead of listening to this nonsense. Charles and Grandpa looked at each other, and Grandpa said, "Charles will answer." Charles began to answer the white man, talking for about forty minutes in Lakota. When he finally finished, he looked at Grandpa and said, "He will translate." So Grandpa talked about the sun and moon and stars, about sleeping and dreaming and dreaming about sleeping, and then waking up, and on and on, and never once mentioned the tree or whether anyone could go up to it and pray. And when he was finally through, Charles said, "Aho," and he and Grandpa looked at each other, very pleased with themselves. I was happy because surely these folks now understood the drill, and we could all go to bed, when out of the blue a second person asked, "Why do men dance in one line and women in another?"

Thunder and I looked at each other and chuckled, and I gave up any hope of sleeping that night. Charles and Grandpa looked at each other, and Charles said, "Grandpa will answer." Off went Grandpa, talking for about forty-five minutes in Lakota in response to this question. When he finally finished, he looked at Charles and said, "He will translate." Charles talked about the sun and moon and stars, and sleeping and dreaming, and waking in the dream only to sleep, and on and on until he finally finished, and Grandpa said, "Aho." I thought, great, and started to go to bed, when from the back of the group someone who was obviously sick and in need of compassion and thought they would get answers out of Grandpa and Charles asked, "Can we pray while we are pierced?" (which is a stupid question to begin with).

Thunder and I looked at each other and burst out laughing, and everyone else looked at us as if we were crazy, and Grandpa and Charles looked at each other as if we were all crazy. They both talked in Lakota to each other for the longest time and then said to us, "What the other said was . . . " and continued to talk until it was time to go into the lodge, at which point Charles said, "And if you understand that, then you know." I was rolling in laughter as I crawled into the lodge. Nowadays, if someone wants to go ask an elder a question, I tell them this story. It rarely stops them, though; they think they are going to get a secret answer and then their world will be fixed.

Charles's brother Phillip once told me that white people think the Indians have a lot of secret answers, and that is why we tried to kill them. He told me this after watching me take flesh offerings for a while. He said that I was a fool for taking the flesh because it tied me to the soul of the person making the offering, but if I was going to take it I should do so in a good way. The good way, he said, involved mainly living in my heart while praying for the people and their prayer while taking the flesh. He explained the way of staying in my heart and then sent me away. Phillip would say that the previous sentence suggests that I now have secret knowledge and it will kill me one of these days. I always used to doubt Phillip on this point until he died in a car wreck.

Charles gave me the opportunity to lead sun dances. He was the one who first approached me about taking a leadership role in the dances. At one of them, after I had just pierced him, and he had pierced me, he looked at me and said, "I love you." The voice was so pure a mix of Charles and Spirit, so complete a mix of the physical and the divine, that it was as if my heart space was completely cleaned and God finally had a home there to arrange as God saw fit. Just as Buddy Red Bow gave me the gift of rainbow eyes, Charles gave me the gift of a rainbow heart—a clean loving heart, a clean space for God to live in. Charles completed the healing of my heart and helped me live in the moment instead of cleaning up debris from the past.

The talk Grandpa and Charles gave occurred in the sweat area behind the sacred arbor. The arbor was located at the foot of a very steep hill, at the top of which was our camp. Since Thunder had a broken leg in a cast, Grandpa Wallace agreed that Jimmy Schulman could drive her down the hill in a four-speed truck with manual transmission, wait for her at the bottom of the hill until the meeting was over, and then drive her back to camp. Thunder and Jimmy created quite a stir driving so close to the arbor in the truck, but since Grandpa had given his okay, there was nothing to be done about it.

When Jimmy started to take Thunder back up the hill, the truck was sitting on a slight incline. He had difficulty getting the truck into gear, and while he was struggling with the gears, the truck began rolling off the incline and into the sacred arbor, finally coming to rest at the foot of the sacred tree. Jimmy was cussing, the other dancers looked as if he had stolen Christmas, and all through the valley, all you could hear was the sound of gears crunching and the laughter of Grandpa, Thunder, myself, and Spirit.

There are challenges to using the heart. Once we get the inspiration and have interpreted it, we must still do it. If the direction is to get the glass of water, I still must get the glass of water to complete the instruction. Once I thought that when I knew what the Original Instructions were, my problems would be solved. For years in my spiritual progress, whenever I hit a problem, I said that the problem was that my definition of God was too limited to allow me to feel safe or secure to let this God handle the situation. For years, I enlarged and tinkered with my picture of God so that God became not only all-powerful but also concerned about me as a person, so there was a personal relationship. I thought that as soon as I got a God who was big enough, all my problems would be solved. One day I hit a glitch and as usual turned to my picture of God, only to discover that God was big enough. This wasn't a God problem; it was a Mike problem. I wanted to do it without God's help, even though I knew God was big enough to handle it and could probably do so better than I. I still occasionally run into a "God is not big enough" problem, but more often my struggles now center around the fact that I still want to do it myself.

Once I hear the instruction, I must follow directions. I played sports as a kid, and I always had a coach. When we went on road trips, the coach would tell us when to get up, and I'd get up. He would tell us when to go to bed, and I'd go

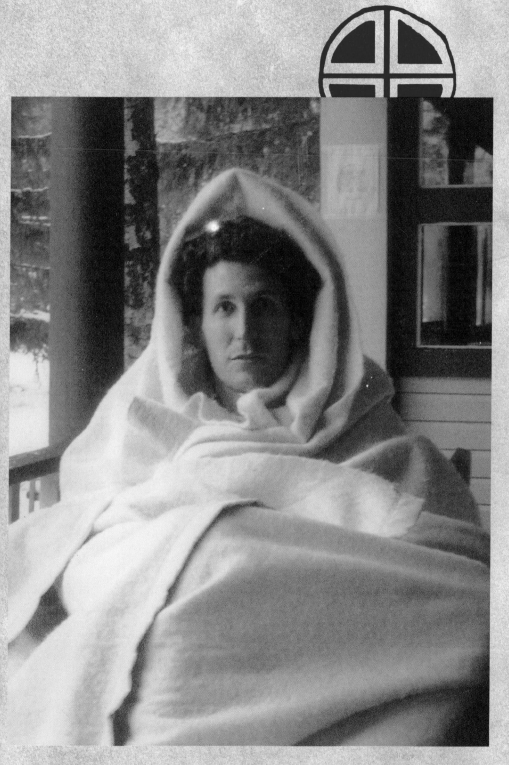
The author in 1987, following his hanbleceya in the snow at Big Indian.

Chief Fools Crow

Mary Thunder

The author and Grandpa Wallace Black Elk, chief of the Oregon sun dance, at the sun dance campground.

The author and Dennis Banks, cofounder of AIM. Dennis Banks is
teaching the author his first Lakota song.

Chief Fools Crow's bonnet

*Buddy Red Bow wearing Chief Fools Crow's bonnet,
blowing the eagle bone whistle.*

The tree of life in the sacred sun dance arbor,
the Lone Star sun dance, 1998.

to bed. He would tell us what food to eat, and that's what I'd eat. He would tell us how much spending money we had, and that's what I'd spend. He would tell me when to go into the game, and I'd go in. He would tell me when to come out of the game, and I'd come out. Everything the coach told me to do, I did. I didn't think about it; I didn't evaluate it; I didn't consider whether he was right or wrong. It never crossed my mind to do that. I wonder why it is that I can do that with a coach, but I seemed unable to do that with God. It just doesn't make much sense. So, in the past few years I've been trying to think of Walter as a coach and me as a player.

When I practice being the player, I sometimes forget I am practicing. When I stumble and fall, I will notice that someone who is fifty years old and has been walking for most of those fifty years will occasionally stumble and trip. Then I realize that if that's true of something we've been doing for many years, how much more true it must be for a brand-new behavior.

As I practice walking the wheel honestly I experience increasing intimacy. The Spirit once discussed intimacy with me and said:

> True intimacy is very rare. It is that external moment when two souls recognize their oneness and acknowledge their uniqueness. It is mutual appreciation that is equal on all levels and therefore the same. It is the shared admiration that makes true intimacy possible.
>
> It is similar to God's appreciation of you. His appreciation of the similarities in that he created you as he is; this appreciation of your uniqueness as you extend yourself. For as you extend yourself, you also extend he who made you a part of himself.
>
> True intimacy holds nothing back because nothing need be hidden or retained; all is known and more will be returned.
>
> True intimacy is gentle except when strength is required. Then it is gentler still.
>
> True intimacy is not restrained by sex, age, sexual preference, race, religion, or creed. It has no boundaries and knows no limits.
>
> To be truly intimate means to be truly alive, awake, and available; open to the moment you are in. One moment fully experienced is a lifetime.
>
> You must walk your walk. We can support your walk on your wheel, but we cannot walk it for you.

Walking the wheel reminds me of my dependence on God. Many of my Lakota friends have a better appreciation than we do that our existence is based on grace. Traditionally, they lived in the natural elements all the time. If the sun continued to heat, they would die. No rain—death. Too much rain—death. They were in daily contact with any number of things upon which they were dependent and before which they were utterly powerless.

I think it is much harder for many of us to develop a sense of that dependence. We get into our car in the garage, drive to work in air-conditioned comfort, drive to a parking garage, and spend most of the day inside the office before we reverse the process and go home for the day. But when we do see that dependence on God, we learn that permanence and continuity are an illusion. We must plan for tomorrow without any assurance of ever seeing it or knowing what it will look like. For instance, our involuntary bodily functions, such as breathing and pumping blood, start with no apparent push from us, and one day they will stop of themselves.

In our day-at-a-time walk around the wheel, we solidify our faith in God, we develop trust in God, and we decide for God. We do this by finding and by living the answer, by walking our talk.

We are so scared to walk so that others see us, so we hide the glory of your creation behind stories and fears and hurts. But what we hide from others we hide from ourselves and you. Help me be willing to let others see you in me. Help me be able to see you in others. And please, God, help me to see you in me.

8 SACRED RELATIONS

Relation is the essence of everything.
—**Meister Eckhart**

*The whole idea of compassion is based on a keen awareness
of the interdependence of all living beings which are all part
of one another and all involved in one another.*
—**Thomas Merton**

*He whom we look down upon, whom we cannot bear to see,
the very sight of which causes us to vomit, is the same as we
are, formed with this selfsame clay, compacted of
the same elements. Whatever he suffers we also can suffer.*
—**St. Jerome**

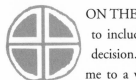ON THE ADVICE OF their teachers, my Lakota friends decided to include people like me in their ceremonies—a controversial decision. But my decision to take the great gamble ultimately led me to a woman named Mary Thunder, who was rolling across America in a beat-up van.

Thunder was living on the road when she accepted me as a student. Living on the road means that you live out of a car or a van, you go as far as donated gas or gas money takes you, you eat what the donations will buy, and you sleep in whatever place puts you up. Being on the road means that you have no assurance but faith about the next meal, the next tank of gas, warm clothes, or a place to sleep. Being on the road means that you accumulate no more clothing and stuff than will fit in a van. Being on the road means that whatever personal stuff you bring into the van is likely to stink there, so you might as well deal with it. Being on the road also means that cars break down, hosts fail to materialize, and sometimes you sleep in less than ideal circumstances.

Thunder was living on the road at the suggestion of her teachers, who had told her that her spiritual growth needed a year on the road, not listening to the radio or reading the newspaper. She had to walk away from her family and friends to do this. She had to leave a husband and three children, a secure and successful job, and her friends to follow the Indian way.

Living out of a van was an act of faith growing from a decision for God. Over time I have come to believe in the power of decision. This issue began to surface whenever I hesitated when offered the chance to assume additional ceremonial responsibility.

There are so many good reasons to quit the Red Road. Travel is arduous; the personal, professional, time, and economic costs are high; the lodges are hot; the sun dance arbor is hotter still; a vigil on a hill is lonely. All of these tests require us to reconfirm our commitment to God and to the holy road, as the North-to-South path is called. Beyond that decision is a sense of peace, a serenity, that I have found in no bottle, no drug, no loving arm, no win in court, or no dollar earned. I continue to be amazed that I know of the peace on the other side of decision, but I still struggle with that commitment when things get tough.

Thunder has said that each time we come to a ceremonial doorway, we have the free choice to turn away from God, and that God will not give us the increased energy or responsibility unless we are sure we want it and have enough discipline to handle it. We have to decide for God and surrender to God.

I believe that in every spiritual process we come to a place, based on internal motivation, to decide for God. Surrender, or deciding for God, is an act of the mind and the heart. We can redefine God to make God safer, and we can step out on faith, but ultimately we decide for God because we do. It is this process of deciding for God that is an act of surrender. When we begin, we don't know whether God exists. Then comes the doubting Thomas phase, when we build a reservoir of faith and trust in our new God, and we must get a reciprocal response back from God so that we can know our new God exists. After that we receive fewer and fewer of those reassurances from God that God exists, and we must decide without reassurance. We believe by choice.

Since becoming responsible for my choices, I often dislike the act of deciding by choice. I can't blame anyone else if I choose wrongly, because I made the choice, the decision. At this point, the feedback from God, the reassurances, become less frequent. Ultimately a time comes when I must act as if God is big enough to handle the situation. In the end, I decide for God without the possibility of rescue by God or even the assurance that God exists.

One circumstance that leads us to deciding is relations with teachers. We carry around inside a circle of our thoughts, beliefs, ideas, and conclusions. By definition, the contents of our circle are "right." If they were wrong, they would not be within our circle. We occasionally put things in our circle that we define as wrong, but even then we have correctly identified them as wrong. For example, I might now say that it is wrong for me to drink. That wrong is still included within my circle because I am right about that belief or point of view.

A teacher is someone who sits outside our circle and forces us to take steps or move outside our circle even when the place to which we are moving appears to us to be wrong. By definition, moving outside our circle appears to us to be wrong, since it is outside our circle and not inside.

Once we move and embrace that point outside our circle, it then becomes within our circle and becomes right. The teacher allows us to see something outside our circle upon which we can have faith or trust, and it is that faith or trust (which is inside our circle) upon which we can rely and that allows us to move toward that point outside our circle.

Teachers are odd ducks. Gloriously human, compassionately divine, they agree to serve a special role in our development into who we are. Teachers teach.

If that seems a moronic statement, compare the teachers in your own life who claimed the title, but did little with it, with those blazing souls who created pathways to masterful lessons that altered the course of your life.

A teacher can take many forms. Sometimes life itself is our teacher; sometimes we are blessed with someone who answers to that title; an overheard remark may teach us; our parents, our friends, and our kids continually teach us.

My teachers rarely taught by specific instruction. Direct teachings rarely occurred. My teachers taught by example and through action. Instead of telling me how to build a sweat lodge, they built one while I helped. Then they had me build them over and over, first for them and later for others, until they were convinced that building one on my own likely would not kill anyone. They made prayer ties and then had me make them—thousands of them—practicing and praying, being of service to the people. My teachers did not talk about the faith necessary to follow Spirit's directive to drive to Oaxaca with no money or gas; they got in the van and told me to drive.

With the passage of time and the benefit of reflection, I have understood that God sent me teachers who taught heart. Other lessons and learning intertwine along the way, but the overarching theme is living in my heart, how to live in love, how to see, how to experience the divine opportunity this life represents.

Teachers value prayer and meditation. The formats and techniques they use will vary, but the importance of the activity is constantly stressed. The teachers say that the cycle of prayer and meditation strengthens our connection with our divinity, with each other, and with ourselves. It is the bedrock of how we heal and how we maintain and foster our growth.

Teachers stress the importance of service to others; in the crucible of service we experience the truth about where we are on our paths. It is through service that we find our rough spots, the places that still need healing. It is through service that we are of and with God. Wherever you are and whatever you are doing, if you take anything away from this book, please go and find something you can do for others in your own community. Our people need it.

On some occasions I have been challenged to distinguish between the principle of the teacher and the personality of the teacher. Our hero-worshiping Western culture tends to place teachers on pedestals. It is a law of nature that they will eventually fall off. This inevitable result leads to confusion, when all that has happened is that the personality has fallen away, like a cocoon, so the principle is fully revealed.

I had many great teachers long before I sat in a Lakota ceremony. My parents, my brother, coaches, friends, and relatives all loved me when a sane person would have looked the other way.

Life is my most consistent teacher. It is always present, always teaching, always providing feedback about the decisions I make. In a general sense, I believe my life is a consequence of the choices I have made. The "we choose our own reality" line is often misunderstood. I remain unconvinced that we are choosing when we don't know we have choice. Spirit does not lead me to believe that we choose all of our outer circumstances—that a six-year-old boy chooses starvation, or a nine-year-old girl chooses incest. I am willing to be wrong about the matter if Spirit so directs, but the concept of choice in this context does not sit easily in my heart. At the same time, it is very clear to me that our conscious choices can affect the circumstances of our life, as with illness, financial circumstances, loving relationships, and so on. The paradox of choice can't be taught but must be graced in the totality of the moment.

Teacher accountability has been the enduring paradox of my spiritual walk. My sober friends tell me that resentments cut me off from the sunlight of the Spirit and led to my death—a principle I wholeheartedly accept. Yet, I have spent untold hours with spiritual masters, the gurus of their way, who were undoubtedly walking in the sunlight of the Spirit yet also drank alcohol, beat their spouses and kids, lied for money, and were verbally abusive, arrogant, and self-centered. How can such people display such glaring faults and still be who they are?

Few people want to talk about these matters. The first time I said something I was roundly criticized for being judgmental—and of course I was. And it is very difficult for a student, sick by virtue of the perceptual prison that brought that student to the teacher, to healthily assess the teacher from within the cell. And the teacher is often accountable to no human. As teachers become teachers, and supposedly more attuned to their own small voice, their job becomes more to listen and obey within the mosaic of their unique expression of truth and thereby become in some way more distant from others and less accountable to them.

It is a hard topic for teachers to discuss. We are still terribly human, full of defects obvious to all, played out on a raised stage inside a see-through house with magnifying lenses for walls. Our frailties are generally so apparent for all to see that to comment on the foibles of another seems hypocritical in the extreme.

Such comments are often perceived as based in jealousy, and indeed they may be.

Yet, we are accountable. We have been offered tremendous trust and responsibility with increasing risk and a greater need for clarity as we grow. Thunder likens the process to moths and a flame: the brighter the light, the greater the attention, the more numerous the temptations.

To address this situation, I continue to make myself open to the feedback of my teachers. I have the responsibility of discernment regarding what they say, but I also have the duty to listen—a duty I discharge with greater and lesser grace.

I also helped create a group of teachers. We are peers in age and experience. We regularly meet in person, over the phone, and via e-mail to discuss important topics ranging from issues with our students to the individual challenges we face. The teachers in this group, many of whom grace these pages in word, idea, energy, and prayer, are a great source of comfort to me, and I am very grateful for their presence in my life.

Choice, to me, means the internal response I make to the external conditions that I am powerless to change. I have a range of options within the given circumstances, and there are tools of development that allow me a measure of freedom over how I respond to those circumstances. I cannot change the weather, but I am responsible for how I feel about it. I cannot change my family, but I can change when or how I am affected by my family.

Ultimately, surrendering to Spirit and the teacher is done solely because we decide to do so. By announcing the intention, the student begins a process where, at some point, he or she must surrender even though the student doubts the teacher and is sure the teacher is wrong, when the act of surrendering runs contrary to long-held and cherished beliefs and understanding. Once the decision is made, the student is free from old, ingrained ways of being that stand between the student and the Spirit.

The student has many reasons, mostly good ones, for avoiding the decision to surrender. The student will have learned that surrender is not safe and will have devised ways of being in control that appear to create safety. However, these ways of being safe must be discarded. Each represents a decision by the student that "Spirit won't keep me safe, so I must do it myself." What once worked and has brought the student to the Spirit no longer works and stands between the student and the Spirit.

Early on, surrender seems easy. We surrender when we agree with the teacher, because of peer pressure, because we don't know a better way, or when we have faith and trust in the teacher. In those situations, it is only control masquerading as surrender. Ultimately, however, the process will lead us to a point where we decide to surrender. We may think surrender is a bad idea; indeed, our whole being may cry out against surrender. Then, we surrender because we decide to do so, with no assurance of safety or a desirable outcome. We jump into the abyss. The student wriggles like a hooked fish as this time becomes imminent. The student will seek distance from the process and from the teacher. Some do so by passively going away; some actively dishonor the teacher; some do both. Whatever method the student chooses will be some type of controlling behavior the student has used in the past to stay safe and secure.

One day my friend Wally approached me and asked to be my student. I perceived him as deluded, turned him down, and suggested he talk to Mary Thunder or someone else. But this kind man persisted and eventually became my first teaching student, because he taught me how to be a teacher.

An attorney I worked with, Dick McCarroll, asked me to handle a suit on sworn account for him. He cautioned me to be careful about the answer that I filed because there were some special rules about sworn accounts at that time. I found a Supreme Court case that quoted an answer and said that this was the proper way to do it. Because the answer that had been used in that case was sufficient, I copied the case, used the exact language of the case in my answer, highlighted the portion of the case that discussed the correct wording, attached a copy of the case to the answer, and sent it to McCarroll for his review with a note that said, "Okay?" He sent back the answer, unread, and the case, unread, with a note that said, "Suit yourself, I was only passing along friendly advice."

In the practice of law, I have often been required to "suit myself." There is always something else that could be done, but some matters simply don't economically justify doing everything that could possibly be done. And I struggle with these questions: What's enough? How much is too much? How much is not enough?

When I was a kid, I used to weed the flower beds, and I'd still face the same question. I'd go in and ask my dad if that was clean enough. Was it enough? He didn't say, "Suit yourself." He said, "Suit me." Although I rebelled against that at the time, there was something comforting about having someone else decide for me. For example, most of us brought up in Christian homes have wondered whether we were saved. But the responsibility for that decision, that state of being, was taken from us because someone told us we were. As we move from youth to adulthood we become our own parent, and we must "suit ourself." So I have kept that sheet of paper from McCarroll because I was really asking him the same question: "Is this enough?" And his answer was, "Suit yourself."

Now I find that if I suit myself about whatever is enough, that is the only way that I can truly learn, because at that point I am living my truth about what I think is enough. If that isn't enough, or if I'm wrong, then I have direct feedback that my view of what was enough in that situation was wrong. I can learn from that; I can learn by the truth being altered. It was also McCarroll who made the same point during trying a jury trial. He said you should always grade your own paper before the jury comes back, and not let them tell you what's enough.

A teacher is a representative of the Spirit, a physical embodiment of what we sometimes perceive as intangible. When we become a student, we announce our intention to begin and continue our process of surrendering to Spirit, which means surrendering to the teacher. I believe that my Lakota friends were surrendering to their teachers when they decided to share ceremony with me.

The word *woLakota* means "peace"—not just peace as an antonym to war, but peace as in peaceful, gentle, a heart-based, strong, inner, self-secure peace. My Lakota friends as a rule are heart driven. Generally, they will feed you before asking why you are hungry. They will laugh with you about your predicament and share some of their own stories long before they pronounce any judgment about why they think you are where you are. If faced with a conflict between justice and compassion, they usually choose the latter. When the guidance of their heart is inconsistent with their beliefs, the beliefs give way to the heart.

My Lakota friends believe that peace is found among the relations. They recognize the interdependence of the relations: we depend on clean air to breathe and fresh water to drink, and our conduct affects both air and water. The Lakota phrase *Aho Mitakuye Oyasin* (Amen to all relations) used at the end of prayer, when the pipe is filled, when the connection is completed, when stones are brought into a hot lodge, when the door of that lodge is opened, in the sun dance, on *hanbleceya* (vision quest), and on and on.

I often think my Lakota friends have shared their ceremony with us out of a place of *Mitakuye Oyasin,* their compassionate view that we all live in the same house and must learn how to live in loving relationship or we will probably die. Understanding that my Lakota friends view the world in relationship terms is critical to having any grasp of my friends and their world. For example, some translate *Lakota* to mean that one acknowledges a relative or family member. In any event, the word has to do with relating to one another, acknowledging each other, being related to others.

An example of the relating piece of the Lakota friendship world are the words used to describe friends. Albert White Hat Sr. has written extensively about Lakota relational words, and I am indebted to him for parts of the following discussion.

In addition to the words for brother and sister, my Lakota friends also have words for male-to-male cousin, male-to-female cousin, female-to-male cousin, and female-to-female cousin. Each describes a relationship. A cousin relationship is considered as significant as the brother and sister relationship. Once you are in the family unit, the *tiospaye,* then you are at least a cousin. Additionally, someone who is close to but not within your *tiospaye* is thought of as a male-to-male friend or a female-to-female friend.

Other examples of the richness of the Lakota language are the words *wicasa* and *winyan.* Although we translate *wicasa,* for example, to mean "man," with my Lakota friends *wica* means "male" and *sa* means "adornment," *sa* being short for *saic'iye,* which means "to dress up." The female cousins of the male who has obtained education, maturity, and responsibility dress him up because they are proud of him.

The *tiospaye* is a group, the *ospaye,* of people who live together. This is the concept of family. Within the *tiospaye,* at least one member has experienced any mistake that will occur in life, and someone has achieved any good one would want to achieve.

The terms for relatives are related to prayer. When a relative greets a relative, that is *wocekiye.* When a relative makes a request to a relative, that is also *wocekiye.* When a group responds to the request, that is *wocekiyapi.* So the word we whites think of as the Lakota word for prayer, *cekiye,* is enlarged by my

Lakota friends to mean asking our relatives, speaking to our relatives or a higher power to the group of the created beings on earth.

Respect for a spouse is shown by the words *maha sanni,* "my other skin." A man might refer to his wife as *winuhca,* a real woman, and a woman would refer to her husband as *wicasa,* a real man. It is a way for each spouse to acknowledge that the other has education, responsibility, knowledge, and experience or wisdom. The word for elder, *wicasa,* refers to an old man whose wisdom has blossomed forth in the final years. A *winuhca* is an old woman whose wisdom has similarly blossomed.

For my Lakota friends, the world and everything in it was created, directly or indirectly, by *inyan. Inyan* was something like the first rock and gave a piece of itself, its *wakan* energy, to create *maka,* the Mother. Over time, the *inyan* gifted more and more of its life to the 405 *oyates,* or people nations, so the people could live. My Lakota friends follow this example when they give a piece of their skin in the sun dance, so the people might live.

When an *oyate* has the *wakan* energy running through it, the *oyate* becomes, in a way, *wakan.* The *wa* is something that is, and the *can* becomes the veins of the body of the people that have the energy of *inyan* running through them.

My Lakota friends recognize the paradox of relationship. We could say, for example, that we are all the same; we all are *wakan,* we all are creations of the energy of *inyan.* But we also can recognize our distinguishing features—that my *oyate* differs from the *tatanka,* or the cottonwood tree. I see this in lodges when we look at the sweat lodge stones, which are all the same, all rocks, yet are also all different in form and size and shape and texture. So when my Lakota friends acknowledge our relatedness, I believe they acknowledge our commonness—that we are all riding on the back of the same turtle without diminishing our unique gifts, all of which are valuable, because without them the tribe, the *tiospaye,* would not survive. They recognize that when we are unkind to one another, we are hurting not just any person but a related person: a cousin, brother, or sister. So my Lakota friends picked me up, a relative, for my good and out of their compassion for the good of the people. We live our lives in community. What we do here affects those there. We are not alone.

Mitakuye Oyasin is such a bedrock view held by my Lakota friends that they have a special place to recognize relatives and a special ceremony to recognize relatives. The South is the place of relationship, and the power of the South is fully expressed in the *hunka* ceremony, the practice of making relatives. For long periods in my life, I was scared of most people and mad at just about everyone else. But the process of being in a sober relationship with the *wakan* has helped heal my view of you. Today I see things differently.

We are remarkable. Our life is a gift of incomparable value. We have the dual charism of mind and heart, the blind paradox of body and soul, the conundrum of life eternal and certain death. We hear of divine love surrounded by illness, starving children, and pain. We experience the grace of inspired paths and watch religious people hurt themselves and hurt others in the name of God. One country produces enough food annually to feed the world three times over, yet sees eighty thousand of its own children die of starvation every year. We build an arsenal of weapons that can destroy us all during an era of peace, and then spend enough to feed those children disarming those weapons. We can move body organs from person to person, yet see people suffer and die from a lack of medical attention. We can now carry eighty or more books on a single disc of plastic, yet produce a hundred thousand children a year who cannot read at a third-grade level. We are a people of contradictions—a living example of what is right and good and holy and wrong and diseased and demonized. The same people who build a home for the aged can drag a man to death behind a truck in the name of God. We are a people searching for a better way at the core and then falling into discord and conflict over exactly how that better way would look.

We are here by divine grace—an expression of creation more vast than we can often see or understand. My limited perception has allowed me to see a love for us that is so profound, so deeply intimate, as to dwarf anything that might stand next to it. And yet our own complexes blind us to that sight and block our view of who and what we are.

I have spent much of my life blinded by my own creations. It took the watery insistence of that love, the compassion and kindness of many, to open my eyes and help me see beauty of the love that is who we are. And now, even as those hurt places in me continue to heal, I spend my time being in love, overflowing with the Spirit that is my nature and my right. I often burst into tears with joy and gratefulness for myself and for you. I jump and dance and wave my hands with the overpowering ecstasy of it all.

John's question "What am I doing here?" sometimes pops into my mind when angry Indians fuss at me for being in, on, or around ceremony. Their fussing hits a sensitive place in me. Ceremony saved my life, so to say that I shouldn't do it because I am white is like telling a diabetic he can't have insulin because he has curly hair. I am certainly not the first to be involved with controversy over receiving the medicine of another culture. Prometheus, for example, gave the medicine of fire to the people and for that transgression was chained to a rock and had his liver pecked at each day by buzzards sent by the gods annoyed by his gift. Nor am I the first to be involved in controversy surrounding my participation in the ceremonial ways of life of another culture. The apostle Paul found that his efforts to take the message of Jesus the Jew to the Gentiles was very controversial and required a special meeting of the disciples to resolve.

Among the Lakota people I find some broad categorical responses to that issue. On the far right are those who believe that white people have no role in ceremony, should not be in ceremony, should not support ceremony, and certainly should not lead ceremony. Next to them on the spectrum are those who believe that white people can support ceremony but do nothing more. Then there are those who believe that whites can support ceremony and perhaps even participate, but there they would absolutely draw the line. Another group would let whites support and participate and even lead ceremony when they have achieved proper training, a knowledge of the culture, and an understanding of the language. On the far left are those who believe that anyone who wishes to can lead ceremony; they wonder what all the fuss is about.

The people who fuss base their claim on the fact that I am not full-blood or enrolled, or that I am white. My Lakota friends make distinctions about whether one is full-blood Lakota or a breed, as in mixed-breed or half-breed. Now, "full-blood" means more than simply 100 percent Native American blood. The term refers to 100 percent Native blood of a particular tribe and band. A person with Lakota and Dakota blood, for example, would be considered a breed, although less of a breed than a person who is mainly Lakota with a little Crow or Apache mixed in. Being full-blood is very rare. More commonly, my Lakota friends are breeds. Breeds can be mixtures of different Native American tribes, but they also might be a mix of Lakota and another ethnic group, such as Mexican or European.

A third category has to do with whether one is enrolled. An enrolled tribal member has a number issued by the Bureau of Indian Affairs identifying the person as a member of a tribe. Different tribes require different blood percentages to become enrolled. One may be a full-blood, yet not be enrolled, or be $1/16$ Cherokee and brought up in a New York penthouse, yet still be enrolled.

Another distinction my Lakota friends sometimes discuss is whether someone is traditional. A traditional person generally follows the "old ways," whatever those are, and is distinguished from everyone else—who presumably believe in something other than the old ways. My Lakota friends also recognize whether someone lives on the "res" or whether someone is a city dweller. Putting all that together, if you are full-blood, enrolled, traditional, and live on the res, you are close to the top. As the other factors change, so does your walking-in-the-door status.

Still another concept is the label "apple," which refers to someone who is red on the outside but white on the inside. Sometimes the word *iyeska* is used here to mean "apple," someone who looks red but speaks white. *Iyeska* is another difficult word because it can also mean a mixed-breed Spirit interpreter. Being an apple destroys all other qualifications; that is, an enrolled full-blood living on the res who is an apple is generally not to be trusted. Some of my Lakota friends say there are reverse apples: white people with red hearts. A Lakota sun dance chief once described me that way, and I rarely have been so touched.

There is a growing thought among some that focusing on blood proportions is not helpful and that the focus instead should be on heritage. Joe Marshall discusses this idea at some length in his excellent book *Dance House*. The term suggests that a full-blood city dweller who lives and acts white, and does not know the stories or the language, may have the blood but lacks the heritage. Personally, I find this concept to be very interesting. Occasionally, Lakotas and other Native Americans will become upset with my participation in ceremony. Often the people who are upset are urban-dwelling Catholic Native Americans who know next to nothing about ceremony, perhaps personally oppose it, and are out of touch with their heritage.

An additional concept discussed among some circles is lineage, which can mean "blood heir," but can also refer to spiritual heirs or descendants or ancestors. I have the spiritual lineage of my teacher Mary Thunder, who claims her lineage from Leonard Crow Dog, Grandpa Wallace Black Elk, and Rolling Thunder, among others. I also stand directly in Leonard's lineage, as I similarly stand with Chief

Charles Chipps and Chief Buddy Red Bow. Further, I have a *hunka* relationship with Buddy, Thunder, Charles, and Horse, all of whom adopted me.

The Lakota idea of nonblood lineage is expressed in the *hunkapi,* or adoption ceremony, wherein one is placed in the ancestors' line by adoption and choice rather than blood. Some of my white friends who become *hunka* relatives think this makes them Lakota, when in fact it does not. This mistake creates ill will among our Lakota hosts and resentment by my white friends. It is enough for me to be in the *hunka* line of these fine people.

The *hunkapi,* or making of relatives, is one of the major sacred ceremonies. My Lakota friends say that the *hunka* rite was a gift of the Creator to establish relations between Lakota and other people of other nations. A consequence of the ceremony is that the *hunka* relations became one.

The *hunkapi* ceremony represents a spiritual principle. The basis of the ceremony quite literally extends a relationship of one person with God to another person. In this way, because both people share a relationship with God, they share a relationship with each other through God.

My Lakota friends say that *hunka* represents a state of peace and oneness through God between two people, two nations, two souls. And that, I believe, is one answer to John's question: What are we doing here? Through *hunka,* the old people are acknowledging a certain peace within themselves and recognizing their oneness with the Creator. And they are extending their peace to a person and a people desperately in need of God's healing touch.

Leonard Crow Dog describes *hunkapi* as creating "a bond stronger than the bond between parent and child, a bond stronger than any physical bond could ever be." He says, "You have to get along with yourself before you can get along with others."

I am the recent adoptee of Charles Chipps, a Lakota medicine man. I was gifted the breath of life and told that the Spirit of his lineage dances in my veins. Charles helped create a space for me at the table of his family, at the table of teachings about how to be in relation to the sacred and the profane, how to be with my cousins (all of us who are created), about ways to be of service to the people.

We are called to serve. It is our nature, as much as the drive to breathe, eat, and sleep. I believe we can no more avoid service than we can another heartbeat. The question is not whether we serve but whom and how we serve. I served my pain for years. I served my misdefinitions of God, my fear, my resentments, and my angers. Those who helped me get sober talked about service as a key to sobriety. Serve God, serve your people, but serve. We are stewards here. We are given things on loan to take care of: our house, our lover, our child, our talents, time, and money. All of it is on loan. Even our life is a gift.

My Lakota friends describe this in the context of medicine. Why the power chooses one but not another is a mystery. The timetable of the power is set to God's watch, and the power itself may leave at any moment. My Lakota friends say that one should act as a good steward of that power, recognizing it as a gift but also as a responsibility to use wisely for the benefit of the community. We have moved away from being good stewards today. We seek individual rewards and recognition, which are not bad per se except that we fool ourselves into thinking we deserve them.

So it is with the *hunka* relation. It is a gift we receive, to sit at the table of my friends' ancestors, to have their breath run through my bones. I have the obligation to be a good steward of my relationship so that perhaps another might receive the charism of grace as I did.

The *hunka* relation ceremony reminds me that we are related, that you are a loved relative of mine, and that we always share the common bond of our life, our death, our joys and sorrows, our faith and doubts, our gifts and challenges. *Hunka* reminds me to be grateful to you and for you, for the work you do, for the love you are. You are a lot less scary when I am loving you, because we have so much in common. You are a lot less scary when I am secure enough in my loving God relationship to celebrate our differences—to recognize and know that our distinctions do not diminish me but rather strengthen the us-ness of the people.

9 SACRED BREATH

INIPI OLOWAN

There's a cold wind blowing outside
Inside the steam warms my bones
As the old man pours the water
Upon the glowing stones

And the Spirit lights are dancing
Inside their native home
Telling us all about our
Loved ones who are gone

And the smell of sage and sweet grass
Is mixing with the steam
And the singer is pounding on the drum
Making prayers as he sings

And the people who have
Crawled into the lodge begin to pray
In their native tongue
All about their ancient way

Across from me is a woman
Who just learned she is with child
She is praying for a blanket
And a place to rest for a while

The man to my left asks
For pity on his life
He asks for health and happiness
For his wife

A little girl is making prayers
For her family and her friends
She asks about her Daddy
When will he be coming home again

Round after round the prayers come
From the old and holy tribe
Who sweat and pray and beat the drum
So we can all stay alive

—Michael Hull

WHITE PEOPLE TRANSLATE *inipi* (sometimes also spelled *initipi*) to mean "sweat lodge." This is a mistranslation but is instructive of how my Lakota friends view this ceremony. The *tipi* part of the word means "house," "home," or "lodge." The *ni* part means "breath" or "breath of the Spirit." It physically refers to what whites call steam. But that explanation is insufficient. Red-hot rocks are brought into the lodge, and water is poured on the rocks. The people believe the rocks are life-giving pieces of the Great Mystery and that water releases the life in the rocks into the lodge. The lodge participants are then enveloped in the life breath of the rock and water. This is what *ni* refers to. So, this is a complicated way of saying that the term "sweat lodge" means "the home of the breath of Spirit." This visible breath is recorded in a song about White Buffalo Calf Woman, which says, "with visible breath she is coming."

An *inipi* looks something like an upside-down bowl. It is generally big enough to hold eight to twelve people. It is made of willow saplings covered with blankets or tarps that keep out light. In the middle of the lodge is a round hole into which are placed heated, glowing stones.

The dirt from the round hole is placed outside the lodge in a mound and becomes the *hocoka,* the altar. Some of my friends call the lodge altar the *unci,* Grandmother. Some of my Lakota friends say that the lodge is a turtle, with the *hocoka* constituting the turtle's head and the lodge itself representing the body. They also say that the inside of the lodge is the womb of the mother, so that when we crawl inside the lodge we rest inside the mother and emerge like a new-born, having been healed by the Spirit's breath and reborn. The line that runs from the lodge door through the *unci* to the fire is called the *inyan chanku,* the path of the sacred rocks.

The lodge itself is half a sphere. Inside the lodge, the other half of the sphere is present, running under the ground, so that we sit inside a great ball. The lodge door generally faces West. But when the flap is closed, you can sometimes see the Spirit breath illuminating the lodge and illuminating Spirit doors in all the Four Directions as well as above and below. Then one knows we are sitting in the middle of the sphere, in the seat of God. Because we sit on the holy ground of God, we have a blanket of fresh sage to purify us for our encounter with the energetic force of the divine.

The rocks are heated in a fire pit. Some of my Lakota friends say that the fire paints the rocks rather than heating them. The rocks are painted in the *peta owi-hankeshni,* the fire without end. When the *oyate* came together in August, a member of the *tiospaye,* called the keeper of the fire, would add his ember to that of the six other bands to start the council fire. When the *tiospaye* left, the keeper would gather an ember from the fire. The keeper had the job of feeding the ember and keeping it alive until the following year. During the year, the keeper would start all the fires from that one ember. In that way, the *oyate* believe that all fires relate to the first and that the ancestors are present through that link. The fire represents the life of the Lakota people and is composed of seven parts: the seven council fires of the seven Lakota bands.

The rocks are placed on a wood cradle, which has four logs running West to East representing the Four Directions. The cradle has a second level of seven logs running North to South representing the seven Lakota bands. The sacred rocks are then placed on the cradle; a conical pyramid of wood is built around the cradle and rocks before this fire is lit.

A horseshoe-shaped four-foot-high dirt wall surrounds the fire pit. The horseshoe is reminiscent of Crazy Horse. Leonard Crow Dog had his children place their handprints on our horseshoe when he came to the Lone Star sun dance. Their handprints connected our fire to his, confirmed our *hunka* lineage, and signified the presence of the people at our dance.

The rocks are called *inyan wakans* or *tunkasilas*. We whites interpret *tunkasila* to mean "grandfather." While accurate, the translation can be incomplete. The *tunka* refers to the first being, the first rock, from which life was given to all the relations. *Sila* refers to being the son of, the child of, the descendant of (the relation of, in this instance) the *tunka*. So here, *tunkasila* refers to the rock as being related to the first rock, the creation. So, in a very literal sense, each rock is a piece of God.

After the people and stones are in the lodge, a water bucket is brought in, a flap door is closed, and cool water is placed on the hot rocks, producing hot steam similar to a sauna. Water is poured on the male *tunkasilas*. Water is the Lakota life-giving feminine principle of life. The male *tunkasila* is infused with the heat of the ancestors. These three elements—the spirit of creation, the spirit of life, and the spirit of the ancestors—intertwine to create the breath of life for the people in the home of the Spirit. All of this is going on within the simple phrase "sweat lodge."

A lodge generally has four doors, or rounds. A round begins when the flap is closed and ends when the flap is opened. Each round has a purpose. For example, the first round is generally used to acknowledge the Creator and its creations, to honor the pipe, and to set the stage for the purpose of the lodge. The second and third rounds are generally prayer and healing rounds. The last round is one of prayer, gratitude, and gift giving.

In addition to prayers, most rounds also include *olowans*, songs. The songs are ancient, vision-gifted expressions of the relationship between the Creator, the created, and the Spirit. Some songs have words and might declare what the Creator has done. Some songs give voice to the needs of the created. And some songs declare what the Spirit is doing in a given situation.

The songs carry an energy with them. The energy makes it almost impossible to learn the song unless one's personal energy level is at least consistent with that of the song. As we struggle to learn a song, energetic healing occurs and allows us to increase our energy level. Then, suddenly, the song becomes easy to learn.

It is a lovely picture. In the presence of the ancestors, the people bring a holograph of the first creation into the womb of the Mother, where the people sit suspended in a holy herb in the center of creation next to the seat of God.

The *inipi* is one of the major sacred ceremonies. Most of my Lakota friends agree that the people used it before White Buffalo Calf Woman brought the *chanupa,* the sacred pipe, to the people. The *chanupa* became the foundation of the *inipi* after it was brought to the people. Nowadays, if my Lakota friends run a lodge without a pipe they call it a cowboy lodge.

Inipis have different purposes. Some are for purification; for example, there are four days of purification lodges before the sun dance begins. I first learned about purification lodges in what I call the lodge of melted knees. At my first sun dance, I sat in for my first of four purification *inipis.* That particular lodge is big enough for two rows of people—an inner and outer circle. I was on the inside, right next to the rock pit. In fact, I am so tall that part of my knees and my toes were hanging into the rock pit. Each time water was poured onto the stones, steam rose to burn my knees and toes. I was sure I was going to die. I decided to leave the lodge and was about to do so when Indie, who was pouring the water, said that anyone who wanted to could leave the lodge but would then not be allowed to dance.

I was determined to dance and made a critical decision. I decided to surrender myself to this new God I have written about and to signify that surrender by my sacrifice of the dance. I decided that if I died in the lodge, I would, but I would die before turning my back on my spiritual commitment. I decided then and there to make God my most important commitment—the center of my life—and that I would allow no interference with that from anyone, especially myself.

Dr. George DeLeon, director of the Center for Therapeutic Community Research and professor of psychiatry at New York University, describes this decision as acting from a place of inner motivation. Dr. DeLeon, an expert in the field of treatment for substance abusers, says that there are ten stages of recovery. One of those stages is external motivation. With external motivation, one opts for treatment because of an external factor: a court sentence, threat of job loss, pressure from family. The person chooses treatment because it is what he or she should do but doesn't want to do.

With internal motivation, the person seeks treatment because he or she *wants* to not because it is a should. The person may want to for positive reasons (to feel better, achieve, be a good provider) or for negative reasons (to avoid feeling bad). But whether positive or negative, the motivation is internal.

This matter of internal motivation is important because it is a process of choosing, of deciding for. In the process of cleaning out our God hole, we decide against—we are taking things out and discarding them. Internal motivation is a process of deciding for (deciding for God, for sobriety), because I want to.

I wish I could say that as a result of my decision the lodge became cooler and my body was no longer burnt. I cannot. I thought maybe it was not really so hot. Maybe it was all in my mind. But Mato, a very tough man sitting next to me, asked for permission to move to the back row. He said that he had a plastic knee and it was starting to melt.

After the third round, Indie said that each of us would be given a dipper of water to drink. That would cool me down, I thought. The first man got his dipper and poured it on the stones, asking for blessings on Mother Earth and burning my knees. As did the second man and the third. When it was my turn, like a fool I poured my water on the stones.

I survived the lodge. Crawling out, I made it about two steps and collapsed on the ground, where I lay for some time unable to move and wondering whether that was what surrender would look like for the rest of my life.

A lodge is a place of prayer. My Lakota friends taught me to pray "I pray to joyfully accept each moment as it comes. To see past the pain and fear to the beautiful and perfect child of God that we are . . . to be that reflection for others and to see that in myself." A kind of beautiful simplicity comes from praying in a lodge. The lodge itself is dark, so the praying voices are just that—voices coming out of nowhere, like the different voices I sometimes hear in my mind. I sometimes think that the combined voices of all the prayers represents my mind, or the committee of my mind.

I laughed when I first heard someone refer to his mind as the committee because it was so true. In any situation, the committee had the voices of my father and mother, my child, my preacher, my coach, and a host of others all shouting to have me hear them. The lodge helps me silence those voices so that I can hear God's voice.

There is a beauty to prayers in a lodge. People say only what they feel is most important, what they are willing to say in the heat. Sometimes there is a type of irony in a lodge, as when someone gives a ten-minute prayer about compassion while the rest of us hope he will soon get some. As my Lakota friends say, "When praying, always remember the person in front of you (who has yet to pray) and the person behind you (who has already prayed)." Because of the darkness, there is a kind of anonymity to the prayers. This may allow people to say prayers on behalf of many others with similar problems or perhaps on behalf of all of us, since we are all affected by those problems. The anonymity also lets people be more honest, as if the darkness somehow is a mask that lets us speak openly about what troubles us.

The lodge is certainly a place of humility. Of course, I keep on getting a lot of lessons about pride and humility and learning my place in the world. Harry Charger told me that my relation to power was a test I would face on the Red Road, and his remarks have been prophetic. Not long after I had danced at Leonard Crow Dog's for the first year, I found myself in Lodge Grass, Montana, in a Crow sweat lodge. The Crows and Lakotas have a long and fairly contentious history. The Lakotas are sworn enemies of the Crows as a culture, and I confess that I had a bit of an attitude about the whole lodge as I went to it. The lodge was in the dead of winter, after a blizzard, and we had to dig out the snow to find the lodge. My opinions about the Crows were sharpened when the fire to heat the rocks was lit in what I thought was an improper way (as if I knew anything), and I had to suppress laughter when all the men stripped and crawled into the lodge. The Crow men I was with were all under six feet, and I am six feet seven inches. The lodges are built to accommodate the smaller Crow people, and as a consequence I had to hunch over. The Crow men, as soon as they got inside the lodge, found spots to lie down on the floor of the lodge. Well, being a sun dancer, pledge and all, I wasn't about to lie down in a lodge, so I sat up. The men all talked around me in Crow, the door shut, the man pouring the water splashed seven dippers of water on some of the hottest stones I've ever seen, and I thought my skin was going to boil off my body. But I sat very, very still and endured the heat, and finally the door was open.

Now, it is my experience that the succeeding rounds are often not quite as hot as the first, so I was pretty sure I could make it. While the door was open the men offered me a spot on the lodge floor to lie down, and I, in my pride and stupidity, said no. The door closed, and the fellow promptly poured eleven dippers on the stones. By the time the eleventh dipper was hitting the stones, I was diving for the ground, lying on top of all these Crow men, trying to wiggle my way into place. These men were kind enough to scoot over, all the while laughing and talking away in Crow, when I discovered an additional problem. Because I was so tall I could lie down, but the lodge was not built for people my height, so my knees were on the ground but my feet were up in the air. Now, the soles of my feet were really not accustomed to all the heat, and I was crying like a baby when those nice Crow men, the ones I had thought so poorly of just a few moments before, were kind enough to open the door. They all had a good laugh at my expense, and I was reminded once again of how pitiful and weak I am, and how pride gets me every time.

In addition to purification and prayer, the lodge is also a place of healing. The lodge is a place to move past blocks to the love we are. My friend LaJeune reminded me that there is an alternative reality. She repeated, as if it were mantra, "There is more. There is a piece you are missing. You can do this. Whatever the question, the answer is love. Whatever the problem or concern, the response is love—to be in love, to be loved, to be loving."

The spirit of loving appears in lodges sometimes as a blue-green sparkly light with a low hum. Jo Todd first explained the sounds and colors I heard and saw. She told me that I was not crazy and these things could be used to heal. She taught me to channel, to understand energy, to meditate, to sense the energy in objects and people, to see, and to admit to what I know. Jo helped me understand that although energy is spiritual, it is not spiritual per se. Energy is a physical fact, a truth of our world. It is also a physical fact that energy imbalances are associated with sickness; that is, if you find one you are likely to find the other. Healing can sometimes be accomplished by energetically adjusting the imbalance.

We are like infants when it comes to our understanding of energy. We all manipulate it and use it, but we do so unconsciously and often with grossly inefficient methods of operation. Energy healing works better on some problems and not as well on others. For example, if someone has a leg fractured in three places, you could channel energy all day, and that leg would likely still be broken at the end of the day. However, you could channel energy to a broken leg set in a cast for days on end and help the patient be more comfortable, speed the healing process, and perhaps help produce a more complete healing. This is not to say that nothing can be done to heal the fractured leg. If God needs that leg to be healed that day, then you can bet it will happen, but that kind of healing is Spirit based and is not energy dependent as I am using the term here.

Energy has two essential components: light and sound. The gospel of John says, for example, "In the beginning was the Word." A Zen koan reads, "If you blot out sense and sound, what do you hear?" The Upanishads offer, "Sound is your essence." And Sufi Khan said, "Sound is the source of all manifestation . . . the knower of the mystery of sound knows the mystery of the whole universe." The authors of Genesis recognized that God spoke and then there was light. I have heard the sound of energy for as long as I can remember. The sound is something like the humming of a high-voltage electric wire. Put enough different voltages together, and you hear the sound of God: OM.

I have seen the energy around people for years. This was not especially helpful until Jo Todd appeared, because I did not know what to do with what I saw, like someone in a blizzard having a match but not knowing the concept of fire.

Energy also has several features that are in some respects diagnostic, namely, color, speed, and coarseness or fineness. Energy can also have a smell, and we can develop a sense of energy, a kind of experiential knowing about the condition of the energy. With experience, one can use information about the qualities of energy to diagnose and treat illness.

Ceremony also has energy lines. In the sun dance, I see lines of energy in the arbor indicating how the ceremony is to be run. When the dancers are placed on those lines of energy, the wheel turns faster, the dancers and supporters receive more healing, and the benefit of the ceremony to the people increases.

The overall movement of the energy creates an energy field, or aura. I can generally find four on most people: one several inches from the body and the succeeding ones farther away from the body. How many aura fields a person has, and their texture and color and so forth, also are diagnostic of that person's health. Our energy presentation has a color, reflecting a certain vibrational speed that we experience in terms of time. Most of us in the Western culture, or at least most whites in Western culture, live in our third energy center. This is generally thought of as the place of the intellect, where we think about things and make decisions. For some of us, it is where we attempt to control things. Sometimes we experience events as moving very fast around us, or we ourselves are moving much more slowly; that is an indication that we have moved above or below our normal energy center and are operating in a different frequency.

Sometimes we live in ceremony time, what some call blue time. Blue time is generally related to the fifth, or throat chakra—the place we speak from, the place of prophecy. Blue time is generally considerably faster than the yellow time we normally operate from. One rather striking example of blue time occurred on one of my trips with Mary Thunder to the Yucatan and the Mayan ruins.

We liked to go to a place called Palenque. Thunder believes that the Mayan world was the center of our world and that Palenque was the heart of the Mayan world. There is a tomb at Palenque where you have to climb up several steps to reach the top of the pyramid, only to walk down more steps to get to the tomb. Thunder believes that she and her husband, Horse, are related to the king and queen who were buried inside the tomb. We had been hoping that someone of Mayan decent would show up to guide us on an after-dark tour of the ruins when a fellow fitting that description appeared. He agreed to meet us at the pyramid after the moon had risen and give us a tour of the ruins. Thunder wanted all of us to climb to the top of the particular burial pyramid and then for some of us to crawl down into the pyramid and do a pipe ceremony honoring the deceased king and queen.

In preparation for our meeting with the Mayan guide, our group had a meeting at which Augusta Ogden, another of Thunder's students, gave each of us a piece of jade. She reported that the person from whom she had obtained the jade described it as originally appearing on a necklace, which was one of the artifacts recovered from the tomb of the king and queen at Palenque. So she gave each of us a piece of this jade, which we wore or put in a pocket in preparation for our visit.

When we arrived, the Mayan guide took us on an after-hours, after-dark tour of the ruins, which we had visited numerous times on other occasions. We then sat at the foot of the tomb for a long time while the Mayan guide told us that many pieces of jade jewelry had been discovered in the tomb when the burial site itself was uncovered. He further related that the various pieces of jade had gone to the museum in Mexico City. The guide reported that several years earlier, the government of Mexico had fallen on hard times and needed a loan to keep itself from going into default. The government had no collateral for a loan of the size it needed, and consequently it had permitted the lender to burglarize and steal several national treasures in the Mexican museum, including several pieces of the jade jewelry recovered from the tomb. Of course, all of us were skittish as we heard this story, thinking that this Mayan knew that we each had a piece of this jewelry in our pocket.

When the guide finished his story, all of us climbed to the top of the pyramid, and several of us prepared to climb back down into the interior of the pyramid to do the ceremony. Thunder elected to stay at the top of the pyramid. She sat there with others and lit a cigarette while I, with Horse and several others, including the guide, proceeded down into the interior depths of the pyramid. We got to the bottom and said some words and had a ceremony. As we were there in the bottom of the pyramid we began to feel an enormous shake. We thought it was an earthquake and feared that the pyramid was about to close in on us. So we completed the ceremony and climbed up to the top as quickly as we could. When we burst out Thunder looked over at us and asked sharply, "What's wrong?" It turned out that she still had the same cigarette she had lit when we started climbing down, and about half of it was left. Our perspective was that we had been in the bowels of the tomb for almost an hour during the ceremony, but according to her cigarette "watch," we had been down there only about three minutes. We later learned that at approximately the same time when we were down at the bottom of the tomb feeling a quake, a tidal wave had hit Japan, the putative burgling lender.

That was an example of blue time. The Mayan guide was in front of us when we climbed the stairs. We thought he came out ahead of us, but the group at the top of the stairs could not confirm our story. We never saw him again. He never came up from the bottom of the tomb.

My Lakota friends believe in keeping energy moving. Indeed, when Albert White Hat Sr. talks about *wakan,* meaning "moving energy," he expresses the belief my Lakota friends have about the importance of maintaining the movement of energy. In fact, they often speak of someone who is depressed or someone who has low energy as being someone who has allowed his or her energy to become stagnant. My friends often point to sickness as an arrest of movement or as energy that is simply not moving at all. They also say that if you move from one energetic level to another, or one way of operating to another, the period of transformation or transference is often accompanied by sickness—a symptom of a change in the speed or movement of energy. At those times, my Lakota friends say it is especially important to keep the energy moving so you don't get caught in the transition and lose the benefit of the exchange.

For example, when I finished the first sun dance at Paradise and was on my way to dance at Grandpa's, we stopped off at the Chipps's house. I was as sick as I have ever been. I was running at both ends, had a high fever, felt really miserable, was extremely dehydrated and weak, and was sunburned. At times I thought I was near death, and at other times I wished I was. We pulled up to the Chipps's place which is outside of Wanbli, South Dakota. At the time, Grandma Chipps was living in a house made of railroad ties. We arrived at the Chipps land, with me being so sick, and Grandma Chipps immediately gave me the job of bringing in the dishwater. I thought this would be a simple task of turning on a tap and filling up water to wash dishes with, but I was mistaken. There they have water that has to be hand pumped from an old well. The hand pump to the well was about fifty yards away from the house, downhill. So getting the dishwater entailed walking down the hill, filling up two five-gallon pails of water, and then carrying them both back up the hill to the house. I had to make several stops both ways to run to the outhouse because of my various ailments. Of course, the more this went on the madder I got. I was spilling water on my pants, on my feet, and in my shoes. My socks got wet, and I was just miserable. All of this was highlighted by the fact that when I finally made it back to the house, the buckets were only about half full, and Grandma would fuss at me for being so careless with their precious water. Then she would accidently bump the buckets over and fuss at me again for putting them in her way, and I would have to go back down to the well to fill up more buckets of water. This must have gone on for half a day. I was fit to be tied when Grandma said, "Well, you're through." Grateful and relieved, I was about to crawl back to my van to fall deep into my own misery when Grandma said, "But you might stop by and ask Phillip whether he needs anything."

Now, Phillip had just returned from Eagle Butte with a bunch of sweat stones the size of watermelons. He seemed glad to see me and was certainly grateful for my help. He handed me a big sledgehammer and told me to start busting all these rocks. There I was, busting these rocks, and between swings of the sledge-hammer running over to the outhouse and making it most of the time. About sundown, I finally finished with the rocks and was grateful to crawl back into my own misery when Godfrey Chipps arrived to announce that his brother Charles would be running a sweat lodge.

So we crawled into a tiny lodge with more rocks than seemed humanly possible, red-hot. I didn't have enough sense not to go in the lodge, and fortunately there were enough people in there to hold me up. After we survived that lodge, I crawled out and was hoping I could make it back into the van and collapse into my own misery, Charles said Godfrey would be running a *yuwipi* that night and we were all invited.

In a *yuwipi*, you sit up most of the night; you can't leave the room once you're inside, you pray the whole time, there is a healing involved, and at the end of it you have a feast, which includes soup, coffee, and donuts. Now I was locked inside a totally black room with a lot of singing going on, hoping I didn't have to race to the outhouse, because I certainly couldn't get out.

Of course, by the time I finally did make it back to the van and collapse in my own misery, I wasn't nearly as sick. Some of the illness lingered on for several days, but I was much better. The next day I could move through much of the energetic transformation that was happening as a result of the dance.

Jo Todd taught me how our energy lines connect us to others. Her focus was on creating or maintaining healthy relations with others through heart connections. Later, Mary Thunder showed me how those energy lines also maintain unhealthy relationships with people and things and institutions and principles. The first ceremony Thunder gave me was medicine to cut the energetic cords we have with others who take our energy and slow our development.

After Thunder taught me how to disconnect, she then taught me how to connect the people in the ceremony. Lakota ceremony emphasizes connection. The connections are like conduits or straws through which energy flows. For example, I was connected to my pipe when I first received it. Now, I know a method to connect to the pipe as I fill it. We connect to participants in the *inipi*. We connect to people through our pipe. We establish a connection in the lodge to people we put out on *hanbleceya*. We connect to people when we do the *hunka* ceremony. The line from the tree to our chest is a visible symbol of our connection. I experience an energetic connection to the people I pierce. In short, connection is important.

One interesting consequence of leading ceremony is becoming connected to ceremonial participants. The connection resembles a golden thread. Through the cord, the leader knows and experiences the thoughts, feelings, dreams, and experiences of the ceremonial participant. If he or she is sad, so am I; if tired, I am exhausted; if laughing, I have the giggles. Being connected to many people creates multiple feelings, so it can be interesting to feel angry, upset, sick, amorous, giggly, and sad all at the same time.

Connection is not limited to ceremony. We connect with people all the time. A handshake, a kiss, a thought, harsh or kind words, and all of our everyday normal activities create connections. If you feel tired around certain people, you are likely being drained by them. If certain people pep you up, you may be draining them.

Connection occurs from our heart to another's, and also head to head, loin to loin, and in many other ways. It is especially significant that we are connected to everyone we have ever slept with. When we do the math and see that they are connected to everyone they ever slept with, it soon becomes as if we are all holding hands. We connect to each other and to the Spirit in lodges. In the better lodges we become of one mind, one body, one heart, one Spirit.

One consequence of connection is that we can become dependent on another person for our energy, for our source of force. Once we see connection in that way, jealousy and codependency become easier to understand.

Ceremony helps us disconnect from old energy lines, from lines we no longer use or need, that keep the focus off God and on people. Ceremony helps us to connect with God as our source and then to share that love with others through our God-directed heart connection.

After the disconnect ceremony, some interesting things happen. The next day a person will get all sorts of unexpected phone calls from people who are not even sure why they are calling. This shows that their connection has been cut, and they are attempting to reestablish it.

Ceremony has energetic consequences. When I explain this, I use the analogy of glasses and water to illustrate the point. We begin life like a water glass. Our glass is small, like a fruit juice glass. Our glass of water is like our container of energy, our aura. If we go through life unaware, then we end our life with a glass about the same size as the one with which we started. Awareness has a tendency, although it does not come with a guarantee, that the size of our glass will increase over time. The quality of our life can affect the condition of our glass. For example, those of us who did a lot of downers have a water glass with a lot of holes in it. Depressed people who have no energy have holes in the glass. Those of us who did a lot of uppers have a very rigid glass. People who are "bouncing off the walls" have a rigid glass. Other life decisions can affect our glass. Smoking, for example, wipes out the glass, and we must use energy to reform it. Some people who smoke do so because they have an abundance of energy and find that smoking will help them get rid of it. Traumatic experiences can affect our glass, creating holes where holes did not exist, or "shutting us off from the world"—a condition of emotional trauma that indicates a rigid glass. People with a lot of energy and a lot of holes leak everywhere, and we say that they have no boundaries. People with closed minds have rigid glasses. Our language is replete with similar examples.

A consequence of the condition of our glass is that water is used in service to our issues instead of in service to the Creator. Where we have holes, the water leaks out and can't be used. Where we're rigid, the water bounces around inside the glass and can't get out. So one way it gets out, but it's not used; the other way it can't ever get out. In either case, it is not used.

Water goes into the glass. Water is energy. Our glass becomes filled with water through life, through our connection to Spirit, to the divine. Many things create water: exercise, emotional attachment, divine connections, substance use (which creates a kind of artificial water), sexual relations, fantasies. Fantasies are an especially interesting example. People who fill their glass with fantasies fill it with nothing and are locked inside the glass without energy to get out. That is one reason why healing them is so difficult. The glass is rigid, and the attention is focused on nothing. Healing requires knocking a hole in the glass and bringing enough energy into it to promote an awareness of the nothingness that is there. My substance abuse counselor friends describe "knocking a hole" as an intervention.

If we go through life in a state of unawareness, we end our life with a haphazard flow of water and a quality of water created by chance, not choice. Awareness gives us the opportunity to improve the quality, flow, and consistency of water.

In addition to wholeness or rigidity of the glass itself, we do things with the water we have. For example, our stuff—our resentments, worries, fears, jealousies, emotions that some call bad and the New Agers call "negative"—all consume a little of our water. They hold onto our water and use our water. Since the water is being used for those purposes, it cannot be used for other purposes, such as the healing of our selves or of others, or being of service to God and others, or being in love. It is the nature of the water to be used, and the water is neutral about how it is used. It is our choices that design the use of water.

For example, jealousy can blow a hole in our water glass. Jealousy is a perversion of the heart. It means in part that I am looking to a limited number of people—or perhaps only one person—to satisfy my water needs. Since we need water to live, we can become very dependent upon someone else to satisfy our needs. If they don't, our needs will not be satisfied, and a need by definition must be satisfied if we are to live.

We can also use our water to make others dependent on us. If they believe they need our water, we become important in their eyes. In some sense, this dependency relationship protects us from our fear of death. When our self-esteem is low, our fear of death increases, and we will latch on to someone else with whom, by association, we perceive we look better, thereby increasing our self-esteem. As our self-esteem increases, our fear of death decreases.

Our addictions, compulsions, and habits both use water and affect the flow of water. So, if we act out of our addictions, our water is flowing to support that choice and is again unavailable for other flows that support love, being in love, and acting out of love.

People try to take our water, especially when they see that we have an abundance of it. People commonly report returning from ceremony only to get into a big unexpected fight with a loved one or a coworker or a neighbor. We tell people leaving our ceremonies to watch this because it is a sign that someone has recognized the infusion of water we got in ceremony and wants to possess it.

The taking of water also occurs when we give and give. People will continue to take, but it is our responsibility to monitor our water level and keep from giving so much that we run out of water. One of our lessons is learning how to give responsibly, at the direction of Spirit and not our ego, so that we have a reserve of water available for use in service to the Spirit.

Our health is a function in part of our water level. Health does not distinguish between a lack of water caused by jealousy and a lack of water caused by being of too much service to others. What our health sees is not enough water, and it takes steps to correct the imbalance.

Commitment to awareness promotes growth and healing of our water and our container. Participation in ceremony, for example, promotes growth. Ceremony is like water being poured into our glass—energy pours out of the holes, healing them. When our holes are healed, then our water glass begins to fill with water/energy, raising the water level to the next hole, until the whole glass is mended. When the glass is empty, then we go back to ceremony and are refilled.

As the holes in our glass begin to heal and our rigid areas become more flexible; as we surrender our negative emotions, addictions, and unhealthy habits; and as we learn to become responsible for the water, three things happen. We can obtain and retain more water, the water we have is more available to use in service to the Creator, and the flow of the water can become consistent with love, being in love, and being loved. How much and the quantity of what we are refilled with I believe is dependent on the purpose and the use to which we put the energy we were previously given. I also believe that over time, if we continue to use the energy wisely, we develop a residue of energy, and so long as we continue to participate in ceremony we always have some residue left over. I think that the residue goes away at the beginning. We don't have a residue; we are cleaned out.

As our glass heals, we trade up, getting bigger and bigger glasses, and then one day we become bigger than a glass and more like a pool fed by an eternal spring. And just as in nature, as we become the pool, the environment around the pool becomes inviting so that other life-forms of beauty begin to surround the pool—other trees and grasses and flowers and animals and fish, all being fed by the eternal spring through the hollow bone that is our pool.

The water itself is impersonal and completely personal at the same time: impersonal in that it loves and serves everyone equally, personal in that it loves me in particular very much.

I learned a few things by sitting through lodges. There are practical things such as where to sit. There is a *catku wanku,* or place of honor, which is opposite the door, next to the rocks, and across from the fire. Then there is the door person inside the lodge, who also tends to be the singer. There are questions about sitting on the inside row next to the rocks, where there is more dry heat, or on the outside away from the rocks, where there is more steam heat. There is a job being firekeeper and one who watches the door. This job is important, and participants do well to cultivate a friendship with the firekeeper. When you call for the door, it is the firekeeper who opens it, and he actually doesn't have to open it if he doesn't want to. We who were sweating in the lodge were taught to pray in a certain order. We were taught to pray for the elders and then the children, family, friends, and ourselves last, if at all. I also spend the time listening to the lodge leader singing songs and to the singer singing songs, and trying to learn them, and learning small ways to help regulate the heat in the lodge, such as covering hot areas with sage water and being careful not to move when it gets really hot.

After I had sat through what seemed like a few thousand lodges, someone asked me to pour water in a lodge. That was a whole different experience. I was pretty nervous the first time. I wanted to be careful not to hurt anybody with the steam and not to take too long. But as I moved into the role of being a water pourer, things began to change. First, I had new battles with my own sense of pride and humility. I worked to remember that I was doing this as a servant of the people and not as a leader. The second challenge was to respond to people's own reactions to me. Some people just assumed that I had "big shot ideas" and was more difficult to deal with, and then others became almost like lodge groupies and began to hang around me. One interesting thing that happens in lodges is that as we sit through each ceremony, the quality of our own energy begins to improve somewhat, and people begin to be attracted to it and want to try to take it from us in whatever ways they usually take energy. Some do that by trying to provoke fusses; some do it through sexual relationships. So I would have all these people, both male and female, who suddenly found me attractive although they had never found me attractive before. I was flattered about this for a long time but finally recognized that it really was not personal and had nothing to do with me, and I had to tell people that regrettably they'd probably get over it.

I also began to develop my own sense of rules about the lodges I ran. For example, it became clear to me over time that I am responsible for my lodges and everything that happens in them. The second rule I developed was the absolute prohibition from having a physical relationship with anyone who comes to my lodges that did not begin before. Sexual relations can become so odd when the energy gets stirred up in ceremony that it is well nigh impossible to conclude whether the attraction is energy related or ceremony related. The better course of conduct for us is simply to not have any relationships like that at all. It has actually helped, I think, because it has made me a person my group perceives as being relatively safe.

The first time I ran a lodge on the reservation was an odd experience. A lot of the people who come to the reservation are urban Indians who are only recently discovering ceremony. Often, although the ceremony is Lakota in style, they are not Lakota at all, or if they are, they are not fluent in their language. So there would be me, a white guy, leading a lodge on the reservation with full-blood or mixed-breed Native Americans with less knowledge about the ceremony or the songs or even their own language than I had. This created some interesting dynamics that we have all had to work through.

I learned about energy in a lodge through an old friend named Jane. We had sobered up together and spent a lot of time together on the road with Thunder. She was diagnosed with breast cancer, had tried alternative methods of healing, and was scheduled to undergo a mastectomy in a couple of days. She asked me to conduct a healing lodge for her, and I did. Jane did most of the work, holding the pipe and praying. The rest of us sat in the lodge and also prayed for her. In particular, I asked that Jane receive a healing from her breast cancer and that she not need the mastectomy. The lodge was pretty exhausting, and we all crawled out very tired that night. When Jane went to the doctor the next Monday, she asked him to do one last test before proceeding with the surgery. He did, and the cancer was gone. He repeated the test, and the cancer was still gone. I can't claim any real credit for this, and my own reaction was somewhat interesting. On the one hand, I accepted the verdict as a matter of fact, a natural outcome of the prayers we had made. I was just as surprised as Jane and the rest of us at this outcome.

I don't want to suggest that people are always cured in the lodge. I once asked Buddy Red Bow about it:

"Can you teach me how to heal folks?"

"Ain't much to tell. When folks are sick, you can love them, pray with them, and be a hollow bone so Grandfather can work on them through you."

"If I do that, will they get well?"

"Hoss, you can't go predicting who gets well. Some do and some don't, and only the Great Spirit knows why."

Purification, prayer, healing—all of these are concerned with people. We learn about relational healing from the lodge. For example, my secretary once said that a federal prison chaplain was on the phone. The chaplain told me that the Native Americans in his prison had asked me to come to the prison, build a lodge for them, and sweat with them. I told the chaplain that I was sure he was mistaken—I doubted that the brothers wanted to sweat with a white guy. He said he would check, but would I please come to the prison to meet with the men.

I talked to Leonard Crow Dog about it and he said I should go. I asked, "What do I say when they ask about me being white? What happens when they say 'What are you doing here?'" He said, "Go and listen to Spirit."

When I cleared security and walked into the room with the eight Native American prisoners, I realized the chaplain had forgotten to mention the color of my skin. They were quiet for a while. Then one fellow said, "Are you Indian?" So I explained that although I might have a little Native blood, I was a white guy. I explained that my father's family had escorted the Cherokee from Georgia to Oklahoma on the Trail of Tears, and that my mom's family was possibly Kiowa and Cherokee.

"So," they said, "if you are a white guy, what are you doing here? How did you learn?" I explained about sweats and *hanbleceya* and Leonard.

"How do you know Leonard," they asked? I explained about dancing with Leonard at Paradise. I explained that Leonard had just left my house on his way to meet Leonard Peltier at Leavenworth Prison in Kansas. This news perked up a few of my cousins, but one fellow said, "How do we know Leonard was at your house? And why are you here, anyway?"

The Spirit spoke to me and I said, "Look, I'll tell you one story, and when I finish, if you don't think Leonard was at my house, or if you think I should leave because I am white, just say so and I will be glad to leave." And they agreed.

"Leonard," I said, "was having trouble seeing Peltier at Leavenworth. The warden wanted him to take a drug test." All the cousins nodded. "What did Leonard do?" "Well," I said, "Leonard said he would take the test, but only if the warden held the cup." We laughed for a long time about that, and no one said anything else about skin color.

The next time I came I brought willow, rocks, tarps, firewood, and tools for building the lodge. The guards were a little nervous watching us bring all that stuff through their security gate. I walked in behind the stuff wearing a name tag with the title "Spiritual Advisor," which my Lakota prison friends had given me.

We marched out into the middle of the prison yard, which was surrounded by two fences topped with concertina wire. We saw the guards in towers spread along the fence with guns pointed at us. We stood next to the exercise yard where the men were lifting weights, and we started building a sweat lodge. And while the sweat lodge was being built we prepared a fire pit, put the stones in the pit, and started the fire. When the lodge was built, we covered it with blankets and tarps, brought the hot rocks in, brought the water in, stripped, and crawled inside the lodge.

I must say that I was a little nervous being inside a pitch-black place with a bunch of rapists and murderers. I didn't know if they were going to kill me because I was a white guy running an Indian sweat or if they were just going to kill me because they liked to kill people. What I knew for sure was that these fellows were never out of sight of the prison guards for long, and we were now going to be inside a pitch-black place for a couple of hours. Also it was really strange to look out the door of this lodge, this church so ancient no one can accurately identify its origins, and see past the fire to a double row of fences with concertina wire and guns pointing at us. I don't know how those fellows make it day after day praying for the people.

What I do know is that I was given another chance to love, to learn to love, to channel God's love, and to find out where my own obstacles to love were located. I was afraid of these fellows. It took a long time to remember that they were just people like you and me, that their conduct had been less than they themselves had desired, and that we were all suffering from the same disease, which is a lack of love, whose symptoms had simply been different from mine.

While I was sweating the men in prison, I also got a call from another fellow who asked me to come up to Waco and run lodges for a group there. The fellow who called was gay, and he held a gathering on the weekend once a month for other gay men to talk about being gay, coming out of the closet, and relating to friends and family and children and work. He was trying to organize the gathering along spiritual lines and thought that a Saturday lodge for the men to pray would be helpful. Now, we didn't cater much to gay people where I grew up; I was quite leery about heading up to Waco to do these lodges. But again, I checked with Thunder and Leonard, and although they had plenty of fun with my discomfort, they told me to go, so I did.

A group of us rode up to Waco and built lodges. As we were filling the pipe, I looked up and noticed a bunch of gay men standing around me naked as jaybirds.

It's probably a gross generalization to say that all gay men are handsome, but frankly, these men were. Every one of them was handsome, well built, and well endowed, and their rear ends were only a few feet away from me. It's hard to describe whether I felt more discomfort crawling in that lodge with those gay men or with the murderers and rapists in the federal prison.

The Spirit told me that these men didn't really know much about lodges and I didn't know much about being around gay men, so it was a chance for both of us to learn. In particular, the Spirit told me to address the various "rules" I had learned about lodges and discover whether they were based on spiritual principles or whether they came from a place of tradition, custom, or social usage out of the culture of the lodges.

Those gay men taught me a lot about love. The personal decisions and sacrifices they had made to remain true to themselves were staggering, and I have the greatest respect for their decisions. Those men loved me through my own discomfort until I was able to remember once again that we are all just people, that God loves all of us, that that is what mattered and the rest is just details.

One day we held a completion lodge with the gay men and expressed our thanks for gifts given, lessons learned, and things given away. I gifted the folks there, as is my custom, and was packing up preparing to leave when the men gave me a gift. The gift was symbolized by a necklace the men had made to resemble the Lambda flag. It came with a title, something I treasure: Honorary Gay Guy.

The gift of those lodges is that before I worked with them, I saw those groups of men as prisoners or gays who happened to also be people. Today, I see people and often don't remember that they are either inmates or gay. Those are simply details of their lives that Spirit has obscured except when it's necessary for me to know them.

10 SACRED SIGHT

In every heart the Lord dwells. Therefore, speak no bitter words.
The one who listens within you also listens within everyone else.
　　　　　　　　　　　　　　　　　　　　　　　　　—*The Kabir Book*

I FIRST ASKED JOHN'S QUESTION—what was I doing there—at a Lakota ceremony when I crawled out of a lodge at my first vision quest in 1986. I came out of the lodge into rain—a big, cold downpour. I was supposed to go out into this cold downpour on my blanket and pray for a vision.

The day had begun with more promise, with the smell of sweet sage and hot sunshine. I was sitting in a circle with several people on the shore of Lake Whitney, just outside of Dallas, Texas. We were passing around an abalone shell filled with burning sage. I had been taught how to pass the smoke around me to purify myself. Mary Thunder sat inside the circle, next to a blazing fire we had just lit that was heating river rocks.

I had wanted to go on a vision quest since I was a kid. At a *hanbleceya*, a vision quest, one is taken to a sacred space to fast and pray for a vision for the people. The Lakota teach that our purpose can be given to us in a vision. My Lakota friends say that ceremony is a way to place oneself in a position to receive direct revelation from God, to be in communion with God the mystery, the indescribable. It is the mystery, it is God, that we seek on the hill.

As with the other ceremonies, *hanbleceya* begins with the *chanupa,* the pipe. My Lakota friends say that the early Indians used the vision quest as a kind of rite of passage. When a boy was ready to become a man, he filled his pipe, gave it to the *wicasa wakan* (holy man), and asked that man to put him out on the hill. The holy man would purify the quester in an *inipi* (sweat lodge) and then take the boy to his sacred space, where the boy would stand and fast, praying for a vision about his purpose and how to live his life. When his time was complete, the holy man would return, and the boy/man would relate his vision to the old man in yet another *inipi*. The old man would interpret the vision and give the young man advice regarding the direction his life would take.

In white society, we don't have a formal, ritualized rite of passage. The closest we get is getting drunk on our sixteenth birthday, trying to have sex, and wrecking our car.

My vision quest started when Jimmy Schulman, a therapist and friend, who was unaware of my interest, called to say he was going to a vision quest near Dallas. Would I like to come along? I had been trying to find someone who conducted vision quests for several years, but no one ever felt right. Now, Thunder does.

Jimmy said that I needed to talk to Helen West, who would tell me how to prepare and what to bring. He and I headed to Galveston to meet Helen, who graciously told me what to prepare, bring, and do.

She spent much of our time discussing prayer ties. A prayer tie is a small piece of cloth filled with tobacco and prayers and tied to a string. Thunder required seventy-seven ties: eleven ties per string, seven strings. The last thing Helen told me as Jimmy and I left was to avoid getting my ties tangled. She said that the condition of my ties would reflect the condition of my mind, and that if my ties were too tangled, Thunder would not put me out on the hill. I assured Helen I would be careful.

I forgot to ask Helen how close together the ties should be, so I placed them one foot apart. Now I had seven eleven-foot cords I was to avoid tangling. I carefully packed those ties in a box, put the box in the car, packed my other stuff, and drove to Lake Whitney.

In addition to my prayer ties, I had also packed a tent—a large old canvas tent given to me by my maternal grandfather. I had taken it on Scout camps when I was a kid. At that time, I was afraid that no one would want to stay with me in my big tent, so I always arranged for tent companions well in advance of any trip where the tent was to be used. Although I had long since forgotten the reason, the habit remained, and I had arranged for Jimmy and his girlfriend, Diane, and another friend to stay with me in the tent.

When I got to the land, I parked and began to pull my ties out of the car and out of their box. At that precise moment, the others informed me that they had brought their own tents and would not be staying with me. My old childhood fear returned. My ties leaped out of my hands and landed in cactus, where they rolled themselves up into a jumbled mess. I had to ask for help untangling my ties so I could go fulfill my spiritual commitment. We sat on the ground, cutting string and retying ties, trying to make it look as if nothing had happened.

I should have seen the warnings right away: that ceremonial lessons are experiential, that I would have to ask for help, and that I would try to hide from God and the teacher what it was I did not want God or the teacher to see (like Adam and Eve covering their nakedness in the garden). I was expressing through my conduct the crazy, parallel belief that God was all-knowing and all-seeing and that I had the power to hide something from God—or at least that God was really busy, with no particular time for me, and might not notice the tangled ties. As I was pulling the tangled ties out of the prickly pear, someone came by and told me that

Thunder wanted to talk to me about going out on the hill. Naturally, I cussed.

Tangled ties actually did reflect my mind. I was only a few days sober and a few days past the longest drug and alcohol binge I had ever been on. I wasn't talking to my parents, I was in trouble at work, and I was having serious marital problems.

I sat waiting for Thunder to fill her pipe and begin the ceremony, and thought about my expectations for this ceremony. Thunder had warned the group against having any expectations. She said we might consider simply surrendering to the process.

Earlier, when we were alone, she had asked whether I had any expectations. I said no. But I lied. My theory was that I would go up on the hill and Jesus, or maybe the archangels Michael and Gabriel, would discuss the state of the world with me. I would enjoy a beautiful view, beautiful stars, and a panoramic Star Wars–type vision at the end.

When the pipe was filled, I was directed to prepare for purification in the sweat lodge. In the lodge, I heard thunder. I was praying and happily thinking about my vision as I came out of the lodge into the biggest rain since Noah and the flood.

Somehow, my bright, hot, dry vision had turned cold and wet. Now I was thinking I would like to get into my car and have a vision some other time. This was another sign, if only I had noticed it: I wanted God and answers to prayers, but only if it was easy. Any discomfort, and I was ready to wait. How little I valued my connection with God and how much I desired ease and comfort, that I would consider choosing my comfort over being with God in a sacred space.

That, in fact, is the teaching. When we move into ceremony, we move into a nonlinear sacred space, and everything that happens there is God directed.

Ultimately, I chose my blanket, where I was wet. My wool blanket was wet, and everything was cold. And I waited for Jesus, and Michael, and Gabriel, and the Star Wars vision.

I waited.

I never saw Jesus there, or Michael, or Gabriel, or a splendid vision. But I did receive an important lesson about God, about myself, and about others. The new God list I had made said that God loved and cared for me personally, that I was not a statistic, and that I could let go of some of the fear I used to protect myself from you because God made a safe world. One way I reminded myself of that was to say that nothing, absolutely nothing, happened in God's world by mistake. As I was sitting on my blanket, cold and wet, cussing everyone and everything, certainly not praying, and occasionally saying that nothing—absolutely nothing—happens in God's world by mistake, I thought: I am in God's world. That is what the sacred space is. The rain is not a mistake; it is here for a reason—that this glorious rain display was created by a loving God. As I experienced this, the rain quit and my blanket was dry, and I knew that God loved me personally and that I never had to walk by myself again.

God also used this time to teach me about relating to others. My Lakota friends use a single phrase to describe relating to others. At the beginning of most ceremonies, when one goes into an *inipi,* for example, everyone says *"Aho Mitakuye Oyasin"* or "Amen to all my relations." This is an especially important phrase to remember in the sweat lodge because it will get the flap open if you get too hot. Newer people sometimes have a hard time remembering *"Aho Mitakuye Oyasin,"* so they will say, "Amen to all my relations."

Everyone except the humans seem to know we are related. A favorite example concerns two boys who found a turtle by the side of the road. They brought the turtle home and put it upside down on the top rack of the oven. They put a pan full of water on the lower level, shut the door, and put the oven on high heat. The boys figured that the water would steam the turtle and make turtle soup. In a little while, the boys heard scratching. Upon investigation, they found that the scratching was coming from the oven. When they opened the door, as the stream billowed out they heard the turtle saying *"Aho Mitakuye Oyasin."*

I was not as wise as that turtle as I sat on my blanket in the rain. I had failed to grasp our essential interrelationship. But when I moved into the space of vision and saw—really saw—the birds and the plants and the trees and the shrubs, the green and the four-legged and two-legged relatives that were around, in this space I could really see and appreciate the interconnectedness of us all, and how we all had our own job, including myself, and how none of us were more or less important than anyone else. We all had to do our jobs in order to make the whole thing work. I had an experience of that inner connectedness that I had thus far only read about or heard others describe.

Mitakuye Oyasin means that we are related to all groups of people and to the four-legged, two-legged, and winged relations—all the ones we don't like or care for, that we're prejudiced against and bigoted about. Thunder says that what I dislike the most in others is what I have the most difficulty accepting about myself. If God can love me, how can I fail to love others? Stated differently, if

God can love me, and God can love others, why can't I love others?

I have been on many *hanbleceyas* since this one. I have put many people out on their blankets. Yet, even after all these prayers, I am still amazed by a ceremony that helps make it possible to wipe out years of learning, to make it possible to directly receive the divine love of God. I will always be grateful for this gift. For just as Jo Todd and Burney gave me a God to love, Thunder gave me a chance to feel God's love for me.

Since my first vision quest was in a monsoon and the second was in a blizzard, I began to get a reputation among the people putting me out as someone who was a little bit of trouble. People began to give me a hard time about expecting a tornado or other bad weather at my next quest, and it became something of a running joke. There is a whole other side to the vision quest, the support process, which is done by the people who do the work and support those who are out on the hill. We like to say that the questers do a great deal of prequest work, emptying themselves out to prepare to go out on the hill so that they are empty enough to receive something when they get out there, and that all the support people—the people who get the lodges ready, tend the fire, work the lodges, and get people out to their site—do a ton of work during the quest and also empty themselves out during the quest. So, when the questers come back full of the Spirit, they can impart some of it by gift to the now empty supporters, who have worked so hard on their behalf.

I enjoy supporting the questers—the physical work, gathering the wood, maintaining the fire, working in the kitchen, late-night talks on security. A special thrill is checking the questers. Thunder likes us to see the questers several times a day, to just make a visual spot check. Since they are walking in holy land, seeing them is maybe a little like seeing an angel.

Checking questers at night is also fun. Especially where the terrain is mountainous, we quietly walk up and down mountainsides at night with no light, trying to see questers. When I started checking, I often tangled with vines, tripped over stumps, and fell into trees or poison ivy or poison oak. I often came back a mess. One of my Lakota friends told me that the trick to night vision was seeing with my heart. Since I was walking at night so much, I began to practice seeing with my heart, letting my heart sense the presence of bumps in the road, of stumps and vines and trees. I still trip, of course, but much less often. My heart somehow senses the dangerous objects and warns my body to avoid them.

Later, Thunder had me help her with talking to people before they went out. This is a real honor, because people share their hopes and dreams, their pains and sorrows. People approach *hanbleceya* as a date with the divine, as a chance to encounter death and rebirth, and they are candid and full of Spirit. Later, Thunder let me help her listen and respond to people after their return. Hearing how the Spirit has transformed that energy, and feeling the change in the energy, is to stand in the presence of miracles. Person after person will return with story after story of a new piece for their life they did not previously have. To see the results of Spirit at work is a gift I cherish.

Often one or more of the questers would bring to their talk an issue they were working on that was very similar to a personal issue I was working on. While helping with their connection to ceremony I would pray for them and that issue, and more often than not, both they and I would come to some resolution of that issue in our lives.

My favorite part of all the support work was sweating people into and out of their *hanbleceya*. After the talk with Thunder, the quester would be sweated into the ceremony, and often I got to be in the lodge or actually run it. Here the people and their prayers, their promise and their pain, their hell and their hope became very transparent. For me to see and experience that degree of honesty was transforming, because I saw the questers on their return, fresh from their blankets. I would sweat them out, and see and experience the calm, beautiful, transformative energy they were after their time on the blanket, inside sacred space, praying for a vision to benefit the people.

I have been involved in supporting many *hanbleceyas*. The process has always worked, without exceptions. The transformative work is always staggering. Even people who somehow sabotage their work always report an empowering experience.

The weather joke became more interesting several years later when I was asked to put people out on the hill for their own vision quest. By this time, I had been helping Thunder put people out for quite a while. She had gifted me with the *hanbleceya* lineage at the Rudi Ashram in New York. Later, she had plans to put some people out, but Grandpa Ellis Chipps died, so she and Horse and others went to the funeral, and I stayed behind and ran that vision quest for her. So the request to lead a vision quest was not out of the blue, but I was not looking forward to it. I told everyone who asked that if it were me, I would go to see Thunder and ask her to put them out, but a few people insisted that I do it. So, after talking with Thunder and securing her blessing and the blessings of my other Lakota elder friends who had a voice in the matter, we had our first *hanbleceya* in New Mexico. Friends of mine—Wally and Glenda, Jo, Burney, and others—helped me do all the support work necessary for the quest, and we had a prayerful and spiritual time.

It is quite an experience putting people out. I connect with people who go out on their vision quest, and I stay connected to them the entire time they are out. The teaching is that whatever they experience, I experience. Whatever fears, thirsts, longings, hungers, concerns, worries, angers, revelations, dreams, and visions they experience, I experience being connected to them. It is a very exhausting process, with no sleep, but hugely illuminating because I go through not only my own process but theirs as well. It is another way in which I think being a leader is a cosmic joke, because I end up getting to do a lot more personal work. It's my experience that those who need it must do most of it, and it seems as if the Spirit has organized it so that I have a whole lot of work to do.

Before the *hanbleceya,* Thunder had told me that although I would have fears and doubts and worries and concerns, I should really practice on my faith, which is always a challenge for me. She said that I would get one gift from the Spirit during the quest; that had always been her experience. I talked with Thunder, Phillip Chipps, and others, and they all said my job was to pray for those questers, that in fact I would always be a little bit connected to them and that I was signing on to a lifetime of prayer for them. Thunder also taught me that if everyone who goes out comes back and nobody dies, the vision quest is a success, and everything else is gravy.

On the last day of the quest, we were preparing the huge feast and giveaway, during which everyone celebrates going out and coming back. Then, from the east, an enormous thunder cloud bean to roll in, heading our way. In the midst of our feasting celebration, the wind kicked up, and it started to rain and hail. We thought our feast and giveaway would be spoiled. So in the midst of the rain, and with the help of many others, and not really knowing what I was doing, I went to the fire with tobacco in hand to pray.

I was taught that four sacred relatives are present in most of the ceremonies my Lakota friends do. Tobacco is used for prayer, sage is a cleansing herb, sweet grass is pleasing to the Spirit and announces what is going on, and cedar tends to call in the Spirit. Standing at the fire, tobacco in hand, praying, I was in an interesting place as the prayor. I had been through thirty or more sweat lodges in five days, I had been praying for fifty people for five days, and I had been prayed for by the support people. The questers had prayed, and I was connected to that by virtue of my connection to them.

So, I stood in that prayer place as the wind and rain and hail came up, and my prayer was more like a conversation with the Creator: "Grandfather, all these people are here. They have worked really hard to establish and maintain and enhance their relationship with you. You have given them all these gifts, and now they stand in this place of celebration to thank you for what you've given them and to pledge and commit themselves to you to stay in gratitude and to give that away to others. It is going to be real hard for them to do that if you dump a load of rain and hail on them." And as I stood there at the fire and watched, the wind shifted, the rain quit, the hail stopped, and the clouds literally blew around us and went to the other side of the mountain, and we could see it start raining and hailing again.

I tell you that story because I came to believe that that was the piece of medicine Thunder had mentioned, and it was an affirmation by the Spirit that prayers are heard and responded to even if they are not always answered in the way we would appreciate. On other occasions, for one reason or another, I have felt moved by the Spirit to pray about weather conditions and the Spirit has always responded. I don't want to suggest by this that prayers control the weather, because they don't. On other occasions I have wanted the weather to be different and have prayed about it, and I wasn't in a state of having prayed for several days but was responding to something that I wanted, and I got absolutely no response. It is only when I have been in a really prayed place, responding to the motivation of the Spirit to pray for something of benefit to others, and asking with all the sincerity and humbleness that I can manage, that the weather has changed.

The sense of magic in prayer is one of the greatest obstacles we face to a fruitful prayer life. Those of us with a Protestant upbringing heard that if you ask in Jesus' name it will be granted. The Lakota version appears, among other places, in the pipe-filling song, which says, "If you do it this way, then everything you ask will come to pass." The simple concept here is that if we ask and ask in the right way, whether it's through the pipe ceremony for my Lakota friends or in a gathering of two or three with a Christian background, we have an idea that we will get what we want. But that is simply not the experience of most of us. So then we began to modify that prayer. "Nonetheless, your will not mine be done." Or "That or something better,"as my New Age friends say. Or we will hear that God does answer prayers and sometimes the answer is no. All of these formulations address the central teaching many of us were given that if we ask for it we'll get it. And that creates a kind of magical thinking: if we act right, we can somehow control God and make God give us those things that we want, because he can do it and has promised us that he will. So if we don't get it, we are left with a choice: either God is breaking his promise, or God is not as we were promised, or God is different or less than or something other than what was represented, or that something is wrong with us—that we are not good enough or strong enough, and that if we just acted better or were different, the prayer would come true. This sense of magic is that if we act right, God will give us what we want; we are somehow controlling God and controlling our situation, and if we don't have what we want, then we can shame and guilt ourselves or become angry with God because God is not acting right.

What we miss in all of this is a willingness to let God be greater and more mysterious than we can imagine. The process my friend Jo Todd gave me of creating some definitions of God helped me develop a trust relationship with the Creator. I've noticed that my definition of God has become more and more vague over time and that I have been increasingly willing to let God be a mysterious force. I have accepted the proposition that a created being cannot fully understand the Creator and that a created being can commune with the Creator by the grace of the Creator. And although I cannot fully understand God, I can define God as something that cannot be fully understood by me. In this way, my prayer life focuses less on the carrot-and-stick approach and instead focuses on communion and union, on our createdness and our relatedness to God and our fellows. This does not mean that we don't acknowledge in our prayer to God what we want, but I think we do so with a mature understanding that our perspective is necessarily limited, and the benefit from prayer flows principally from the act of connecting with and communing with our Creator. The benefits over time are incremental.

I was finally gifted a song by the Spirit on a later vision quest. I love Lakota songs; I love the words, the tune, the beat, the rhythm, the way I feel when I sing or hear them. I had been going out for a couple of days and was sitting on a hill overlooking a pond of water. The time had been quiet, with a little praying and singing but not much else. On the last day before I was to come down, a cloud rose from the south. It was a west Texas front cloud; I could see the front line coming, and all day it passed over me so that I could see exactly how long the front line was and how big the cloud was. The wind was blowing, and I really enjoyed it. The cloud looked like rain, but it never did rain; there was just wind and blowing. While it was all going on, I moved into a sacred space, and the Spirit taught me a song, which translates something like this: "Grandfather, have pity on us; we're sitting here praying; have pity on us." I must have sung that song a thousand times that day, over and over and over, guided by the Spirit.

In the evening, the last of the cloud passed over me and kept on going. It was twenty or thirty miles to the north of me, so I had seen the entire cloud from top to bottom, from front to back. Then the wind shifted and started blowing from the north back to the south, and the cloud started coming back my way. It began to rain, and it just rained, and rained, and rained. I was soaked, cold, pitiful, and miserable. What I had to keep me company was that song that the Spirit had given me. And the song became a part of me because I was praying and was pitiful and in real need of God's grace.

My time on the blanket during vision quests has led me to recognize several spiritual principles. I believe we have a need to believe in God. I believe we have a need to believe in a true God and that life and our experiences continually give us feedback about where our beliefs incorrectly reflect the metaphysically real nature of God. I believe we have a need for times of communion with the true God: times to sit, be refreshed, be renewed, be filled. I believe we have need to express our worship: to speak, laugh, dance, sing, cry, talk, draw, paint, sculpt. I believe we have a need to actively communicate our joyful experience to others. I believe we have a need to relate consciously and compassionately with our relations: to humans, the four-legged creatures, the creepy crawlers, the green growing things.

I believe we have a need to live with love in integrity and to be guided by a sense of social justice, defined as making sure the children get what is due them. I believe we have a need to practice our communion with God and our fellows through ever deepening relations with others.

We should approach the divine with a sense of awe. We are created beings. Since every cause has an effect and every beginning has an end, that which is born must die, and that which dies must be reborn. By ourselves we can do little or nothing to resolve the most important problems we face. Suffering can't be avoided; in fact, the more we try to avoid suffering, the more suffering we endure and the more we impose on others.

We are alone. We think we are not; we dress in our aloneness and beliefs and thoughts and opinions and emotions and feelings and things and people and relations, but at the end of the day we are created beings standing alone in relation to our Creator at the same time holding hands with all the other sentient beings.

11 SACRED GIFT

God had better be there
—**Burney Fuller**

IN JUNE 1998, CHIEF LEONARD CROW DOG, in the presence of my teacher Mary Thunder and with the help of our Lakota friends, presented me with a sun dance chief's bonnet and authorized me to run sun dances. As I stood in the arbor I thought of how things had changed since my first dance at Paradise, when Leonard was not sure whether I could dance because I was white.

The sun dance is the high ceremony of the Plains Indians. The form of the ceremony will vary slightly with each intercessor's expression of his vision, but generally the dancers pray and dance for four days and nights without food or water in a sacred arbor. At the center of the arbor is the tree of life, a cottonwood tree with a *can ojikata* (fork) at the top of the tree. A collection of chokecherry branches is tied to the tree just above the fork, forming the nest of the *wakinyan*, the thunder beings.

The tree is described differently by each intercessor. Today, "tree of life" is common. Some of the older explanations describe the tree as the "enemy" or as "darkness." (Interestingly, when the Christian missionaries first described a person who hung on a tree of life on Calvary two thousand years ago so the people might live, the story received a warm reception as being already familiar.) Ropes or thongs are tied to the tree of life and are also attached to wooden skewers, which are pierced through the breast skin of the male dancers. Male dancers "break" on the last day of the dance: they pull away from the tree in such a way that the wooden skewers break through the skin. Some of my Lakota friends say that it is our flesh, not the tree, that is ignorance, and we give that away when we gift our flesh. Traditionally, only male dancers pierced, but now women also pierce, although typically not at the breast.

Piercing and breaking are the part of the ceremony that most commonly grabs people's attention. Dancers also talk about it. A few special phrases are used to describe the experiences: "How you going this year?" "You dragging?" "You hanging?" "Going by a horse?" "You just pulling this year?" "Those eagle dancers are looking strong. You going that way this year?" All of these comments refer to the methods of piercing and breaking. Pulling from the tree involves being connected from the skewers to the tree by a rope. The dancer then pulls against the rope until the flesh rips and the dancer is free. Someone who goes by the horse is pierced somewhere, often on the arms. One end of the rope is tied to the pins; that end is threaded through a fork in the tree, and the other end is held by a man on a horse. At a given signal he rides the horse toward the East gate. Standing in the West gate, the man has his pins ripped away from his arms. At least, one hopes this is what happens. I have seen people whose pins did not break free, and they were dragged into the tree. My Lakota friends say that going by the horse produces lightning power.

Some people hang. Hanging involves being pierced in the back or chest and then being lifted by a rope tied to the pins and tossed over a tree branch; the person then hangs suspended in the air until the pins break free. Some people break quickly this way, but I have seen some hang for a long time. Leonard Crow Dog himself once hung for four days.

Some people eagle dance. Eagle dancers pierce on the second round of the first day and stay connected until the end of the fourth day. They are very brave, and their sacrifice is substantial. My friend Shari Valentine has eagle danced every year of our Lone Star Dance, and hers is a tremendous gift to the dance. An eagle dancer I greatly admire is Chief Luciano Perez. He eagle danced at Leonard's while I was completing my four-year commitment. His energy was so strong, powerful, and serene that even though he was eagle dancing he was carrying us. Chief Perez has modeled a sober spiritual ceremonial lifestyle and is very committed to caring for our children. He also serves with Leonard as a chief at my dance. Those who are in ceremony with Chief Perez are blessed.

Some people drag the skulls. Ten or more buffalo skulls are tied in a line and then tied to pins in the dancer's back. The dancer pulls the skulls around the outside of the arbor until the pins rip free. My Lakota friends offer different explanations for pulling the skulls. Some say it is done as an act of contrition; others say it signifies a willingness to carry or shoulder the burdens of the people.

People ask for a description of being connected to the tree, pulling the skulls, hanging from the tree. To me, the sense of being connected to the tree is one of great peace. I feel as if I have a direct connection to the Creator, as if we were in direct and total communion. Dragging the skulls feels like shouldering a great weight, and breaking from the skulls feels like being released from a great burden. I always feel a sense of sadness when I break from the tree, as if I have somehow lost some connection—although in truth, the connection I walk around with in the everyday world today is probably greater than the connection I felt the first time I pierced. Hanging from the tree, to me, is an abject lesson in permanence. One experiences a whole range of emotions, everything from "I wish

I'd come down" to "I could stay up here forever" to "won't I ever break" to "I wonder if I will really start flying while I'm up here."

Several years ago, I started the horse pull piercing, and a couple of interesting things have happened. First, through the process of prayer in the piercing, I become so rooted in the ground that I think a bulldozer could come up and not knock me over. Second, a couple of years ago, while waiting for my turn with the horse, a chant, "help us, help us, help us," sort of just erupted from me, and that prayer has stayed with me over time and seems to come from the seat of my being. Now, two years later, when I'm filling the pipe, or in the lodge, or in the arbor, or walking down the street engaged in prayer, after I say what I have to say, the seemingly unconscious part of me will take over, and the chant of "help us, help us, help us" will come forth.

Sometimes I am asked about the blood sacrifice associated with the dance. Blood is sacred. Blood represents the Spirit; it represents life; it represents the gift of life. Losing blood represents death, but it can also represent the gift of life to another. When we are reborn, we are reborn from a blood-based life into a Spirit-based life born in blood. When we sacrifice our blood in the sun dance, we are purifying our blood—our life—and offering it to Spirit, who infuses it with life and permits us to offer it for others. Leonard Peltier has written: "To give your flesh to Spirit is to give your life. And what you have given you can no longer lose. . . . When you give your flesh . . . you are given a wordless vision of what it is to be in touch with all Being and all beings."

The first dance I attended was run by Grandpa Wallace Black Elk. Grandpa's dances are different from some others in that he dances two "day days" and two "night days." So, in a dance that begins on Thursday morning, the dancers will dance Thursday, Thursday night, Friday, and Friday night, and the dance will conclude on Saturday. The first dance I saw, we arrived on the first night, and I support danced while someone pierced and broke. When that dancer broke from the tree, I felt it in my chest without ever seeing it, and I was captivated.

So, the next year I asked Grandpa Wallace for permission to dance. My desire to dance was so strong, and Leonard Crow Dog's AIM dance seemed so closed, that I looked for another place to dance. Grandpa Wallace is a tall, elegant man, a former AIM member, and part of the Wounded Knee takeover crowd. He is one of the first Lakota elders to have the compassion to share his traditional knowledge with other races, including whites. Whenever we whites sing a traditional song, or sit in a lodge, we do so in part because Grandpa helped open the door for us.

Asking Thunder if I could dance anywhere was novel. When I met Thunder, she was completing her own commitment. The idea of a white guy like me dancing wasn't in the picture. Nonetheless, I asked Thunder if she would sponsor my dance.

A sponsor acts as an advisor during the four years a pledge makes and completes his or her commitment. The sponsor also promises the intercessor to complete the vow if the pledge is unable or unwilling to finish it. So Thunder agreed to sponsor me, and we both went to see Grandpa to ask whether I could dance.

Grandpa readily agreed, although he warned me that my life would forever be altered. He told me I was committing to the spiritual life in a permanent way. I did not especially appreciate his comments at the time, although I have come to believe that a dancer steps over a line into the responsibility to be a new person, someone visibly committed to being remade in the Creator's image, someone who agrees to place serving the people ahead of other interests.

One of the first lessons I learned while dancing related to being in the now. Ceremony keeps me present, living fully alive in the eternal now, the place I want to be because it is the home of God. At that first sun dance in Oregon, I was standing next to the chokecherry bush, which had next to it a hive of ground-dwelling wasps. These wasps would on occasion land on me and bite or sting me. I was very grateful during that dance for the presence of Mato the bear, a person dressed as a bear who, it is claimed, becomes a bear during the ceremony—at least for those inside the sacred circle. When I was attacked by those wasps, Mato would come over and fan the wasps away from me.

While I was dancing in the dance, I was transported to a place that I call the place beyond knowing—a magical place of knowing where something is simply true because it's true and not because of any other reason. There's a place beyond that extent of knowing where things just are. In the place beyond knowing, I had experienced the same presence that had come to me after the auto wreck. On this day of the dance, as I was attached to the tree, the Spirit would take me from the dance to the place beyond knowing. When I was there, Mato would come over and fan me, and I would come back to the dance.

I also went to this other place I call the place of paying bills. I would be standing there dancing and praying, worrying about whether or not I had paid my bills or turned off the electricity in my house. When I was in the place of paying bills, Mato would come over and fan me, and I would come back.

I eagle danced at Grandpa's my first year, so during the dance I went from the dance to the place beyond knowing, back to the dance, to the place of paying bills—back and forth and back and forth. I am grateful to the Spirit for taking me to this place beyond knowing, because there is now a path with identifiable landmarks along the way. Now I can find my way to the place beyond knowing and find my way back, and it's not scary to me but familiar. One of the barricades to getting to the place beyond knowing is fear, because it involves such a complete loss of control.

After the dance was over, I went up to Mato to ask him how he had known to come fan me at those particular times. He told me that I simply wasn't there. I said, "What do you mean I wasn't there? You could look and my body was present and my mind wasn't?" He said, "No, you just simply weren't there. Nothing was there. So, when there was this empty space, I just came over and fanned until you showed up." Within the last couple of those years, I have come to realize that for me, most of the time, the dance is where I need to be. The place beyond knowing is wonderful. But the real spot for me today is in this world—in the dance. It is the place of coming down from the mountain and living in the marketplace, chopping wood and carrying water.

The next year, I decided to ask to dance at Paradise also. I arrived there in the company of Thunder and Buddy Red Bow and others to ask Leonard Crow Dog for permission to be in his sun dance. I don't claim to be the first white person to have danced there, but I suspect the list before me is a short one.

Thunder and Buddy agreed to sponsor me at Leonard's dance. I went with the two of them to speak to Leonard, gifting in the traditional way—a Pendleton blanket for Leonard, dress material for his wife, tobacco and fresh sweetgrass, gifts to address specific needs for the ceremony, and cash to help defray the cost of the ceremony. Thunder and Buddy both spoke on my behalf and Leonard ended the meeting without committing one way or the other. He said he would need to talk to the other traditional chiefs about our request and would let me know. Several days passed and I heard nothing from Leonard, although I continued to participate in the purification lodges. The morning the dance was to start, I was sitting by the fire feeling a little depressed, talking with Thunder and Buddy and laughing because I had never gotten the go-ahead from Leonard. We were all saying that it was funny we were disappointed and sad that I would not get to dance, given how hard the dance was. In some respects it seemed we ought to be happy that we could avoid it. As the dancers were lining up to go into the arbor, Leonard came running into the camp. He told me to grab my stuff and get in line. I was going into the arbor.

Going into the arbor at Leonard's is quite an experience. I have been doing it for years now, and it still sends chills through me when we start. The music begins (*Kola le miyeca wauelo he, Kola le miyeca wauelo he*—Friend, this is me that is coming). The drums are pounding, eagle bone whistles break the morning air, a hint of sunlight creeps over the peaks, and we walk on still dew-wet morning grass around the circle and then to the arbor. I did not have an eagle bone whistle when the dance started. I just stood in line, tall, curly-headed, big-nosed, very white and wide-eyed, standing next to my Lakota friends walking into the arbor. At the end of the first day, when the dancers retired to their camps to rest, I went back to my camp to find everyone gone. Thunder, Horse, her son Richard and his wife Star, and her family had all gone to the Chipps's place to see about a healing for her grandson. I spent a very scary night there; I wasn't sure I would make it through that night or the next day or the next night. No one spoke to me.

Late in the third day, Buddy returned. Everyone knew Buddy by sight. He was big, funny, and wore a huge black hat. He and Thunder discussed the hard time I was having. He walked into the front of the shade arbor, where we were resting, and talked around long enough for everyone to see him and know that he was there. Then he motioned for me to come up to the front. He offered me the chance to leave the dance, which I refused. He didn't say much else, but he put a leather thong around my neck. Attached to it was an eagle bone whistle. The whistle had been given to him by Grandpa Bill Schweigman when Buddy first sun danced. The eagle to whom that particular wing bone belonged had broken its wing, and there was a buildup of calcium over the bone where it had healed. Buddy then said good-bye and left, and I stumbled back to my place. But everyone there had seen Buddy talking to me, and it was his way of introducing me to the group without forcing me on them.

When someone pledges to sun dance, the commitment is to dance for four years, with a fifth year of dancing in gratitude for the gifts of the first four. During the first four years, a dancer is a pledge and does not identify himself or herself as a sun dancer. Instead, people speak in terms of years, as in, "This is my first [or second or third] year." Or "I'll be through after this year and my giveaway year."

I was taught never to refer to myself as a sun dancer until after completing my fourth year. Even now, I rarely apply that label to myself, preferring instead to say that I dance, or that I sun dance. I also wear a shirt most of the time. These days, some of the dancers walk around without shirts outside the ceremony so people will see their scars and know that they dance. I was taught modesty about this and still follow that rule.

Some people say that a completed dancer is a pipe carrier. There is substantial dispute about who or what is a pipe carrier. I myself do not use the term even though I am a sun dance chief. I was taught that we have a pipe we take care of, again referring to our role as trustee for the benefit of the people. I was also taught it is better to follow the pipe than carry one around. So, I generally say I follow the pipe, or I might say I take care of a pipe.

I was also taught that a completed Sun Dancer generally becomes authorized to pour water for *inipis* and put people out on *hanbleceyas*. This is a responsibility a sun dancer fulfills in service to the people. I have met a few sun dancers who believe they are God's gift to the spiritual world because they have the ostensible authority to lead ceremonies. I always feel sorry for them because I know a major humbling is likely headed their way. I always hope their attitude changes before the humbling and before too many people get hurt by it.

I was also taught that the ceremony marks us. It is a way to be identified as a person who is dedicated to being of service to the people, who places the needs of the people ahead of his or her own wants. The scars identify the person as one who follows the pipe. The scars say, "Here is a person dedicated to the four virtues: generosity, bravery, wisdom, and fortitude. Here is a person you can trust, a person who is willing to die trying to do it right."

I was also taught that a completed dancer could dance additional years, and that just as a four-year dancer has danced one year in each direction, some choose a full cycle: four years in each direction, or sixteen years. And then some dancers have danced every year since they started and plan to dance the remainder of their life. A four-year dancer, although completed, often does not possess much spiritual wisdom. I equate a four-year dancer to being in the fourth grade in terms of spiritual maturity. Certainly better than kindergarten but still not safe to be left alone.

A sun dancer can sponsor others to dance. But there's a catch. The sponsor agrees that if the pledge does not complete the four-year commitment for any reason, including death, the sponsor will complete the pledge. This rule is one of those eminently practical spiritual rules my Lakota friends follow. One does not lightly agree to sponsor someone, and the system fully supports completion of the pledge if it is at all possible.

I have now completed my thirteenth year and my twenty-first dance. In some ways, that seems like a lot, but really it is not. I know one Grandpa who danced thirty-eight years asking the Creator for one piece of medicine to help the people. I myself equate my experience to being a freshman in college—someone who is more mature than a first-grader but still with much to learn.

I generally receive one spiritual piece, one nugget, at each dance. I want something big. My ego is such that I still want something that will make me important in your eyes. My compassion has grown through you so that I want a cure for cancer or AIDS. What I "got" one year was the directive that I not eat something I was unwilling to kill unless it would be embarrassing to the host. About all this applied to was meat, so I have largely quit eating meat. I don't judge those who do; in fact, I often hunger for red meat, but I confess to being unwilling to shoot for my food. So, no meat. Shortly after this directive I was invited to some friends' house for supper, and they served elk the fellow had shot on a hunting trip. I was glad for the latter part of the directive since it would have been embarrassing to my host if I had declined the main course. I could just see myself telling a partner in my law firm that Spirit had told me not to eat his elk. And it was tasty.

The years follow a generally predictable pattern, at least for most of those I know. My first year of dancing was a wide-eyed, "what is coming next" rookie year. I then began to battle my lack of humility when I received attention for sun dancing. I also began to "lose" the non-God things in my life: friends and family; possessions; job; religious beliefs; and attitudes about money, sex, and power. For example, by the time I finished my fifth year, I went from being single living with one person to being married to another. I moved; changed jobs; lost one family member; resurrected relations with others; lost most of one set of friends but gained others; and changed my eating and spending patterns, how I spent my "free" time and what I thought about. Then came a time of consolidating the new additional battles with pride and power, all the while growing compassion for my people who walk the road.

I continued dancing at Leonard's but also began to attend a dance hosted by Chief Charles Chipps. One day when I was at the Chipps's waiting for the sun dance to start, Charles walked up to me. He is a big fellow, very tall, with a wide grin and a big voice and a huge heart. I hadn't spoken a lot to Charles; I was actually afraid of him and tried to stay out of his way. He walked up to me with a big bag of scalpels and said, "Do you know what these are?" I said, "They look like scalpels," and Charles said, "Well, the Spirit has spoken." And he turned around and walked off. I was standing there with a bag full of scalpels and didn't really know what he meant, so I went back and sat in my chair and tried to stay out of the way and remain inconspicuous. In a little while, a man came up to me and said, "I think I'm supposed to do the piercing at the sun dance." I said it surely was fine with me and wondered to myself why he was talking to me about it. He said, "To do that, I'm going to need those scalpels that Charles just gave you." I said, "Oh, well, fine. Here, you can have them." So I returned those scalpels to that gentleman as quick as I could.

In a little while, Charles came back with the man in tow, and the man handed me back the bag of scalpels. Charles said, "Do you know what those are?" And I said, "They look like scalpels." And Charles said, "The Spirit has spoken." The man and Charles left, and I stood there for a while and was beginning to realize what this might mean, but decided I would go back and sit in my chair. A little later, another man came up to me—a different man, a man more senior to me and probably wiser and a lot smarter—and said, "Well, we've all been talking, and we're quite sure that I'm the one that needs to do the piercing." This time I wasn't slow on the uptake, and I said, "I think that's a great idea." I just handed that bag of scalpels to the second man, and he left pretty happy. I was very happy to see him go. But in a little while, along came the second man with Charles, and Charles said, "Didn't you understand what I said?" I said, "Not really." Charles said, "What could be confusing about the fact that the Spirit has spoken?" The second man handed me back the bag of scalpels, and off they went.

As you may have guessed, I did the piercing at that sun dance and at several dances after that. I have found that it is a big responsibility to pierce the people. I become tied to their heart and soul. Charles was kind enough to give me increasing responsibility for the ceremony as time passed, until finally one year I ran the sun dance at the Chipps's when Charles was called away.

The change that occurs in a person leading a ceremony such as the sun dance is phenomenal. The spiritual responsibility to the Creator and to the participants is staggering. I began to see and know and understand things that had been hidden from me, and I was confused about how to interpret them. As I was trying to understand these things, Leonard Crow Dog came into town. I was talking to him about these things, and before I got very far, he started to laugh and looked at his wife and said, "See—I told you." She kind of laughed and said, "Yeah, you did." Then he looked at me and said, "The Spirit has spoken," and I thought, "Oh, my God." Leonard said, "You're going to run a sun dance here in Texas."

Now, running a sun dance here in Texas was not high on my list of priorities. Aside from the more obvious problems, such as the fact that I'm white, I'm a lawyer, and I work in a prominent firm in town, it would also be a controversial thing, it would be off the reservation, and so on and so forth. But Leonard was adamant that I would lead the dance in Texas and that he would authorize it. So we spent about eighteen months while I wrestled with those questions. Meanwhile, friends helped us get all the grounds ready, select the tree, build the arbor, build the lodges, and collect the wood and rocks and all the other things that are needed for a sun dance to take place.

I don't want to make light of the challenges. One significant challenge was my work. I started my professional career as a lawyer with a significant insurance defense firm. My professional career has changed over the years, but I have and still do represent several very traditional clients. Corporate America, Fortune 500 companies, and the lawyers I work with tend to be more establishment oriented, although there are certainly exceptions. There is certainly nothing wrong with being that way, but the fact remains that the concept of an "Indian" religion or being in a sweat lodge or a sun dance or anything like that is foreign to many of my lawyer friends. I had some substantial concern about how they would perceive me and who we would be in relation to one another. It was one thing to do a dance in South Dakota, hundreds of miles away, where the dance was unknown to those in Texas and my presence at it was not likely to raise an issue of any consequence among my lawyer colleagues. It was another thing to do a sun dance in my own backyard.

The same, of course, could be true about my family, who while supportive of my efforts to pursue this path, have chosen not to follow it for themselves. Again, I am exposing them and my wife's professional career to some degree of risk, much as my own participation was a risk for my career.

Doing the dance in Texas was a statement of sorts. It said that yes, I was doing it; yes, I was doing it publicly; and yes, this was who I was and I wasn't hiding that or doing it alone, far away, but rather doing it here with my own family and my own friends. The decision also required me to face my own direct conflicts with those who raised the wanna-be issue and who wondered why a white man was participating in Native American ceremony. The dance was going to be very public, and the fact that I was leading it would also be public. The dance also required me to face my lingering doubts about whether this was something I really wanted to believe in, something I really wanted to do and follow and pursue.

I was very skeptical about the prospect of leading a sun dance in Texas. It is true enough that I had a vision about doing so and that the topic had been a subject of discussion in our group for several years. But I was doubtful that Leonard would actually gift me the sun dance medicine and recognize me as a sun dance chief. There were so many good reasons for that not to happen. I also questioned whether there was an actual call for me to lead a sun dance and whether there was sufficient support for a Texas dance—support from people and in material terms. Rather than deciding whether the dance was something I felt called to do or wanted to do, I delayed that decision to see whether the Spirit and Leonard would conspire to produce events to make the dance happen.

So I set up a series of tests, in a way, that either Leonard or the Spirit would have to pass as evidence of the call to do this. That may not have been the best approach, but I felt so conflicted that I was doing the best I could. The first test consisted of obtaining a letter from Leonard to my community, acknowledging that he wanted me to run a sun dance in Texas and asking them to help me. I figured that the prospects for getting such a letter from Leonard were somewhere between slim and none. But in fact, I got not one letter, but three. One of those letters is in the appendix.

There were physical preparations. Building an arbor is an extraordinarily ardrous and difficult process. It is labor intensive and requires special kinds of materials, not the least of which are long posts with a fork at the top to support the actual arbor. In Paradise country they use pine trees that have a natural fork, but in my part of the world we would have to use cedar, and finding one hundred sixty or more cedar trees long enough, with a fork at the top, that someone was willing to donate was, I thought, an impossible task. Of course, some people called and offered us the opportunity to clear cedar from their land. River run-off had produced a marshy area, which in turn had produced hundreds of tall cedar trees with a fork that were just ours for the taking. Harvesting the trees produced all the firewood we would need to run the sun dance lodges.

People poured in from a variety of places to prepare a kitchen; build the arbor; plant the grass; build the sweat lodges; and donate the tarps, blankets, pitchforks, shovels, sweat lodge rocks, and all the various things requiresd by a sun dance, so that the physical preparations were handled by our community.

I should digress for a moment to describe our community. When I first started pouring lodges, there were four of us who attended with regularity. Over time, my one student became two and then three, and now numbers thirteen. Some of my students have students; many friends also participate in and support ceremony. Some of us purchased 170 acres in Texas where we offer ceremony to the people, includng the sun dance. Today, our community has well over three hundred members living across the United States and in several foreign countries. Our community has also joined with other like-minded communities so that a gathering involves a good number of people.

It was with the help of many folks that the logistics of this first Texas sun dance began to come together. Then I told Leonard I wanted to delay everything for a year. I thought surely that would change things, but Leonard said that my request was just proof that the ancestors were listening, that that was the traditional old way of doing things, and that in fact he had been testing me to see if I would delay things a year to let everything get done just right. He said he would come down to Austin and help dedicate this ceremonial space. I thought for sure that would never happen, but of course, he did come down and did ceremony at the site of the arbor and did a *yuwipi* to bless the land and our efforts.

The last hurdle involved Leonard's transmission of the sun dance lineage and gifting of the sun dance bundle to me. He told me he would do that on the last day of his dance at Paradise. This, to me, was the biggest hurdle of all. I simply never believed that he would make that transmission and offer that gift during his dance when all of the Lakota people who attend the dance and the other Indian nations represented there were actually present. I thought something would happen so that the presentation would occur after the dance was over on another day, or at another location, or not at all.

But instead, in 1997, on the last day of the dance, in the afternoon, Leonard got on the microphone at Paradise and called me out to the center of the arbor.

He had me walk all the way around the arbor wearing a star quilt, a chief's quilt as he called it, while the drummers played a slow drumbeat and sang a song. I walked around the circle and came to a stop near the tree in the center of the arbor, as he directed, while all the dancers and supporters and chiefs looked on. He called all of the supporters of the Lone Star dance to come out and stand next to me. And then he walked out into the arbor and prepared and gifted me with the transmission of the lineage and the sun dance medicine. He presented the lineage and bundle to me and then called for all of the dancers and chiefs and supporters to file past after the gift was made to shake our hands. After the ceremony was over and we had returned to our camp for the evening, I asked everyone in my camp to independently record their own recollection of what Leonard had said over the loudspeaker to me and us during the ceremony. Later, I read our notes back to Leonard to make sure we had correctly recorded his words. This is what he said:

Relatives! Listen. Look at the sacred tree. Listen to this drum. This is a sacred way of life.

In the arbor stands a man who knows this sacred way. He has been coming to Paradise for a long time.

He has danced at Paradise for many years.

He is a relative to Frank Clearwater, who gave his own life at Wounded Knee so the people might live.

The ancestors have said for a long time a sun dance in Texas is coming. My dad and grandpa talked about this. They said the ancestors have been praying for this for many generations.

And now, the Spirit has given a man a vision to answer the prayers of the people and bring the sacred sun dance way of life to the people of the Lone Star Reserve.

This man, Mike Hull, holds this vision in heart. He is the person my dad and grandpa spoke about so many years ago.

The people you see out in the arbor around him, Butch, Jo, Wally, Glenda, his friends, and others will help him bring this vision for the people to the people.

And so I, Chief Leonard Crow Dog, authorize you, Mike Hull, to perform and lead the sacred sun dance. You are authorized by me, the chiefs, members of the tribal council, my dad and grandpa, and the ancestors. All of them stand with me today. All of them will be with you when you lead the dance. I give you this sacred bundle, this holy earth, sage, cedar, tobacco, sweet grass, chokecherry, sacred stone, buffalo, and tree.

I give you the medicine for this sacred way of life.

I authorize you to bring the tree to Texas. It is a good tree, a sacred tree, a holy tree.

I authorize you to dream the dream and vision the visions that will help the future generations through this sacred sun dance way of life.

I recognize you as a sun dance chief and present this bundle from a sun dance chief to a sun dance chief because the Spirit wants it this way, the ancestors pray for it this way, my dad and grandpa saw it this way, the old man inside of me says it this way.

I will come to Texas and present you with the sacred sun dance bonnet.

If anyone has questions about you, or your sun dance, or your authority, tell them to come see me. I will tell them about you. I will help them listen to the ancestors.

Relatives, help him. We need to protect the sacred way for the children, for all of the children, for the future generations.

I give you this medicine and this song.

You have many followers and will attract many more.

You will save souls and change lives through the dance.

You will dream the dance.

You will heal the people.

You will help the children, many generations, and the unborn.

You will help many babies be born.

The dance will heal the soul of the people.

It will be the cause of the healing of the future generations.

It is right and good for the people to support you, to support this vision, to support this sacred way of life.

Be happy.

All my relations.

I was frankly skeptical about the whole thing, but in the end I felt that I was being led to follow through on Leonard's suggestion and agreed to lead a dance in Texas. I finally decided that all of the effort, all of the risks, all of the potential heartache would be worth it if there was a healing, or if somebody got up and walked, and if we could help the people.

A man named Rick came to the first Texas sun dance in 1998. He had some movement in his legs but had been confined to a wheelchair for the past year because of a degenerative condition in his back. His legs were atrophied. Rick had been going through a series of healing lodges with my friend Butch in an effort to walk. He had experienced some increased movement and strength in his legs but had not been able to walk on his own. On the third day of the dance, Rick was assisted out to the tree, where he lay on the ground because that was all he could do, and he prayed. And then Rick got up and walked out of the arbor. At first it was a halting kind of walk, a stuttering puppetlike walk. About an hour later, he was still walking a little better and seemed a little stronger. By the end of the day, you would never have known that Rick had spent a year in a wheelchair. We needed help, so I told him to start chopping some wood.

On the last day of the dance, Leonard and others presented me with a *wapaha. Wapaha* is short for *wanbli pa,* meaning "eagle head skin" or "eagle bonnet." The bonnet acknowledges a man's education, knowledge, and experience, which all create wisdom, one of the four virtues. The person will supposedly also demonstrate the other three virtues: generosity, fortitude, and bravery.

I struggle with the burden of the bonnet. In one sense it reflects a continuation of the gifting of the sun dance to me—a process that began long ago, continued with Leonard presenting me with a star quilt and a sun dance bundle on the fourth day of his dance, and ultimately supporting the creation of that dance in Texas.

Does being a sun dance chief make me a Lakota, or a Lakota chief? Emphatically not. I am not Lakota. What it does do, it seems to me, is recognize that I have publicly committed to the Creator, the Spirit, the people, and to myself that I will diligently endeavor to grow into wisdom, to become generous, and to grow into fortitude and bravery. It means, perhaps, that my community is entitled to watch me struggle as I grow in these areas. It does mean that I am accountable to these virtues, and accountable to the people and to God in how I discharge those duties.

I also had a vision about why the ceremony was entrusted to my care, and about whether I was worthy, since I was white, to accept the responsibility. On the third day of the Lone Star dance, I saw a stream of buffalo running from the West through the East gate, running for the tree. Standing outside the circle but around the East gate, I saw many people, each having possession of one of the many reasons why the Lone Star dance was not a good idea. Each person was yelling his or her particular reason at the buffalo as they thundered past: "Don't go in there—he's white, or not red, or off the reservation." The buffalo never slowed down. They stopped to eat the grass growing around the tree. It was as if the people were asking the buffalo to deny their basic nature to feed, or as if the buffalo were interested in the life of the grass, not the philosophical reasons why the grass should be avoided.

To me, the grass sustained the people and was used by the buffalo for that purpose. There was no judging the people as wrong; it was just desire for the food that overpowered everything. Today, I am convinced that we are the grass, that our function or role is to feed the people, that the people will be fed because the food is good and healthy and life giving, that the opinions are all of a class that the food should not be eaten, not that the food is bad. The food we provide, the food we are, is spiritual food, and it is available and sustaining to all who would eat it.

12 SACRED TEACHER

White smoke.
Look. Can you hear it?
—Michael Hull

OF ALL THE JOBS I HAVE been entrusted with, none has been more difficult than that of piercing Vincent, a Lakota child. This is what I wrote about that experience.

It's the skin of the boy I will always remember. The pale, innocent skin of the boy, as he reclines on the sacred buffalo robe. The skin covering the chest of the boy moving up and down with his shallow breaths. Little sighs of breath, really. Tiny breaths that move supple skin not yet marred by age. Gossamer hairs shining in the sun cover fine skin as the boy bites down hard on fresh-cut sage.

I see his skin through gray smoke. I can smell the cedar burning in a rusting coffee can. Gray smudge smoke drifting over innocent skin, obscuring what I am about to do.

Pale, rusty skin. Not red really, any more than mine is white or hers is black. Penny red is good. Penny skin moving up and down, up down.

The boy's eyes are peaceful. He knows what is coming, and he is calm. Trusting. Big, brown, calm, peaceful eyes envelop me, hold me, trust me. His eyes hold me; my hand grasps metal. Sun-warmed metal. Surprisingly heavy. Aluminum and steel, I think. A dull chrome finish. A No. 3 handle, a No. 11 blade. A sharp, pointed No. 11 blade. Moving soft skin. Up down. Up down.

I wonder how much of this Abram felt? Abram with a boy. An innocent boy with soft skin and trusting eyes. His boy, Isaac. His favored child. Did he cover the boy's eyes? Close his mouth? Was that boy bound, or did he lie, as this one lies, on buffalo skin, looking up with brown trusting eyes?

The boy's breath moves in rhythm with the drum. A steady beat, a strong beat, thump, thump. Dancers sway with the wind in the hot sun, blowing bone whistles with parched throats in time with the drum. Whistles begging God to hear us. Crying whistles. Beating drums. Singer's voices carried on cedar smoke and beating drums:

Wakan Tanka. Unsimala ye (Grandfather have pity on me).

Wani wacin na lecamu welo (I do it this way so the people may live).

And how many people do it this way for that reason? How many people dance for four days with no food or water, gazing at the sun? These men behind me. My sisters around the circle. And this child, who assumes the burden of a people worshiping a mysterious God, a nation ravaged by the cruelty and indifference of white time.

Here there is no time. Just movement. A continuous moving cycle of up down, up down. Our movement is up. We lift the sacred tree. We raise fervent prayers with parched throats. Our hands point skyward. Swollen eyes gaze at the blinding sun. Chanting voices, crying whistles, gray smoke all ascending to a great mystery we believe something about and know less of. And all of our ups are met, overpowered really, by one down. A great golden sun pounding down, down, down on us. Gentle when we are strong. Relentless when we are weak. But whether gentle or relentless, the sun is always steady, steady as the drum. Up down, up down. Thump. Thump.

The drum beat begins to move through me. The beat raises me above the boy, past the gray smoke and crying whistles, above the sacred tree, beyond the circle and pine boughs through the sun to a cloud. A small cloud really. Not much bigger than a porch. A vista where I look down and see the circle, the sacred tree, the boy. Faint whispers of crying whistles, of the drum, reach my ear. Thump. Thump.

I see my friends, my brothers and sisters. I see them as if they have no clothes. No skin. Just bones and form in space, decorated with personal ornaments of choice and chance. The skin is on the ground crawling to the tree. Anger. Bravado. Arrogance. Nervousness. Fear. All of the skin we show to hide ourselves. All that is skin that we see every day long after we quit looking at bodies and hair and new shirts and dresses.

And then the bones and form fall away. Here a sadness, there an anger, a history of abuse, an abusive history. There is fear and sickness and hate. There goes a happy disposition, tumbling off a skeleton of "they won't like me." There go jeans of anger thrusting, thrusting, "keep away," "keep away," yet always connecting, touching, reaching out for more.

And when all the skin we see, and all the bones we hide, fade away, I see coming up from some place deep and buried the hopes and dreams and glory of who made us and of what we are. And what I see is so breathtakingly beautiful as to pierce the profane and reveal the beauty of all we are or ever will be. It is the beauty of a people who are made in the image of a mystery too profound for us to understand or even behold. And this beauty is fragile, fine, so precious, that we hide it away. We hide it with clothes and skin and bone and form lest it and we be trampled by some ill-perceived demon, and our hearts trampled along with it. I see fragile hope, uncertain joy, glimmering faith, unrealized dreams all displaying their aura of beauty. It is this hope, this faith, this holiness that clutches my heart with gnarled hands and squeezes and twists and pulls until I think I will drop, only to be released and caressed, to rest and wait for the next time. "Remember this," I hear. "Remember thump thump," says the drum. Remember your birth. Remember you are much loved.

Remember the boy as the cloud fades away and the drum brings me back down to a sacred tree and a No. 11 blade and my steady hand looking at trusting eyes and soft skin moving up down, up down. Thump. Thump. And then I see two spots on the chest of the boy. Not big, really. Penny size. One just above each nipple. About two inches above. And behind me are other boys, men now but still boys, still some mothers' boys, dancing naked in their clothes, swaying before the God sun, with chests and skin, and skewers stuck through their penny holes, by my hand, my hand, my hand.

Blood streams down sweating skin, and my boys are pulling, pulling, skin skewer rope, dancing with the tree. Each friend pulling and ripping and tearing his skin and my heart. Bone whistles cry to the Creator to hear us, see us, reach down and touch us your people, who give all we have to you. And what we have is our skin, our bones, our robe, and it is not much, yet it is everything we have to offer that is ours to give. We stare at the pounding sun through swollen eyes and pierce and dance, and beg you to look down and see us, and help us see you. Look up. Look down. Thump. Thump.

Finally one boy breaks free, and then another. Breaking free of tree and rope and old clothes, skewers pulled through ripped skin, my boys are led around the circle back to the tree, beautiful in their hopes and dreams and joys. And while the singers pray and the whole arbor moves up and down, the little boy with the beating heart waits and breathes and looks up at me with those piercing brown eyes as if to say, "Come on, let's get on with it."

Any other time they would put me in jail for what I am about to do. Rub, pull, cut, stick. Anywhere else this is front-page headlines. Man cuts boy, man pierces trusting boy with brown eyes using a No. 3 handle and No. 11 blade. But here somehow that is not quite right, not "appropriate." A funny word, "appropriate," meaning proper, or to take possession of. So is it right, is it proper, to take possession of the skin of the boy? The twelve-year-old boy with the brown trusting eyes and the soft skin? *Tunkashila. Unsimalaye.* Thump. Thump.

Let's start with this side. Rub that skin. Rub that penny. Rub round and round with fresh-cut still-wet sage. Focus on the skin. On the penny. And from somewhere a tunnel comes. A tunnel of sight and sound. A tunnel of slow motion so that all around me drops away. The music fades, and all I see is the boy. Only the boy. Only the skin. Only the penny. Pull up the penny skin with thumb and finger. Stop. Where are the pins. Here.

Here are the pins. The skewers. Lovingly made by someone. The size of my finger. Pointed. Sanded. Smooth virgin wood. Prayed over. "Quick, hold them here." Hold the smooth, sanded, prayed-over pins right here while I slice open the young skin of the rusty red boy with brown trusting eyes and calm shallow breaths. Grab that skin. Hold it. Pull it up. Stick the scalpel through. Cut. Cut. Up down. Up down. The boy's hand tightens. His toes curve around. His heart is like the drum: thump, thump, thump, thump. Quick. The pin through the cut. Through the hole. Now the other side of his bleeding chest. And he is done. Or nearly so. He is frightened now a little. Doe eyes, the breath a little quicker. But his family sweeps him away. Cheers. Yells. They carry him away to his rope. His rope tied to the tree. The sacred tree. The holy *wakan cha.*

And there I sit. Under the tree with a bloody blade. And gray smoke in my eyes, and a hand squeezing my heart. Twisting and pulling. Twisting. Pulling. A twelve-year-old boy by my hand, my hand. Up down. Up down. Thump. Thump.

How many years now have I done this? How many pierced? How many cut on, pins in, take him away? The smell of blood. Of offering. Of life spilling on the sacred buffalo robe. Why do we do this, you ask, they ask, I ask. And then another lies down on the robe as the drum beats and the bones cry and the boy pulls on the rope tied to the tree tied to the boy tied to me.

I will never forget the skin of the boy.

13 SACRED BALANCE

It is always a mistake to be led by power, even to God. Let weakness be your guide. Let illness and craving and fear show you where God's love is needed. Then go and be that love.

—A. Attansio

Love proceeds from wrong to wrong.
Only an absence requires miracles.

—A Course in Miracles

A *WAPIYE WICASA* is a medicine man. A *wapiye winyan* is a medicine woman. *Wapiye* means to fix something that is broken; for example, a body. It comes from the root *piya,* meaning to mend or redo. Learning to heal, learning how to heal, is something we can only be just so good at. It is such an art that about the time we get decent at it, we die. Learning to heal is tough because there are few textbooks and lots of quacks. So most of us learn on a hit-or-miss experiential basis.

I did not start out believing I was a healer. My mom was the first to describe me that way. Later, my counselor LaJeune claimed that gift for me. During a visit at my home in the early 1980s, she became very ill and asked me to lay hands on her. I did, and she recovered. She was healed, and I was scared. Poor Jo Todd listened to hours of denial from me about healing—I denied it, yet secretly wanted to believe.

Sometimes I think God called me to be a healer because I was so sick. For somehow, in the process of healing, as the healing energy of God's love pours through us to our client, we are healed in the process. Jamie Sams taught me that the heart can be healed, that we can live past the hurt. She taught me that two things the heart fears are pain and death, and that the fear of pain prompts the heart to work to avoid pain. After I learned that the heart cannot die, I understood the risk was one of hurt, and that the hurt would heal.

Jamie Sams is another bigger-than-life, big-hearted woman. I met her in Austin when she was here on a book tour. We hit it off and parted with a promise to get back together. Sometime after that, I saw Grandpa Fools Crow and Buddy Red Bow. They both recommended that I go see Jamie to promote further healing of my broken heart. Jamie was kind enough to invite me and several others to her house, a lovely spirit-filled home in New Mexico. After we visited for a while, Jamie announced that I had poison in my heart. She said that the poison prevented my further recovery and I would have to be healed if I wanted to expand my capacity to love. Jamie did a ceremony to remove the poison and heal my heart. I distinctly sensed something coming out of my heart, and Jamie fled the room to throw up the bad stuff. A year later, I married the love of my life.

Jamie's teachings are so powerful that she could not teach enough people fast enough without wearing herself out. So, the Spirit directed her to record her teachings in books so they could reach more people. Her materials are listed in the bibliography, and they are well worth the read. Those who meet her are likely to have an experience they will always treasure.

If I have learned anything in the world of healing, it is the importance of the decision to love. The decision to choose a perspective works something like picking the kind of oil we will use for our engine. Pick anger and hate, and that oil will run through our engine, and we will become anger and hate. But choose love and it is that oil we experience. And if we love, if we choose to love, then we become love over time, as God's love heals us.

One of my best teachers about healing was my friend Sarah, who had a form of cancer since she was a child. This particular form of cancer is considered incurable. It creates small tumors just beneath the skin that quickly spread to other body systems. The only known treatment for this disease is to detect and remove the tumor before it spreads. When I began to work with her, Sarah had not gone longer than six months without undergoing the surgical removal of one or more tumors. She had undergone surgery nearly a hundred times.

Sarah was in my therapy group, and I had known her for several years. She loved snakes and butterflies. Boa constrictors and monarchs were her favorites. I had grown fond of her, and had also become impressed with my own abilities as a healer. So, I violated the first rule of healing: that healing must always be by request. I violated the rule by asking Sarah whether she would like for me to heal her of cancer. She agreed. How arrogant I was.

Sarah and I began to meet weekly for a healing session. I cautioned her not to expect a sudden healing. In my experience, a sudden, dramatic healing generally occurs only when such a display would benefit the community.

As we began our healing sessions, I also worked with Sarah toward developing a new God—a God that would keep her free of cancer. I should have gotten a yellow flag for another violation, because I never asked Sarah what healing would look like for her. I assumed that healing was life here as I knew it. How was I supposed to know what healing looked like for her?

As we worked on healing and a new God, I asked Sarah whether she wanted to live. Her answer was ambivalent. If living meant living free from cancer, then yes; otherwise, no. I should have seen that we must decide to live, and have faith that God will let us if we ask, if we are to live. We began to work to fill Sarah's God hole with the new God and clear away the clutter that was there. One day, Sarah hit an issue, and fear of that issue, that was bigger than her new God. So she began to use the process less and less. By that time, Sarah had been cancer free for almost two years. I was so proud of my success that I quit asking God to heal her.

A short while later, Sarah developed a new tumor and died.

I have spent many agonizing hours pondering Sarah. Of all of the teachers I have had about healing, she made the greatest impact. For a long time, I thought Sarah would be alive today if I had acted better or differently. If I had had more faith. I doubted my new God and all that I had learned. In a very real sense, Sarah had become my grandfather, and I was reexperiencing my struggle over his death.

I was still at the stage where I wanted to control God and avoid my fear of pain and death. I failed to see the healing process as another opportunity to promote union with a God who loves us past our fear and pain. I failed to see the reality of life and worked instead to create my own reality. I failed to see the teaching of being wrong, of having my illusions dispelled by life experience.

The teaching of being wrong is a powerful and painful way to learn. As I heal, as the layers of mistakes become uncovered, I discover at increasingly deeper levels what false beliefs I have and how these errors create harm in my life. This teaching puts me into the East with the freedom to vision new ideas to address old challenges.

Sarah's death fueled my doubt and made me question the widsom of living in my heart. Her death had prompted a kind of rage at God and a renewed sense of my own powerlessness over my life. My family, some of my friends, and many of my Lakota friends kept asking me why I was going to ceremony. Wasn't I wasting time? Didn't I realize it was for red folks? What was I doing there? The question was beginning to seep in: What am I doing here? And as my depression deepened the question turned into "What am I doing anywhere?" I was desperately seeking some kind of answer, some kind of response that I had not gone off on a huge mind trip. I decided to take a trip to the coast to clear my head. Is there anything to this ceremony? I wondered.

On the trip, I decided to ask God for a sign. Jo Todd, Burney, and Mary Thunder, separately, had all suggested that perhaps Sarah had been healed and that it was my definition of healing that had been in error. I thought, but what about the people who have crawled into my sweat lodge with cancer and have crawled out cancer free? What about the person now free of kidney disease or the one with AIDS in remission? That, I thought, is healing. But, ultimately, I asked God whether my teachers were right. I asked God to teach me about healing and about Sarah. As these thoughts flowed through my mind I swerved to avoid a snake, and a monarch butterfly splattered across my windshield.

I stopped the van, got out, and gathered together the various pieces of the smashed butterfly into my left hand. I closed my hand and got back into the van. Driving away, I said, "God, make me a channel of healing life energy." I started humming a healing song taught to me by my Lakota friends. In a moment, I felt something in my hand. I opened it, and there sat a big, beautiful monarch butterfly, flapping her wings. I stopped the van, opened the door, got out, and watched her fly away.

All the ceremonies are actually driven by songs. There is a song for filling the pipe. There are sweat lodge songs, sun dance songs, *yuwipi* songs, and other ceremony songs. People today often fail to appreciate the role of songs in the ceremony. In the first place, all of them are very heart-won. They were generally given to someone on a *hanbleceya* and then passed down to others with authority to sing them. My Crow friends, for example, still identify specific songs with specific people, and only those people are authorized to sing certain songs. Still, when sweat lodges are held these days and people sing songs, they do so without appreciating the fact that the song exists in the first instance because some person spent a long time standing on a hill without food or water, praying to the Spirit for a vision to help the people.

The songs themselves identify us to the Spirit. They let the Spirit know that we are here and that we are asking for a piece of help for our people. We ask for a healing, or food, or finding a lost object, or finding our way, or some other kind of help. This tells the Spirit that we have been here before and that we are asking for that kind of help.

The elders' concern about the training of those who lead ceremony is well founded. It arises out of the purpose and nature of ceremony. Most ceremony is described as having a transformative purpose, a kind of death of the old and birth or rebirth of the new—a denying to disease and a rebirth to life.

Some traditions use words like those but tend to describe a symbolic transformation death of an old lifestyle, thought pattern, or way of conduct. My Lakota friends recognize physical death and rebirth as a potential aspect of ceremony. Thus, one of them describes vision quest as a process of death and rebirth centered on a prayer for a vision to benefit the people.

The physicalness of the ceremony recognizes death as a distinct possibility of the process. One really is in a hot lodge for longer periods of time than a sauna manufacturer or physician might recommend. Skin really does blister in there. People really do dance for days on end with no food or water, staring at the sun. People really do stand on a hill for days with only a blanket and a pipe, and maybe a knife for protection from unfriendly relatives. People really endure lack during these ceremonies. And yes, people really do die, even with an experienced, trained, authorized intercessor. Every few years, someone will die during a sun dance. People can die on a quest. A friend of ours was put out by a Lakota man on her vision quest. She was tired of living and tired of life. She was praying for a transformation. And when the intercessor went to retrieve her, she had died.

Not long ago, the papers ran a story about someone not traditionally trained who conducted a "vision quest" by burying people in sand up to their necks, putting plastic bags around their heads, and giving them straws to breathe through. My Lakota friends were outraged that someone would do such a thing in the name of "Indian" ceremony.

It is odd, ironic even, that such an interior ceremony should have been the ultimate arrow that broke open the issue of whites and ceremony. The history of this issue represents a curious underground mix of politics with principle, power, money, pride, and possessiveness. I first heard about the issue long ago. Whites, it was said, do not participate in ceremony and are not invited to. The societies are closed. The medicine is forbidden to whites. Whites should not own a pipe, carry a pipe, pray with a pipe, or for God's sake even be seen with a pipe. But the issue is not necessarily that clear. My Lakota friends point to no tradition, oral or written, prohibiting whites from participating in or with ceremony. In fact, the opposite is true. Everyone from Father Buechel, who settled in Lakota land in the early 1900s and wrote the first Lakota–English dictionary, to early settlers had contact with ceremony. The early Lakotas presented President Ulysses S. Grant with a pipe. Coach Phil Jackson was adopted and given a Lakota name.

No, what kicked off the problem were a few people, mainly not Lakota, often with no training, who adopted silly names and started offering to lead other people through "Indian" ceremony, often for a fee. This was offensive to my Lakota friends for any number of reasons. The purists were offended that the ceremonies were being offered by people with no training, who were bastardizing the sacred in the name of the sacred. There were those who objected to a white guy calling something made up "Indian" (whatever that means) when in fact it was not. Then there were many people who charged fees, often exorbitant, for the privilege of leading an Indian ceremony. Meanwhile the real Indians who had been trained and authorized to lead ceremony froze through the blizzards back home on the reservation.

People who properly lead ceremony act from a position of trust and are viewed within the community as a fiduciary of the sacred. The leader is called by the Spirit and is recognized by the community who then watch the person to see whether and how he or she responds to the call. A person must undergo many ceremonies, arduous tasks, and numerous sacrifices before leading ceremony. This is a far cry from a self-styled shaman deciding to hold a sweat lodge or lead a vision quest and placing a magazine ad broadcasting the event and the price.

As interest in ceremony grew, an Indian who likely had few possessions, who perhaps lived at or below the poverty line in a traditional way, and who had received a pipe made in a traditional way (which can take over a year to make) would suddenly find himself sitting next to some white guy who had purchased a pipe the weekend before. The Indian had perhaps grown up with the songs, with the traditional stories about how the pipe came to be and how to care for a *chanupa*, knowing the pipe songs, while the white guy just had another toy.

All of the resentment seemed to boil over when ads for vision quest began to appear. Nonauthorized white people would offer to put you or me out on a "Lakota vision quest" for some ungodly fee. And my Lakota friends rebelled. No whites, no pipes, no ceremonies, no participation. Some even went so far as to draft resolution on the topic (see appendix). The Pine Ridge tribal government passed a resolution in 1998 prohibiting white participation in sun dance. The *Lakota Times* often runs articles condemning whites and the Lakota people who allow our participation in ceremony.

The whole issue of plastic medicine man Indian wanna-bes hit a peak of sorts several years ago. Leonard Crow Dog had come to visit Mary Thunder for a prayer ceremony and had stayed for several days. One remarkable evening, he got us into a big group, gave a long talk, and presented several of us with eagle feathers. We then ended the evening with a long group sing. The evening was photographed by a friend of ours, and there were several pictures of Leonard sitting next to Thunder and a woman named Augusta Ogden, who played the drum while we all sang. That picture got out of our group's hands in some way that is still mysterious to all of us, and on the day purification started at Leonard's dance, the new edition of the *Lakota Times* came out. Who should show up on the front page but a picture of Augusta Ogden sitting next to Thunder and playing the drum, with Leonard cropped out. Underneath was a caption about plastic medicine people, including Thunder. The article went on to say that these people would arrive at lodges in limousines and feed people caviar at the sweats. Now, having been in almost all of Thunder's lodges for several years, I knew that both of those charges were untrue. But the paper apparently did not bother to check the accuracy of the statements.

There are many valid reasons for and against whites participating in ceremony, but the issue is simpler for me. Ceremony saved my life. Vision quest saved my life. I refuse to believe that a benevolent Creator would show me the way to health but prohibit my walk down that road.

My work and its demands constituted a major factor in how I chose to develop my healing practice. By the late 1980s, I was a partner in a major law firm, I was maintaining a one-on-one style healing practice at a Healing Alliance in Austin, run by my friend Jo Todd, and I was participating in, sponsoring, supporting at, or helping to lead numerous pipe ceremonies, sweats, vision quests, and sun dances. I was also trying to spend time with my stepchildren, family, and friends; maintain the kind of personal spiritual discipline that allows everything else to work; and spend a weekend a month with my teacher if all the other activities didn't take up the entire time.

Of course, most of my friends from the healing side of life could not understand how I could get up every morning, put on a coat and tie, and go to work. Most of my lawyer friends thought the healing practice was just very strange—if they knew anything about it at all. My work demands were significant, my legal career was back on track, and I was beginning to have some success as a lawyer. As a follow-on to the vision I had in Grandpa Wallace's sun dance arbor about moving from the place of paying bills, to the place of knowing, to the place of today's world, I often had the experience of leaving a major or significant ceremony on a Sunday and—despite my injunction to others that they give themselves several days of rest and gentleness after a major ceremony—needing to appear in court the next day. In fact, one memorable sun dance saw me completing the dance in the evening on Sunday on the West Coast, flying all night (through Las Vegas, an interesting place to stop after a week in quiet ceremony), arriving in Austin about six, and rushing home to clean up, tend my wounds, and appear in court at nine that morning.

I believe my world presented this challenge as a continuation of the lesson about staying in today's world, and also to help me learn that the divisions I imposed between the secular and the sacred or between the sacred and the profane are self-imposed divisions and that, in fact, all we see is sacred.

I learned that I would characterize some things as secular or not sacred as a way to justify conduct in myself or others that I would not permit myself or would discourage in others in a sacred world. Harshness, going for the jugular, being aggressive, being judgmental—all traits occasionally viewed with favor in the secular world—are not necessarily high on the list of approved virtues in the sacred. As my worlds began to merge, I had to address my points of view about what belongs in the secular and sacred worlds. What I found is that some of my attributes in the secular world really did have a place in the sacred and that some of my secular traits were really just the old ugly "I want" disease hiding out in a new place.

As more people in my law world found out about my other life, I found that most of them just didn't care. They were so absorbed in their own dramas and traumas that my own unique form of weirdness was just not that important to them. Only my self-centeredness had led me to believe that my world would be a center of theirs. Of course, some people did and do care, but as my secular world has continued to merge with the sacred one, my success as a lawyer has increased, not decreased.

I also made the decision to address the time problems. The heavy time demands of all of these activities required me to either quit doing some of them or speed them up. In that regard, all the teachings about blue time became helpful as I learned that some things could be done more quickly and often better.

Another decision I made was to deemphasize my individual practice and to work more with groups of people. About that time I began leading groups at the Healing Alliance and also began a steady practice of leading sweats. Of course, being a hollow bone or a channel of energy for ten people instead of one requires a greater emptiness, a greater flow for me to do my part, which in turn requires cleaner sacred space and more personal work. Later, when I began to lead *han-*

bleceyas and lead larger groups, the process repeated itself: more personal work to create a greater sacred space and sacred area, to be a clearer hollow bone for the Spirit to channel through to heal and be of service to the people.

A few things about healing are relatively clear from my experience, and I offer them to you for what they are worth. I think of them as the guidelines or boundaries that help create sacred space and also as steps to secure the healing I believe we are promised by virtue of our existence in life.

It is important to know the persons being healed: their likes and dislikes, their patterns, their history, their parents and grandparents, where they came from, what kind of work they do, their marital status, whether they have children and siblings. I believe having a general sense of this information is vitally important. Illness does not just happen; rather, it happens in the context of a life and of relations of people, places, and things. It is important to understand where the person has come from and where he or she wants to go while entering into the healing process.

It is important to have an appreciation of what is to be healed. Broadly speaking, perhaps all healing is the same because all illness is the same. At the same time, it makes some difference whether the focus of the healing is on a broken leg or on a broken leg that won't heal. Are you addressing the cancer or the harmful effects of the chemotherapy? Are you treating depression? Accident proneness? An increased incidence of illness? Anger and grief? Not all physical illness is necessarily the result of some underlying trauma, but most physical illness has emotional trauma associated with it, and the emotional trauma can on occasion drive physical illness. It is also apparent that both physical and emotional illness can be driven by spiritual disease.

It is important to understand the patient's commitment to the healing. Has the patient come to you after being badgered into it, as a function of curiosity, or as a deep-seated commitment to healing, which you can facilitate? Inspiring or helping the patient to find a deep-seated commitment to his or her own healing is a huge piece of the process. Without that, many healings cannot occur. It is the first hurdle that a patient must jump over on the road to recovery. Sometimes our role as healer is simply to inspire the creation of that desire to tend it while the person goes through the healing process. It also seems to be true that even those with a deep-seated desire for healing sometimes do not heal and other measures are required.

In that vein, it is important to appreciate not only the commitment to healing but the motivation for healing. Is it a fear of death, a longing for life, a desire to avoid pain, or a desire to heal in order to be of service to others? I will accept any strongly driven motivation for healing, since it has an energetic push behind it. I know healers who prefer more positively driven motivations, and I generally think those are preferable, but a person who is ill to begin with may not have them.

It is helpful to have some understanding of the mechanics of the illness or injury. Despite my own desire to believe one walks across water simply by virtue of one's own holiness, we live in a cause-and-effect world, at least on some level, and healing has cause-and-effect attributes and consequences. So it is helpful to know that a cancer of this or that type has this or that origin, has this or that expected course, or this or that expected end result. And I believe it is also helpful to know how medicine would treat that particular illness or injury or disease.

It is important to have an appreciation of where a person is spiritually and emotionally. The healing process is a great opportunity to assist patients in doing a spiritual inventory and to encourage them to take steps to promote their own understanding and faith, to assist them to examine some of the larger emotion-based processes that drive their life, and to help them understand the energetic consequences of those processes and what role they play in their life. Those whose lives tend to be based on fear or sex or possessions all have different outlooks on life, and all are driven by different intentions.

It is also important to know, if possible, how the patient perceives a healing would affect the person's significant relationships with people, places, and things. Are there aspects of the environment that would hinder the patient's healing or promote it? The patient can be helped to engineer an environment that will support healing, or limit his or her contact to people whose influence could be detrimental. I spend a fair amount of time trying to gather this information directly from the patient and indirectly from others, acting as a kind of investigator by talking to family and friends and also through my own meditations and conversations with Spirit. Sometimes I use a large bag for this process, made by a friend, that two people can comfortably sit inside. It is pitch black inside, and this helps me see the aura of the person I am working with. It seems to provide a safe environment for some conversations with people about their processes. I do not think of myself as a therapist and don't encourage long sessions; I simply do my best to find out where the person is and where we are going in the healing process.

Once I have an understanding of the person, of the disease process, and where the person wants to be or what the person considers healing, then I can move forward to the next phase. I like to spend a fair amount of time gathering this kind of information. After the information is gathered, the paradoxes become more important. I think it is important at this time, for example, to develop with the patient a clear understanding and intention regarding healing, while at the same time having no expectation about the healing and, in fact, being willing to achieve some other result than what was intended or antici- pated. This is a huge part of being willing to ask for something without demand- ing that something be given.

It is also important to have an appreciation of personal work that the healer must do as called for by the patient. The patients who come to see me always strike certain responsive chords, or I have similar experiences or similar emotional processes or similar doubts or lack of faith—or, on occasion even similar physical ailments. I believe that it is difficult for a healer to take a patient further than the healer has gone, so patients sometimes require the healer to be very willing to do their own personal work. And so in the process of loving, of removing my obsta- cles to loving, I have the opportunity to lay on hands, to sink deeper into who they are. It is tricky to continue the descent past the patient's own defenses to the cel- lular level where the sickness exists, and to become so small, yet so focused in the energy, that the organism of disease becomes a visible symbol that can be under- stood and expelled by the host. In fact, I often believe that people are healers because of the tremendous personal work that they need to do. Their desire to see others heal becomes their deep-seated motivation for personal healing.

The format for the healing is also critical. As I learned to work with energy and auras, I began to work with people on a massage table and try to manipu- late their energetic patterns and help them learn new patterns or restructure old ones. Over time, I learned how to do that in some other ways, and yet the sense of contact seems to be helpful to the patient. My Lakota friends do the same kind of healing through prayer in lodges and with the assistance of objects and in ceremonies. All these ways offer advantages in terms of patient acceptance, and create options for inviting the patient to believe that there is an opportunity for healing in the work.

I believe that healing requires a balance of male and female. Kim McSherry, a friend and a fabulous astrology teacher, once explained a theory about this, which I have found to be accurate. She believes that the patient occupies a place in the unconscious landscape, and that part of the job of the healer is to go to that place. The person who is ill is stuck in this mysterious place—lost, so to speak—and healing metaphorically involves bringing the person back. She believes that it is a function of the male aspect of us to go out and find the person, but that it is a female function to bring the person back. Our function, in her view, is to go find such persons and bring them back.

What is the instrumentality that does the healing? Many of my Lakota friends will speak of healing by the Spirit. The Christian tradition speaks of the Holy Spirit. Almost all of the healing traditions I am familiar with name "spirit" as the active aspect of the spiritualness of the tradition involved with healing. Some of my Lakota friends have a more broad-based understanding of Spirit, a sort of all-encompassing Spirit similar to the Christian expression of the Holy Spirit. Others of my Lakota friends have a more narrow view. They describe particular spirits or say that a particular Spirit has a particular attribute. An eagle spirit might have one attribute or a badger spirit another, and the healer has the ability to harness those particular kinds of healing attributes but does not have ability to harness all healing attributes.

I come from the Christian tradition, of course, and understand the Spirit to be a more encompassing term. When I think of Spirit, I have come to believe that I am praying for assistance of the Christian Holy Spirit, or the active aspect of the divine. Once we are into the healing process, whether in a lodge or on a table, in a ceremony or otherwise, we enter into that process with a clear intention but no expectation of achieving healing. We have been careful to understand that healing itself has a unique connotation in a healing universe. For example, sometimes healing is death of the physical body, and sometimes healing is a loss of an organ or a loved one. Healing can take all sorts of forms, and we have to be careful not to limit our understanding of healing to a traditional medicine-based or Western model. I often encourage my patients to do a fair amount of personal work if I perceive that there are physical habits or emotional traumas or abuse patterns or spiritual obstacles to healing. All of this personal work must occur before the actual ceremony. We then enter into the ceremony relatively cleaned out, with a clear intention, a willingness to encounter a Spirit and to renew connection to the divine, and we simply ask in faith and trust for the the Spirit to facilitate the healing. In the process I was taught, I go to find the person or the disease or the disease process, and bring the person back while leaving the disease process there, or healing it or discarding it or doing whatever else is appropriate.

I tend to do a minimum of four sessions to ensure a complete healing, but that is not the end of the process. After the healing itself has occurred, I help people avoid sliding back into old patterns and expressing their gratefulness to Spirit for the healing that has occurred. I work with them as they return, changed, to their relationships with people, places, and things.

We often tell people to be very careful of their energy for the next several days after a healing, because others will be aware of the shift in energy without knowing the reason for it, and they may try to sabotage the healing out of a desire to have things revert to the status quo.

Hopefully this book will further stimulate discussion along these lines. To that end, I have started a discussion group at www.pilamaye.com to see what we can do. Drop us a line with your ideas. We need your help.

14 SACRED TRUST

When an alien resides with you in your land, you shall not oppress the alien. The alien who resides with you shall be to you as the citizen among you. You shall love the alien as yourself for you were aliens in the land of Egypt, I am the Lord your God.

—Leviticus 19:33–34

The fruit of the Spirit is love, joy, peace, patientce, kindness, generosity, faithfulness, gentleness, and self-control.

—Galatians 5:22–23

FOR MANY OF US, coming back from ceremonies constitutes a kind of running joke. Most of us who travel to South Dakota to be in ceremony with our Lakota friends lead a relatively pampered existence. We have homes to live in, we get up out of bed in the morning and have food to eat. We live in air-conditioned homes, walk into our garages, crawl into our air-conditioned cars, drive to our parking garages, and spend a day in our air-conditioned offices. If we go out during the day, it's often for a limited time to go to a meeting or grab a bite of lunch, and our comments are often about our brutal experience with the weather. Often our material needs do not include whether we will eat or whether we have a roof over our heads or a car to drive or money in our pocket, but where to go eat and how to get more money and how to drive a bigger and better car and own a nicer home.

So it is from this mind-set that you must understand the group of us, generally twenty or so, as we plan for our annual trip to South Dakota: a distance of some fifteen hundred miles and a drive that might take twenty-two hours or so. We spend weeks planning our menus, buying the food, gathering camping gear, and getting fresh batteries, flashlights, sleeping bags, warm blankets, the right clothes, mosquito repellent, and all the other camping accessories we think are necessary to go spend a week in South Dakota in "primitive" conditions. When the day finally comes, our bags are packed, the cars are loaded, we have a little money in our pockets, our hopes are high, and we get on the road for that grueling twenty-two-hour drive.

Once we get there, we live outside for two weeks or more. We get up with the sunrise and stay up very late with the ceremonies. We get tired working outside when we are used to being indoors. We're subject to all the elements. We generally come back exhausted and broke, sunburned, and sometimes injured or sick, often without much of what we took up in terms of material goods. Somewhere in the midst of all this (I call it the Saturday night seminar syndrome, that syndrome that sets in when you're sure the seminar won't take this time), someone says, "Why do we do this? We could be Methodist or Baptist and go to church once a week on Sundays or maybe be extra-spiritual and add in a Wednesday night or two, and we could spend two or three hours a week doing that, but we wouldn't come back from church broke, or sunburned, or injured, or bug-ridden, or ill, or other things like that." So, it's a running joke among us to say, "Yeah, gosh—I wish I could be a Baptist or a Methodist or something like that. Why am I here?"

Another way to interpret the question is to ask what am I doing here, with Lakotas, as opposed to the people of my own Protestant lineage. Given how clearly sick I was, given how far I had sunk, why did I look outside my culture of Baptist Protestantism for help?

The question goes far beyond me. A whole generation of white people is looking outside our culture for spiritual direction. And we are looking to oppressed cultures for help. Generations of other-than-white cultures have historically been mistreated by us. The Native Americans certainly have their story, yet so too do the blacks, the Hispanics, the East Indians, the Japanese and the Chinese. And yet, these cultures, which have been oppressed by us, have flourishing religions that are being embraced by whites. Just forty years after forced internment of the Japanese, Japanese Buddhism is flourishing in the United States. Chinese Buddhism and Taoism flourish here. Eastern physical disciplines are eagerly embraced by the white culture. East Indian Hindus have numerous white followers, with growing vibrant ashrams that dot the landscape. Black churches remain the backbone of the black communities and attract a growing number of followers. The oppressed Tibetan Buddhists now count many American followers among their ranks. Louis Farrakhan and his Nation of Islam, the Muslim, all count a growing population of American whites. Countless magazine stories boast about the promise of religious systems other than our own. Even systems with a unique place in America, such as the Mormons and the Church of Scientology, claim a growing number of converts.

I believe we are looking for help because our old answers don't work. I believe we need God just as we need air and food and water, and our historical sources of nourishment are insufficient today to keep us alive. That was certainly true in my case.

We live in troubled times; perhaps all times are troubled. The quantity of homeless, malnourished, ill, poverty-stricken people increases daily. The distance between the haves and the have-nots increases daily, and the percentage of those in the middle steadily declines. HIV, AIDS, hepatitis C, and other diseases run rampant among the people. At least 80 percent of Africans are HIV positive. We stand to literally lose the population of an entire continent in one generation. Ethnic war rages; starvation is on the rise. At home we become increasingly self-absorbed as we exercise, meditate for health, gorge on vitamins, eat expensive health foods, and undergo plastic surgery—all in an effort to feel and stay young, to cheat death for a few more days or months or years. Our distrust of our political system is at an all-time high. Our leaders are less than complete human beings. Our culture is in many ways hitting bottom. So, given the troubled times in which we live, the fact that we are reaching out for help, if unsurprising, is certainly gratifying. Both cultures are troubled. One does not have to drive through too many downtowns to see the evidence of white decay. Like others, I feel and experience the illness and oppressive resentment when we travel on the reservations. To argue about why things are this way is, it seems to me, to argue about why someone is choking to death instead of dislodging the ham sandwich.

I did not start ceremony because of our troubled times. I think I have long held a fascination with the Indians, even though I am not convinced that the Native American of my youth ever really existed. We were fed such a clear picture—either a complete savage, replete with torture, or a noble savage, full of native wisdom. But in either case, a savage.

One component of the romantic idealization related to healing. From somewhere I developed an idea that the Indians were experts in healing, who could heal anything, at any time. The fine points of how this occurred were fuzzy to me, although I do recall having an early awareness that healing had something to do with a medicine man and "ceremony."

The medicine man concept was also idealized. It involved a kind of Jesus-like figure in animal skins, bone, and bits of feathers who could heal with a few words, perhaps a song, and a drumbeat or a whistle. The ceremonies were similarly shrouded in shadow. I have an extremely early memory of a vision quest as being some kind of rite of passage where someone stood naked on a cliff for many days praying to God and having a spectacular kind of vision. In my early teens I was aware of the *inipi,* the sweat lodge, and I saw a ceremony called the sun dance in *A Man Called Horse.* But the details of those ceremonies, or how performing them related to healing, remained unclear. Nonetheless, when I was given an opportunity to participate in ceremony, my interest in healing provided an early motivation for accepting the offer.

I wish my early motivations had been fueled by a crystal-clear vision, or that my intentions had been clear and pure, but such was not the case. Curiosity, for example, prompted me to ask to be a student. The ego desire for personal glory, for ego self-gratification, for an understanding of myself factored into my motivation to learn how to heal. I wanted to be with friends who were already pursuing the ceremonial road and to obtain their approval.

Yet, sitting beside all of those mundane, personal considerations were other attractions. A desire for a personal relationship with my Creator and a path with some promise of providing one. An access door to learning alternative methods of healing. An opportunity to learn the mysteries of the universe, to participate in the path of the heart, to heal and be healed, to gain an understanding of my own heritage by looking at it from the outside. All of these factors played a role in my decision, and perhaps some were also factors in the decisions of others to walk a path outside their own lineage

I do ceremony to sit with God. My Lakota friends taught me a way of filling my pipe that opens my heart space and allows me to rest in God. So, ceremony not only gives me life but also keeps me fully alive in the loving embrace of my Creator.

I do ceremony to learn how to live with God all the time. Often when I go to ceremony, people ask what I do for a living. I say I am a lawyer, and they look at me. They always say, "How can you do this?" (meaning Native American ceremony, which is good) and "that?" (meaning being a dirty, unethical, money-grubbing lawyer). The real answer is that there is no difference between the practice of ceremony, and the practice of law. All of life is a ceremony. It took me years to learn that. I have learned that any person or thing that teaches me about God teaches me about me, that anything I learn about myself teaches me about God, and that what I've learned about God and me applies equally to you and to our relations with each other.

For example, I had a vision at the pipe house. In the vision I saw land, followed by a tunnel, followed by a heavenly land. The tunnel had four parts to it: the East was the *wakang wacipi;* the South was the *inipi;* the West was *hanble-ceya;* the North was the *nagi wacipi.* The old land is my life without God, without Original Instructions, without ceremony and friends. The new land is life when I know how to live in my heart, but not with my heart. The bridge between the two lands is ceremony.

I do ceremony to be reminded God made me. I hear people express concern about doing ceremony because they claim they aren't worthy. The Spirit has told me that worthiness or the lack thereof is an illusion. We are worthy by virtue of our creation and existence in this world. We are worthy because God made us that way. We cannot do anything to become more worthy, nor has anything we have done made us less worthy.

We do ceremony to be healed and to be of service. The quality and quantity of our service are somewhat dependent on us, on ourselves as a vessel, and on the energy we have to give in service to the Creator.

We also do ceremonies for the elders and the children in order that the people might live. My Lakota friends emphasize the value and importance of elders and children: the elders because of their experienc and the children because of their innocence. Both are close to God, the elders about to return to God and the children just having come from there. The elders say the children fulfill another important role. My Lakota friends say that when their elders and wise people made decisions about the future of the *tiospaye* as to what they should do or not do, or where they should go, or whatever, they always based that decision upon what would be best for the children—the seventh generation down the road. I think we also honor the elders because they preserved the way of life from a very hate-filled, prejudicial, brutal, dishonest, murderous system designed to destroy the ancient language and culture and heritage and ceremony. It is the elders who held ceremonies in secret places at secret times so the way would be preserved.

When we are in ceremony we must be grateful to the Spirit for the gift of the ceremony, we must be grateful to people who followed the way long before the white man appeared on the scene, and we must be profoundly, tearfully, joyfully, grateful to the elders who sacrificed so that the ceremonies could live.

I do ceremony because I love it. I love feeling alive, feeling you, feeling the connection to God, hearing the glorious sounds of the divine silence. I sit in ceremony to heal and be healed, to love and be loved, to know and be known, to experience fully the totality of the forest. The lodge door is the magic barrier to the fullness of life. The flap is open. Come on in.

Ceremony also keeps me present, living fully alive in the eternal now, the place I want to be because it is the home of God. For example, a friend went to vision quest. He spent his time inside his ties and was totally bored. He had no vision of any kind, or even interesting birds to watch. He was really angry. When I went to get him, he took one step outside his ties, fell to the ground terrified, and rushed back inside his ties.

Inside his ties, praying, with God, he had felt safe for the first time in a long time and had let down his defenses. Only when he left the safety of his ties did he feel the terror that he normally felt every day. He was so accustomed to the terror he felt for the world that he had forgotten it. Dealing with that terror changed the man.

Many things stand in the way of ceremony. Fear of seeing our stuff is a big obstacle. So is the fear of doing it "wrong." I see this especially where there is a "right" way to do things as expressed in the Original Instructions. There are certainly different schools of thought; my friend Jo Todd says that if you are trying to express your heart then it can't be wrong. Butch says you can't do it right no matter how hard you try. I think that they are both right and the correct rule is that the universe rewards action, and that it probably isn't right or wrong but just is.

Ceremony heals pain. Pain is not necessary for development but growth is necessary to experience pain. Maybe being underdeveloped spiritually made us unable to handle pain and so we drank. My diary said: Pain is the touchstone of spiritual growth.

I find it somewhat more difficult to discern why my Lakota friends picked me to share their ceremony. My Lakota friends are, as a rule, an easygoing bunch. They tend to laugh or cry, or do whatever they do, in the context of the moment they are in. Yet, with all the coolness, there is also a serious presence among them that lives just behind that easy humor. And this mixture is well exhibited in the giveaway ceremony.

I often think my participation in ceremony was a part of someone's giveaway. After most ceremonies, Mary Thunder would give something away to each of the participants. After every pipe, many sweats, following *hanbleceya* or sun dance, on her birthday or my birthday, on holidays—gifting, always gifting. Of course, Thunder was always given a lot of stuff too, but most of those things she would turn around and give at the next ceremony. The process of giving like this created a whole currency of things people could have for a while yet still also appreciate the gift of giving.

My Lakota friends really enjoy the giveaway, which often completes a ceremony. Sometimes symbolic and sometimes real things are given away to the community as evidence, and in honoring of, and in gratefulness for, what was received or given away during this ceremony. This giveaway is done for others, for the elders and the children, for the relations. And it is a gift. Sometimes we give up something in the sense of having it taken from us when we really don't want to gift it.

In the sun dance, we gift out of choice. We choose to give a personal sacrifice for the good of the group. This giveaway is important in the sense that it recognizes that the survival of the group is important; survival of any one individual is not.

One of the four virtues that my Lakota friends recognize is generosity, so the practice of gifting and giving is a deeply held and cherished value in that society. There are many occasions when the society and culture call for things to be gifted: marriage, death, return from a successful *hanbleceya,* or a naming ceremony. One of my early experiences with gifting was the occasion of Thunder's birthday, when the process I was accustomed to as a white was reversed and she gifted us on her birthday instead of the other way around. My Lakota friends say that when gifting occasions arose, people would often give away everything they owned: their clothing, *tipi,* horse, everything. The culture, of course, reinforced this because people would then give the giver new things, so the couple would have a new *tipi* to move into or the quester would have new clothing to wear signifying his spiritual rebirth and return from the spiritual way. The whole process of gifting created a kind of currency where no one ever had too much, no one ever had too little, and everyone got to have new things from time to time.

I have done two major giveaway ceremonies. One followed the completion of my sun dance commitment in my fifth or giveaway year, when I gave away all of my "spiritual" items to people who had helped and supported me along the way. I gave everything from feathers to buffalo skulls to dancing regalia— everything I had except my pipe. On the occasion of my marriage, I gave away almost everything I owned, including clothes, personal possessions, music, books, family-related mementos, my van—everything except my pipe.

There is a giveaway and feast at the end of every ceremony, whether it is a pipe ceremony or a sweat or a sun dance or a vision quest. A big celebratory feast is put on by the person or people sponsoring the ceremony. Then there is a gifting: sometimes large and sometimes small items are given away to whomever it seems appropriate. The giveaway sometimes occurs at a sun dance when somebody needs money for the ride home. A blanket will be put out in front of the drum, the singers play a song, and people can walk by and drop money into the blanket to help the person get home. Sometimes people will bring huge piles of blankets and material and other things and gift everyone there. Sometimes this is done for a successful birth or a healing.

The feasts are also important. My Lakota friends place a high value on food.

This value begins, I believe, with an appreciation of the food itself. Most white people sit down at a table where every item on the table was grown, gathered, and prepared by others and then purchased at a supermarket. With many of the items, such as canned peas or canned corn, the only investment we have to make into that meal is to turn up the heat on an oven. My Lakota friends have a different perspective on that food because they have worked so hard to gather food and prepare it, and there is a direct relationship between the work they do and the food they see on their table.

I see something similar to this from time to time when I watch a white person attend a sweat lodge fire and then watch one of my Lakota friends attend a sweat lodge fire. A sweat lodge fire will consume a certain amount of wood, and in fact, it may have taken a tree twenty or thirty or more years to produce enough wood to make one lodge fire burn. My Lakota friends often have gathered that wood, hauled it to the place of the lodge, and then chopped the wood to the proper size for the lodge. So they have a real appreciation of the work that went into gathering that wood and it is judiciously used for the fire. Some of my white friends attend a fire with precut wood that was delivered to the lodge site by another white guy in a truck. Those white people have wood they have purchased already cut and split, and they do not have the same experience of the energy and effort that went into gathering that wood. Consequently, as a rule, my white friends will use substantially more wood for a fire than will my Lakota friends.

My Lakota friends put great stock in that food that has been gathered. They gather everyone around the table and make sure that everyone has whatever there is to eat, and they are always proud to offer whatever they have. It's freely available to all who gather at the table. My Lakota friends easily understand transubstantiation as it was explained to them by the Catholic and Episcopal priests, because they believe that if you eat a piece of the buffalo or the deer, you somehow are infused with some of the energy of that animal. So they honor it for its bravery or cunning or courage or whatever characteristics they attribute to it. The idea that wine and the wafer somehow are the essence of God was not new to them and was easily accepted.

Often my Lakota friends push away from food because they don't like the way it feels. The spirit of the person who prepared it was troubled, or it wasn't lovingly prepared, and that translates into the food not tasting right somehow, and my Lakota friends won't eat it. Sometimes they complain about getting stomachaches or other illnesses because they believe that the person who prepared the food was not in the right frame of mind while preparing it.

Thunder told us that the kitchen is the heart of all the camps, and I've accepted that as true. We work really hard on our kitchens to make sure that they serve wholesome, tasty food. We have learned that when we sacrifice the vitality of the kitchen to make it an efficient one, the camp as a whole suffers. Only when we have a vibrant and efficient kitchen does that energy radiate into the camp and into the ceremonies the kitchen supports.

I once asked Buddy Red Bow and Mary Thunder about John's question: What was I doing there? The question came up in the context of my reluctance to return to dance a second year. Both of them said, independently of each other, that if I did not return I would merely reconfirm the red view of the white man and make it that much harder on the next white guy to enter the ceremony. They told me that I represented the opportunity of reversing the flow of negativity surrounding the white man. And, lest I feel too much about this, they also told me that someone was going to fill this role, that prophecy predicted it, and that I was merely the latest in a long line of people to give it a try.

Both of them told me that Leonard Crow Dog believed a healing between red and white needed to occur. They said that most of the chiefs and dancers and supporters were watching me to see if I returned, not really believing that I would. They said most people assumed I was like the other white people: although I had vowed to dance four years, they figured I would break the treaty. They said one of the reasons the dance was so hard for me was that I was dancing to help heal the hatred of the whites, which, however justified, was still killing the red people, since that is the nature of hate.

I also think I have a part in eating the energy of the people. As the painful energetic feelings of my Lakota friends are sent my way I have the opportunity to accept that energy as a sacred gift and transform hate into love, judgment into compassion, and so on. It is an interesting experience to be a white man and to also feel hatred, to know the effects of discrimination, to be judged—indeed prejudged—by race, skin color, language, or clothing as being one kind of person, in this case a lying, cheating, stealing, greedy, threatening white person.

The discrimination includes assuming certain qualities of character about me because I am white. Indeed, not just assuming but having an unshakable faith that the assumptions are true. And the discrimination is active. It is a discrimination that says, with regard to a ceremonial way of life, don't let him participate because he is white and will steal it; he is white and cannot understand it; he is white and will lie about it. It is the kind of discrimination that reduces me to an object, a representation of all bad experiences any member of the culture has ever had with a white man. It is the kind of discrimination that says I should not take care of a pipe because I am white. It is the voice saying I should not run an *inipi* because of the color of my skin. It is the kind of discrimination that says I can do all the grunt work surrounding a ceremony because I am white, but cannot lead the ceremony for the very same reason. It is the voice that says I must surrender my leadership role in a lodge to a Native American unqualified to lead a sweat because he or she is Native American. It is the blind eye of discrimination that says I cannot pray the Lakota way, pray with a pipe, pray in the *inipi,* pray on a *hanbleceya,* or pray in the sacred sun dance because of the color of my skin. It is the discrimination that tells me not to walk alone on the highway in broad daylight on the reservation, since I might be attacked or killed because I am white. It is the experience of discrimination that says the women in my group should never be alone, since they might be attacked, raped, or killed because they are white. It is the kind of discrimination that says someone might borrow my car and not return it because I am white and need to be taught a lesson or reminded of my place. It is the kind of discrimination that says I must be taken advantage of, since I do not know the cultural ways because I am white. And then there is the still more powerful reasoned discrimination that says I must be denied life-saving ceremony because I am not Indian, despite all my efforts to live the Native way, while a white-living red person can sit in a lodge because he or she has a defined quantum of blood. There is the discrimination that says ceremony is reserved to reds alone because God gave it to them but to no one else.

The sad thing, of course, is the huge part we whites have played in creating this barrier. Our bad acts are not limited to ancient history or to white government misconduct. My Lakota friends can rightly point to more specific instances of misconduct. White folks running ceremony without authorization or knowhow, doing it incorrectly, charging money, waving crystals through the air, muttering strange incantations, conducting sexual healing lodges where love is free but religion is $100 a weekend. We whites lie about our tribal membership or enrollment or lineage, we lie and take and don't give back to the culture to which the ceremony was given, we dishonor the elders who sacrificed life and limb to preserve the way, we dishonor the spirits, we are not right and not honest, and we do it in their name. And then when some Lakota objects, we talk in huffy terms about how "they" don't understand, can't control religion, or God, or access to God.

Of course all of this is a great reflection for me. Every time I rebel against the Lakota discrimination and say, "Oh no, that is not me," I recall, as I must, the times I have lied, cheated, and stolen, the times I have been less than. And when I look at my white friends acting in such a disgraceful fashion and say, "Oh no, that is not me," I think of all the times I have disgraced myself and my relations.

Some of my white friends think the Lakota are open to me because I can help them. I certainly reject this view to the extent it suggests the Lakota need any more white help. Our "help" came very close to eradicating the Lakota people, and they are probably better off without our kind of friends. I do hope that I am of service to my Lakota friends, at least in the sense that one friend is helpful to another.

Grandpa Wallace once told me the Lakota need the help of people like me to be a translator as a person of the white culture, who can accurately and gracefully translate the experience of my Lakota friends into white language, or lawyer language. He told me that much of our problems relate to our mutual misunderstandings and that although the Lakota can speak on their own as a culture, the day is still distant when the white culture will listen.

Some of my Lakota friends say they let me hang around because one of these days our white culture will tumble from inner decay and that they, who have maintained their cultural integrity, will be there to pick us up. I feel this is closer to the truth, although this view also tends to paint a picture in tones of black and white.

Buddy once told me I was destined to help protect the ceremonial heritage. Heritage is one area where my Lakota friends are way ahead of me. Family connections are somewhat loose for many whites. We likely do not live in the same town, or perhaps even the same state, as our parents or grandparents. Aunts, uncles, and cousins are often distant relatives. Family reunions occur one weekend a year, if that.

Our sense of place is also reduced. We often live someplace other than where we grew up, and we certainly do not live in the same house, or on the same land, or even on the same street. We don't have family stories about our place, about what happened on our place, about the history of our land.

We also don't have a sense of our family stories. We might know a few things about our parents or siblings, or perhaps a nugget here or there about other relations. But we lack a story of our whole family—what we are, what we have lived, what has brought us here.

Buddy Red Bow talked to me about heritage after a radio show he did. He was asked about the Wounded Knee massacre. As Buddy began to tell the story, he told it as it had been told to him by survivors of the massacre and by family and friends who had lost relatives at the massacre. And as he told it I realized Buddy was telling the story as if the massacre had just happened the day before, as if he were there. That is the sense of heritage we have lost.

My Lakota friends who are still on their reserve land allotment likely live with their grandparents and within sight of their extended family. They probably live on or around the land where they have been for years. Perhaps they live in a house their grandparents built. They have a story about this depression in the land, the fall of that tree, the winter when the snow was high and the wind did not blow. My Lakota friends have a sense of family as a close, cohesive unit, not some huge, disjointed mess.

Those who lose their history, their sense of heritage, their sense of place in history, and their stories are, I believe, very ill. Without a family history we lose our past, our roots, and our stability in the world, and we risk losing the whole entire tree.

I also think my Lakota friends are following directions. They tell me that the genetic blueprint for survival here on Turtle Island is entrusted to them, and they have a responsibility to the Creator to ensure its propagation. The Lakotas I know will share oral history with more than one person. We who listen are like seeds. The hope, I think, is that enough seed are spread to enable a few to survive and later sow their own seeds.

A white friend recently received a call from an elderly, respected Lakota woman who had received a dream the night before. The old woman believed the dream was a medicine dream, a dream for the healing of the people. She told several people, including my white friend, her dream in the event she died before the dream was fulfilled. The old woman believed the dream important enough to take steps to ensure that the dream survived her.

My Lakota friends are concerned about the survival of ceremony. They hasten to point out that many Indian ceremonies have been lost, many medicine bundles stolen, destroyed, or locked away in museums. They point out that not all the young people know the language, ceremonies, and culture. They believe that the survivability of the culture is at a crossroads. And like my white friend and the old woman and the dream, I believe that is another reason the ceremonies have been entrusted to me, to help ensure the continuing survival of the ceremonies themselves. In some ways, my Lakota friends are more concerned with survival and less concerned with ownership. They have an interesting sense of ownership, one I find missing in my white culture. They value things in relation to their use to the tribe. So, if Fred has a knife, the knife is a thing of value as it relates to the survival and quality of life of the tribe. Fred's importance is that he is a trustee for the tribe in relation to the thing Fred has. Fred takes care of the knife for the tribe. Fred receives honor as knife protector on behalf of that position within the tribe. In other words, the position of knife protector is valued by the tribe and is honored by the tribe. Fred may be respected for the way he fulfills his job, but the tribe honors the job he fills regardless of the respect anyone has for Fred.

The tribe values its historical knowledge and its stories, games, and past experiences. The tribe assigns the elders the job of preserving and propagating the culture. The position of elder is thus honored because the position is a job the tribe values. The elder may be entitled to respect because of the way in which he fulfills his role, but honor is due in any event. The examples are boundless. Hunter, tracker, gatherer, singer, sewer, arrow maker, *tipi* builder—all possess skills the tribe honors because they promote the survival of tribe and improve its quality of life.

The same is true of the keepers of ceremony. They fill positions the tribe honors. The tribe values its historical collection of healing medicines to its *pejuta wicasa*, its medicine man. The *pejuta wicasa* maintains and expands this tribal asset and eventually transmits the information to a student. But it is always clear that the knowledge itself belongs to the tribe and the *pejuta wicasa* merely caretakes it. Likewise, the *yuwipi* man, or the *olowan wicasa*, all possess knowledge for the use and benefit of the people.

Our culture rarely does this. Our culture is so diverse that what we value or why is hard to pinpoint. We may, for example, honor the position of the presidency without necessarily respecting the man who fills the job. We in our white culture don't hold things as trustee for the benefit of the people. And we certainly don't honor the position and recognize that we have a responsibility to the people because of the gifts entrusted to our care. If our societal members thought that their gifts and talents and possessions were not theirs, but only theirs to take care of, what a difference that would make in our white world.

The risk that whites believe to be inherent in this approach is that someone will benefit from my work without doing his or her fair share in return. But my Lakota friends recognize that everyone must work, and that there is a job for everyone to do. Even a single person doing less than expected is detrimental for the tribe.

All of this is relevant to the sun dance medicine I carry because it is not "mine," as my white friends would say, but only mine to take care of. It is a responsibility entrusted to me to preserve and expand the medicine, and a failure by me to do my job will be detrimental to the people. That is one reason why many of my Lakota friends consider carrying the bundle a dubious honor. The people have entrusted their care to me and one misstep could be fatal to them. Why did they trust a white man to do this?

Responsibility for the ceremonies has been entrusted to several people. I am not alone by any means. I think some people have been led by the Spirit, by their dreams and visions, to entrust me among others with a responsibility of preserving the ceremonies, in the same tribal sense I spoke of earlier. This responsibility is a community one I fulfill for the people. It is not a personal honor and carries with it fundamental obligations.

I want to be as clear as possible here and avoid creating any wrong impression. I am not saying that I think the future of the Lakotas is in my hands. I don't. I do not believe and emphatically reject the notion that I in particular, or any white person, holds the key to the survival of another culture.

Sometimes I think the answer is compassion. My Lakota friends recognize four virtues. The first is bravery: a kind of firmness in our heart, mind, disposition, and conduct in the face of those things we fear. The second virtue is fortitude: patient courage under affliction, privation, or temptation. The third virtue is generosity. The fourth virtue is wisdom: what is true or right coupled with just judgment as to action, sagacity, prudence, or common sense.

I am sure that the white man caused much of the disease and destruction I see among my Lakota friends. I believe our systematic, ruthless policy of destruction almost killed the *cangleska*. But I also believe that love is stronger than hate, that life is stronger than death, that hope is stronger than despair, that prayer is stronger than anger, and that water is stronger than wine. In short, I believe that all we did could not eradicate a people of the heart and that their heart will ultimately play a part in saving our own. I believe it is as if my Lakota friends have been on a one-hundred-year sun dance, sacrificing for all of us to learn the lessons we need to save ourselves. I believe the ceremonies help the youth to live in responsible ways and the young men and women to work to preserve and nurture the cultural heritage. My job, along with others, is to ensure that the ceremony survives and also thrives. That the way is not lost.

I also believe I am a test case, a by-product of the Lakota decision to follow their path of the heart, when they had every good reason to make other choices. My Lakota friends are compassionate, gentle, fun-loving, God-adoring, laughter-filled, generous people. I think they see a culture that is in deep trouble and needs help. I also think they know that if we go down, the sacred hoop dies. I believe they could stand idly by and watch us fall to our own death. Indeed, I think there is much energy behind a movement to do that. But in the end I think that such a destructive impulse will fail because the hoop is not complete without both red and white.

My Lakota friends often pray for health and happiness for the people. They will say that ceremony is life giving, that ceremony is life. Ceremony promotes, prolongs, and enhances the life of the people. Ceremony creates and enhances connection to the divine.

15 SACRED COMMUNITY

My brother, we must be of one heart.
We are all indigenous. We are all Earth People.
Pray for me just as I pray for you.
—**Charles Chipps**

IT HAS BEEN ALMOST THIRTY YEARS now since a small frightened boy, grieving over a grandfather dying of cancer, turned his back on God, family, and friends. Thirty years of hard lessons, painful memories, injury to others. Thirty years of finding God, being loved, living in community. I have two personal gifts of love medicine in my life. Mignon, my wife, is an inspiration, a source of truth, and a constant reminder to examine my future and my arrogance. She is a gift of love in my life. She is a living example of heart living. She walks with grace and beauty. She is my half-side, the part that completes me. We have a daughter, Michelle.

Michelle is an example of what loving from the heart looks like. Michelle may prove to be my greatest spiritual teacher. In the first place, although I've heard a lot of conversation about staying in the moment, there is nothing quite like a three year old to make sure that happens. With her, everything is here, right here, right now. She is very present and accepts nothing less from me.

Michelle is also a great example of love. It is my aspiration before I die to have just one moment of love for another as pure as Michelle has for me and anyone who enters into her world. Seeing the childlike love of a three year old is a gift beyond compare. The trust that Michelle has is also staggering. She is immensely trusting of the people she loves, and even when disappointed is immediately willing to trust again without fear or hesitation or worry. She does not hesitate to continually put her heart out there to be held, and she just expects that it will be.

When I think about the love that Michelle has for me and realize that even this love comes from a finite place, I can't help but reflect upon the great love that God must have for us. Realizing I am only seeing a fraction of that love with Michelle, I appreciate that God's love for me is truly phenomenal and that I can-not even begin to comprehend or understand it.

Sometimes, when it is late at night, when Michelle and Mignon are sleeping, I will look at the two of them and experience the fullness of my love for them. Then I will go outside and say a little prayer of gratitude for my life.

Our community has grown. The small group of people who sat with me on *hanbleceya* in New Mexico has grown to a thriving community from all across America and several countries. I, for so long a student, now have students who have students. Our groups meet to pray, sweat, and cry through the night for a vision for the people. We have friends both young and old, male and female, of

181

many nationalities, from all walks of life. We have our own land now, where we have sweats every Saturday, host visiting teachers, pray, and learn about gracious, grateful, graceful communion with a Creator whose love for us is more than we can know.

Our community gives back to our Lakota friends with gifts of clothing, food, money, and time where and when we can. We strive to discharge the trust bestowed in us by our Lakota friends by carefully taking care of the gifts given to us.

We are not alone. Our community has joined with other like-minded communities who also pray in our old way. The pockets of people are dotted all across the country in groups of ten and fifty and one hundred. We all practice living like good neighbors. Some days are good, some days we know we have more work to do.

And now, on the second Thursday in June, we gather together as in the days of old to practice the communal vision known as the sun dance.

I often wonder how much of this was foreseen by my Lakota friends: how much they guessed at, and how much they find surprising. I wonder about my own family: what to tell my daughter, or my mother or brother. I wonder about the community we have formed, how it will grow or change in the future.

Not long ago, I began to pass on to others many of my community responsibilities. My friends are ready for the challenge. I am ready to be with my family and friends, to hold my daughter's hand, to see my wife's smile. I wanted so much as a younger man; now I want good health for my family, food, a home, and a chance for all to know the gifts of the heart available to all of us.

Another change that occurred on my road was the death of my father. My Lakota friends have another giveaway ceremony that relates to transitioning death, giving away our relatives to the Creator. It is the soul ceremony. After a family member passes over, the family has a ceremony to release the soul to God. I had some skepticism about this ceremony until one year, while I was dancing on the third day at Leonard Crow Dog's sun dance, my father, who had been dead a month, appeared in the arbor.

The year before, my father had been diagnosed with cancer that spread to his bones. It was a painful way to die. I had prayed for his healing, whether through life or death, and for gentleness in his healing. The doctors said he would likely die within a year. I talked to Buddy Red Bow, Mary Thunder, and Leonard about how to proceed and all three suggested I drag the skulls. They said that by dragging the skulls I could perhaps shoulder some of the burden of my father's disease. And so, on the second day of that dance, in accordance with their suggestion, I dragged the skulls around the arbor until the pins ripped from my skin.

My father worked for eleven months, until he went into the hospital on a Saturday. He died on Tuesday. My father had relatively little pain during his illness; bone cancer patients often live their last few months in agony and doped with morphine. My father was able to work relatively free of pain and to complete his life before he died.

I was also protected during my father's illness. When I learned of his diagnosis, I was at the sun dance; when he went into the hospital I was in a sweat; the *wakinyan* raged outside while he died, reminding me I was not alone. And then after the storm broke, in the stillness of the after-storm morning, he died as the sun was breaking through the clouds in one of those glorious Texas panhandle mornings God created just for us. On the Saturday following his death I was in a sweat. Then I was at the sun dance to say thank you for answered prayers, to complete with my father, to give away. In many ways, I have come full circle. My grandfather died of cancer and I left God. My father died of cancer and affirmed my faith in God.

My drinking, drugging, self-centered ways and my slide into agnosticism created a difficult schism between my father and me. My new God healed my personal life, and I spent a fruitful year participating in the healing of our relationship. I let God and my father define healing. I did not interfere. I did not even presume to know what healing would look like. I grieved for the loss of my father. The soul-releasing ceremony asked me to go a little further: to give away, to step out on faith and surrender my father to God.

You can always tell who has died since the last dance. The grieving family will place a lawn chair in the arbor with a blanket, the loved one's pictures, perhaps a few personal items. We dancers will walk past the chair for the four days of the dance, praying for the dear departed. Sometimes the family will stand at the chair, and the dancers will pat them with eagle fans, trying to fan away their grief.

My Lakota friends handle death as a community event. When Buddy died, there was a four-day wake before his service, then the service itself, and then a big feast and giveaway afterward. We all stood watch with Buddy for those four days. And then four years later, there was a memorial feast where Buddy and family were again remembered, and all of this was done by the community.

We whites suffer from the loss of our lost ones. We don't have the sense of extended family shared by my Lakota friends, and we are the worse for it. We miss out by not having a collective grief: the sense that my father's death affects many through relationship—me as a child, others as spouse, uncle, cousin, and friend. This sense of relatedness to family is a quality I admire in my Lakota friends. It helps them remember to be kind to friends and family, to the earth, to our old ones, and to our kids. It is a thoughtful way to live.

All of this is a way of creating a memory of significance for the deceased. After my father's funeral, our family and friends stayed at the grave site and filled in the grave, stopping every little while to change shovels, take a break, or tell a joke, all the while telling stories about my dad. Each of those dumps hurt my heart a little when they hit that hollow casket, but somehow I liked his friends doing it a little better than a bulldozer. It felt as if we were tucking him in.

After my father's death, Leonard told me to bring a picture of my father to the dance. Also, he said, find a *wichaske,* a spirit stick, the height of my father when he was seven, and prepare a *wanagi wapahta,* a spirit bundle, and attach it to the stick and decorate the stick a certain way. Leonard said my father would come to visit me through the stick while I looked at his picture when I was pierced. For two days I danced with the stick. During breaks, I believed it was a stick; I let it rest on the ground. I did not believe the stick was *wakan,* I did not honor it as an instrument of connection with my father. I didn't really believe it would work.

Then I was pierced while holding the *wanagi wapahta* and looking at my father's picture, and he was there. He stayed there for the rest of the day. I cried. We talked and said our good-byes. I yelled at God for taking my dad, and I asked God to take care of him.

After the dance, Leonard took me into a *tipi.* Inside the *tipi* was a fire. Leonard told me I could give the *wanagi wapahta* to the fire and release my father to God, or I could hang onto it and keep my dad. Giving my father to God was hard—probably my single largest act of faith—because even then I could not risk giving my dad to God the Jerk.

I had come full circle. I stood on the precipice with a new God, a new way of relating to myself and others. God had taught me about healing and about my purpose. Once again, to heal I must step out on faith. I placed the *wanagi wapahta* into the fire. As the smoke drifted out of the *tipi* I gave my father to God. I bet he and my dad had a good laugh about it all.

Thunder sometimes explained maintaining sacredness and then giving it away as a statement of gratitude. She expressed gratitude through creating clean space, or cleaning space by leaving places and things, and often people, cleaner than she found them. Just as she helped us clean out the clutter of our hearts so that we could be more available in relation to God and our brothers and sisters, so too would we work on the creation of physical sacred space, working hard to leave it better than we found it.

I believe the giveaway is an expression of gratitude originating from a joyful release of the loving gifts that we have been given that are ours to be responsible for but not hang on to. I suspect that if we went back in ceremonial time far enough, we would find that much of ceremony relates to gratitude.

Wopila is the place of being appreciative or the place of expressing gratitude. Sometime that is joined with *wowanka,* which is a thank-you ceremony or a ceremony to thank the Spirit. As my Lakota friends explain it, in prayer we might not ask our relatives to fix our problems; we might decide instead how it is that we see the problem should be fixed and then ask our relatives to help us do that. Then, if the relatives help us do that, we might have a *wopila* to express our thanks.

Expressing our gratitude releases a healing energy into the world and tends to clean the world's energy and in turn creates an attitude of gratitude in others. When I'm really living in a place of gratitude for life, for my life, for breathing and for seeing the trees sway in the wind or a ripple of water on the lake or the smile of my child or the touch of a loved one, then my heart is full, and it is this love that is so wonderful that I want to share it with others.

Ceremonies are designed in part, I think, to help us fill our heart with that kind of gratitude which is healing to us because we experience it and also healing to others because we get to help them experience it. This space of gratitude that fills our heart is healing and is the space that exists in the middle of the *cangleska*. It is, I think, the spirit of the divine, the Great Spirit, the active hand of God, it is what we seek desperately in so many ways at so many times and through so many methods and avenues. It is my heart I lost and then found.

If my point of view is that every moment gives me another opportunity to love God and God's creations, then I am grateful for that opportunity in whatever form it may take. If my point of view is that my purpose here is to share with you in a way you can see that every moment is a chance for us to love God and our relatives, that my business is to see that God's light shines so brightly through me that you see it and are attracted to it and want some of it, then I am grateful for every moment regardless of the circumstances out of which the opportunity arises.

And so I am grateful for new ideas, for the chance to be in relation to others, for the chance to sit quietly, for the chance to learn from you and from my teachers and elders and children. I am grateful for the chance for my heart to learn, grateful for the chance to sit in my heart, grateful that I have a chance to love you and grateful that you love me, grateful that God loves us both, and grateful for the opportunities we have to share a relationship with one another through our Creator.

The giveaway is a great example of the emphasis my Lakota friends place on good completions, which is a way of ensuring that what was once proper in sacred space does not overstay its welcome. When Thunder completes her ceremonies, she separates her pipe bowl from the stem and says, "For good completions, so we don't have to come back and do this again." My Lakota friends will complete ceremony with the *Mitakuya Oyasin,* prayer, blessing their relations. Thunder often speaks of causeless karma, her phrase to recommend that if you catch karma, let it die with you and don't be a cause of harm to others. The cord-cutting ceremony, cleaning the van, and leaving land cleaner than we found it all describe a process of good completions. The phrase *"Hoka hey,"* attributed to Crazy Horse, is interpreted by Albert White Hat Sr. to mean "I am ready forever at any time." I am complete. My friend Butch says *"Hoka hey"* means "you could die right now and everything would be finished." Good completions is your mother telling you to always wear clean underwear, or the counselor telling us to resolve our marital difficulties each night before we sleep. It is Jesus telling us to make amends with our neighbors before we come to worship, or my father telling me to put stuff back where I found it.

Good completions have an energetic consequence. Good completions closes my energetic connection to a person, place, or event and restores me to energetic wholeness. It means I cannot rely on you as an energy source, and that I am unavailable to you for that purpose.

Good completions is hard work. It takes a consciousness, a discipline, a willingness to encounter the pleasant and the unpleasant. It is also a great gift to those you complete with, and to yourself. As my dad would say, It just leaves a nice taste in your mouth."

For me, one obstacle to good completions is the grief that comes with completions. I have been surprised by the constancy of the principle that completions and grief work in tandem. It is easy to acknowledge that the completion of things we enjoy is sad, but the principle seems to extend to things we don't like and that might be bad for us. I think the desire to avoid feeling all the way through grief encourages us to avoid good completions, which in turn means that we hang on to the people involved in the interaction.

Thunder once taught me a ceremony called a house cleaning. The need for a house cleaning arises when the inhabitants believe the house is inhabited by the spirits of dead people—what we could call a haunted house. Through the ceremony, we talk to the living about the ghost, what the death was like, why the spirit might be hanging around, whether something was left undone. Inevitably, the story includes an enormous sense of incompleteness, something the deceased left undone, or something a loved one of the deceased needs to finish. The ceremony then includes some type of opportunity for that completion to occur, and then all energetic ties to the house are ceremonially severed.

After I began to do house cleanings, I took Jo Todd with me. Jo was a channel and would give a voice to the disembodied entity that stayed around the house. A spirit once told us that our grieving was important to his healing. The spirit explained that our act of grieving created a kind of energy that helped the spirit complete his work here and move to another realm. Apparently, the spirit's work and our grief had to work together to push the spirit out of this realm and into another.

I separated from my second wife about three months after I became sober. She walked in one day to announce that she was leaving. I think the years of mutual abusive drinking finally helped her to her own completion. I decided I would use the time to fully grieve the loss and to give myself a year to do it. And I did. When sad, I cried; when angry, I ranted or raved. I cussed and moaned and hurt until there was nothing else there. It took me two years to complete the process. Along the way I fully appreciated the cleansing, healing power of grief. I came to identify with the pain of those who day after day lock their grief inside—a process that causes the hurt to leak out little by little, littering their sacred space, poisoning all their relationships with the grief resting on their altar.

Some people tell me the grief is theirs to do with as they please. And it is, of course, in a sense. But we do not get to pick or choose what we share from our altar—once we let people connect to our hearts, they get whatever is there, all of it. And since we are all related, since we are all of one heart of our Creator, our grief spreads to our relations. So, the simple fact that it is "ours" does not mean we have the right to keep it or not to dispose of it properly. We see this on a huge scale today with toxic waste. The waste may "belong" to Company A, but it affects all of us, and its disposal is the business of all peoples. Just as that waste is not toxic in its initial form, so too is our grief not toxic. It is only through not being used that our grief presents a danger to us.

I was in a therapy group when I divorced and stayed in it until I felt I was finished. I checked with my therapist, who agreed, and then gave my month's notice to the group and began to plan my completion with the group. On my last group day, I gave each group member and the therapist a gift, something of mine that reminded me in some way of that person. It was a great completion and a fine example of pulling my ceremonial world into day-to-day life.

Not long ago a friend came to a lodge and gave me tobacco to pray for him. He did not identify the particular item he was praying for. I became lost in conversation with another person and later looked at the fire where my friend was offering tobacco to the fire, lost in prayer. I interrupted his prayer, in violation of one of my rules, to tell him the gift-giving therapy story. He broke into a big grin. He was leaving his job for another and wanted to leave his old boss on good terms. He later told me they had a very satisfactory completion.

Once we have created this clear sacred space and stand inside it with our heart in the place of gratitude, being related to all of our relations, then we enter into a sacred conversation with our Creator. Some may call this an entering into; others might call it a deepening of, a recognition of, opening of. But whatever we call it, we maintain or create or enter into a sacred conversation or union with the divine through prayer and meditation or through speaking and listening. And somewhere in the process of prayer and meditation, of speaking and listening with the divine, we begin to establish or recognize or become aware of our own relation with the divine, and it begins to deepen and grow, sponsored by our spirit of gratitude and our open heart standing in humble relationship to all of our relatives. And in this place of wholeness and oneness, we move toward a beingness that neither enlarges nor diminishes our place in relation to ourselves, other nations, or the Spirit.

And in that place of beingness of oneness, we begin to experience the Spirit and the Creator deeply and more deeply through the process in place of silence.

Our union and communion with the creator grows and expands as we prayerfully enter into a sacred conversation and a sacred space that we are responsible for maintaining in a clear and clean way. Through this process of creating and maintaining, and opening and communing with the sacred—whether in a pipe ceremony, a sweat lodge ceremony, a vision quest ceremony, a sun dance ceremony, or any other kind of way that permits us to create and enter into a sacred space and a sacred conversation with talking and listening with sound and light, with heart-based participation and the wholeness of creation—we can directly experience the beginning of the ending of the way of the sacredness of the world. We can see and know who we are in relation to ourselves and to others. We can cellularly experience the moment-by-monent fresh creation of the universe and of our relatives in it. We can see our original face or know our original nature, and we can be of service in communion with our brothers and sisters in a way that promotes health and happiness for the people, as the ceremonies intend.

Knowing what to permit in our sacred space is an exercise in discernment and reflects our wisdom. Knowing what to give away is an exercise of discernment and reflects our generosity. On some occasions we have to put things in our circle that scare us or that we don't like, so that we can pray for them or discover the problem within ourselves that makes relations with them difficult. This is a reflection of our discernment and our fortitude. On some occasions we must accept things into our space that are frightening or scary, that threaten our desire for ease and comfort, our place in the world, and our worldviews so we can see them close and come to know them and understand them. This is an exercise of discernment as a reflection of our bravery.

What I have noticed about my own story and about the people I've worked with and the people I have seen working with others is that the first phase of someone's development, once he or she decides for God, is related to cleaning out sacred space: completing relationships, making amends for past harms, harmonizing financial relationships, initiating and maintaining a time for spiritual communion with the Creator, healing relations with family and friends. Doing this is a lot of work. It requires a huge amount of time and an enormous commitment. It creates a need for substantial change as we amend ways of being in the world, our thoughtforms and emotional patterns that initially created the difficulties based on our misconceptions of God and our own willfulness. The entire process of cleaning out the past helps many of us to return to that divine sense of wonderment, that simple faith of our childhood. It helps us balance our wants with the wants of others and helps give us a sense of patience about where we fit or belong in the grand scheme of things. This phase, whatever its merits, is still self-centered. The changes are beneficial in that our self-centeredness previously fueled our faults and now supports our recovery, but it is still based on me.

With hard work and continued grace, we eventually get to a spot where we are relatively clean. By that I mean we are relatively current with our thoughts and feelings, our hidden agendas have become known to us, our processes are abundantly clear to us, and to a large extent we are living in the present. At this point, a second major shift occurs: we gradually shift out of the way, and the divine becomes the dominant center of our life.

The first phase often relates to my definition of God; that is, in some fashion or another I believe that God is not big enough to keep me safe in the circumstances I face, so I develop alternative conduct to maintain my safety. This conduct is based on a false premise, a godless premise, so to speak, and ultimately harms myself and others. But once I feel I have a God strong enough to keep me safe so that I am willing to surrender the middle of the *cangleska* to God, then the nature of the struggle changes to one of continuing surrender of the middle to God. The problem becomes that even though I know God could keep me safe, the "I want" part of my disease shows up. I learn that in some instances I want what I want, when I want it, just because I want it that way, and it has nothing to do with my perception of God. In fact, I think God is perfectly capable of keeping me safe in this situation, but I want to do it my way anyway. At this stage, I began to see and have the chance of surrendering all of my processes that would have me be in charge.

One purpose—or perhaps benefit—of maintaining clear, clean, uncluttered space is that we reach and maintain a kind of mental and emotional equilibrium, a clear pool of water that can receive the divine communion that's available to us. Many of us are so conditioned that despite, or perhaps because of, our efforts to both obtain and retain peace, our sense of self can be easily disturbed by a kind or harsh word and by an approving or disapproving thought. If I think I am doing well, or if I think you think I am doing well, then I think well of myself and feel good about myself. If I think poorly of myself, or if I think you think poorly of me, then my sense of equilibrium and inner peace is greatly disturbed. If you say kind words to me, I feel good about myself; if you say harsh words to me, I feel bad about myself. All of these things trigger some response, maintained by some piece of clutter in my space. As that clutter is addressed and removed I have a greater ability to maintain that equilibrium. I think that when Jesus was telling his disciples not to enter into worship if they held something against their brother, he was speaking about this sacred space and bringing that clear sacred space to the Creator as an offering for the communion with the Creator that was about to occur. Any clutter inside our space defiles or diminishes or reduces in some way the sacredness of that connection. It pollutes our ability to appreciate the fullness of what is offered.

"Hoka hey" means more than that it is a good day to die. It means also that it is a good day to live. It means recognizing one thing and staking yourself to live gloriously, fully, openly, completely, intimately, passionately to the one thing that is important because you say it is. It is saying that I will risk everything for one thing, because I want to. Now is the time. We are healers, We came to heal ourselves and those around us. We have spent a lifetime preparing ourselves for this task.

We have searched different pathways to a power greater than ourselves: Christianity, Judaism, Hindusim, Islam, Zen Buddhism, Taoism, Sufism, and Native American spirituality.

We have learned about ourselves. We have been psychoanalyzed, grouped, encountered, ESTed, supported, Insighted, Grofed, Rolfed, and Hellerized. We have taken workshops, gone to lectures, studied with teachers, read from, talked about, listened to . . . We have discovered our child, honored our elders, analyzed our dreams, contacted our rage, walked through our fears, and faced our addictions.

We have studied ways to heal: crystals, nutrition, tarot, massage, herbs, astrology, numerology, reflexology, channeling, bodywork, prayer, mediation, yoga.

Now is the time to give away what we have learned. To teach. To heal. To understand and move beyond understanding. To make a difference in our lives and in the lives of those around us.

We lose the "high" of a weekend workshop because we do not give away what we have learned. The information remains locked inside of us. Gradually, that wonderful experience fades away, and we again encounter the same problems with the same feelings, the same attitudes, and the same beliefs. We remain essentially unchanged except for a faint longing that tells us there is more out there. So we wonder what is wrong, we take another workshop, and the cycle repeats itself.

Now is the time to break the cycle, to do what we have learned to do, to be who we are. Now is the time to learn what we have been taught by teaching what we have learned, to reveal ourselves and thereby receive revelation, to empty ourselves so that we have space to receive; to give away what we have learned in order to learn what we have to give, to risk saying, "I am a perfect child of a perfectly loving God who wants me to be happy, joyous, and free." Now is the time.

When my friend John asked, "What the fuck are you doing here?" I did not realize how profound the question was. Just trying to stay alive. Just trying to see past old Gods, false ideas, misunderstandings about you and me. Living past fear and grief and mistrust, living past all the things that would have killed someone not made by the loving and graceful hand of the divine. Doing my part as called on by the elders to ensure the way of life of the ceremony. Doing my part to clean up the messes up our past. Learning to be in union with the Creator, to love and be loved, and to have a little fun along the way.

Grandpa. Thank you for this time and place to pray and for these people to be with. Thank you for the chance to tell Your story about healing and love and waking up a dead man. Thank you for having pity on one of Your creations and gifting all of us with life and love and healing laughter. Thank you for this chance to restore the hoop to its glory. Thank you for this chance to be with my friends and relations as we walk forward hand in hand with You. Thank you for carrying us over the rough spots and helping us stand when things are tough. Grandma, help me every day to love and be loved more and more so that Your loving kindness and gentleness can flow through me to the people You created. Help us to know what You would have us do, and please give us the willingness to do it. Please bless this story and let it help one person, clothe one elder, feed one child, comfort one person. Help this story give to someone else the gift of life You have so generously shared with me. Help all of us fall deeper in love with You.

Aho Mitakuye Oyasin.

APPENDIX: PAPERS

January 4, 1996

To all my relatives,

I am writing regarding the sacred sundance of the Lone Star Gathering of the Sacred Peoples. I have asked my nephew, Mike Hull, to have the ceremony in Texas. The first year will be in June of 1998 around the full moon. Please help Mike and all of us as we prepare for this sacred ceremony.

Chief Leonard Emmanuelle Crow Dog

Relatives, Friends, and Relations:

The Sun Dance is coming to Austin, Texas, the Lone Star State, in the State of Texas, in this land known as the United States of America, in 1998.

I have spoken to Mike Hull and the Sun Dance Committee about this ceremony. A lot of people want to have a Sun Dance and have pledged their support. However, you cannot rush into such a sacred ceremony. I have explained that there is much preparation which needs to be done for this sacred ceremony. I explained about how to present tobacco, the Sun Dance way of life, the sacred tree, the buffalo, the man, and the sacred *chanupa*. I explained about all the things which must be done in preparing the support of this Sun Dance way of life and the things which need to be prepared. I will take care of the eagle feathers and other things.

There are many things which must be prepared a year in advance. The Sun Dance Arbor must be prepared. I shall be there to be part of the ceremony. You must prepare the sacred eagle bone whistles and the sacred spotted eagle feathers and the spikes.

Prepare a place for the sacred lodges. One will face east and the fireplace will be in the shape of a horseshoe in memory of the great leader Crazy Horse.

Relatives and Relations, you have been introduced to the sacred Sun Dance way of life. In that spirit, you need to help each other and support each other. It does not matter the color of the skin so much as the color of the heart.

The Sun Dance will be in June, that time when everything is pure and green. Help each other. Support each other. Prepare your hearts and the sacred Sun Dance grounds for this most sacred of ceremonies.

Relatives and Relations, I ask you to support this Sun Dance. It will be part of a sacred site.

Mitakuye oyasin,

Chief Leonard Crow Dog

At this sacred time, I, Chief Leonard Crow Dog, Sundance Chief for 89 sovereign nations, joined by 21 Sundance leaders, recognize and authorize Sundance Chief Mike Hull and his Lone Star Sundance as the only authorized Sundance in Texas. After Mary Trail dances for four years, and supports for an additional four years, she can ask me about sponsoring a second Sundance in Texas.

Chief Leonard Crow Dog

Chief Leonard Crow Dog
SSN # 504-38-4888
Enrollment #14322
Chief of the Lakota Nation
605-747-3381

MARTHA K. BATISTE
NOTARY PUBLIC
State of Texas
Comm Exp 01-19-99

Martha K. Batiste

August 8, 1989

TO WHOM IT MAY CONCERN

As spiritual Sundaneers, the eagle feather and eagle bone whistle are used in this most sacred of ceremonies. Many races of men and women participate in this ritual. The eagle feather and eagle bone whistle play a major role. Therefore, as a Sundancer, you, Mike Hull, are entitled to have in your possession eagle feathers and eagle bone whistles.

Chief Buddy Red Bow
Oglala Sioux
Pine Ridge South Dakota

SUBSCRIBED AND SWORN TO BEFORE ME on the 7th day of September, 1989, by Chief Buddy Red Bow to certify which witness my hand and official seal.

Delaine S.
Delaine S.
Notary Publ⋯ and for
The State of ⋯s

My commission expires: 12/23/89

TOUCH THE CLOUD

Once there was a great leader
  of the Sioux
Though a man of small stature.
But he was a man who did many
  great deeds for our people.
A warrior, a medicine man,
A leader, and a great war chief.
His name was Chief Crazy Horse.

He had a loyal friend, a brother,
That stood beside him.
  Fought many battles with him
  who shared the victories
  The hard times too,
  But always a friend.

He stood tall and lean
Like a pine tree in the sacred
  Black Hills.
He was strong in heart
Gentle in soul
His name was Touch The Cloud

On this day of August 8, 1989,
I, Chief Buddy Red Bow,
Sundance Chief of the Oglala
Sioux Nation, am honored to

present you, Micheal Scott Hull,
with this name.
For I like Crazy Horse
consider you my brother
And loyal friend.
From this day forward,
Michael Scott Hull, you
will be Known as
TOUCH THE CLOUD.

Chief Buddy Red Bow 89

APPENDIX: DECLARATION OF WAR AGAINST EXPLOITERS OF LAKOTA SPIRITUALITY

WHEREAS we are the conveners of an ongoing series of comprehensive forums on the abuse and exploitation of Lakota spirituality; and

WHEREAS we represent the recognized traditional spiritual leaders, traditional elders, and grassroots advocates of the Lakota people; and

WHEREAS for too long we have suffered the unspeakable indignity of having our most precious Lakota ceremonies and spiritual practices desecrated, mocked, and abused by non-Indian "wanna-bes," hucksters, cultists, commercial profiteers, and self-styled "New Age shamans" and their followers; and

WHEREAS with horror and outrage we see this disgraceful expropriation of our sacred Lakota traditions has reached epidemic proportions in urban areas throughout the country; and

WHEREAS our precious Sacred Pipe is being desecrated through the sale of pipestone pipes at flea markets, powwows, and "New Age" retail stores; and

WHEREAS pseudo-religious corporations have been formed to charge people money for admission into phony "sweat lodges" and "vision quest" programs; and

198

WHEREAS sacrilegious "sun dances" for non-Indians are being conducted by charlatans and cult leaders who promote abominable and obscene imitations of our sacred Lakota sun dance rites; and

WHEREAS non-Indians have organized themselves into imitation "tribes," assigning themselves make-believe "Indian names" to facilitate their wholesale expropriation and commercialization of our Lakota traditions; and

WHEREAS academic disciplines have sprung up at colleges and universities institutionalizing the sacrilegious imitation of our spiritual practices by students and instructors under the guise of educational programs in "shamanism"; and

WHEREAS non-Indian charlatans and "wanna-bes" are selling books that promote the systematic colonization of our Lakota spirituality; and

WHEREAS the television and film industry continues to saturate the entertainment media with vulgar, sensationalist, and grossly distorted representations of Lakota spirituality and culture that reinforce the public's negative stereotyping of Indian people and which gravely impair the self-esteem of our children; and

WHEREAS individuals and groups involved in "the New Age Movement," in "the men's movement," in "neo-paganism" cults, and in "shamanism" workshops all have exploited the spiritual traditions of our Lakota people by imitating our ceremonial ways and by mixing such imitation rituals with non-Indian occult practices in an offensive and harmful pseudo-religious hodgepodge; and

WHEREAS the absurd public posturing of this scandalous assortment of pseudo-Indian charlatans, "wanna-bes," commercial profiteers, cultists, and "New Age shamans" comprises a momentous obstacle in the struggle of traditional Lakota people for an adequate public appraisal of the legitimate political, legal, and spiritual needs of real Lakota people; and

WHEREAS this exponential exploitation of our Lakota spiritual traditions requires that we take immediate action to defend our most precious Lakota spirituality from further contamination, desecration, and abuse;

Therefore we resolve as follows:

1. We hereby and henceforth declare war against all persons who persist in exploiting, abusing, and misrepresenting the sacred traditions and spiritual practices of our Lakota, Dakota, and Nakota people.

2. We call upon all our Lakota, Dakota, and Nakota brothers and sisters from reservations, reserves, and traditional communities in the United States and

Canada to actively and vocally oppose this alarming takeover and systematic destruction of our sacred traditions.

3. We urge our people to coordinate with their tribal members living in urban areas to identify instances in which our sacred traditions are being abused, and then to resist this abuse, utilizing whatever specific tactics are necessary and sufficient—for example, demonstrations, boycotts, press conferences, and acts of direct intervention.

4. We especially urge all our Lakota, Dakota, and Nakota people to take action to prevent our own people from contributing to and enabling the abuse of our sacred ceremonies and spiritual practices by outsiders; for, as we all know, there are certain ones among our own people who are prostituting our spiritual ways for their own selfish gain, with no regard for the spiritual well-being of the people as a whole.

5. We assert a posture of zero tolerance for any "white man's shaman" who rises from within our own communities to "authorize" the expropriation of our ceremonial ways by non-Indians; all such "plastic medicine men" are enemies of the Lakota, Dakota, and Nakota people.

6. We urge traditional people, tribal leaders, and governing councils of all other Indian nations to join us in calling for an immediate end to this rampant exploitation of our respective American Indian sacred traditions by issuing statements denouncing such abuse; for it is not the Lakota, Dakota, and Nakota people alone whose spiritual practices are being systematically violated by non-Indians.

7. We urge all our Indian brothers and sisters to act decisively and boldly in our present campaign to end the destruction of our sacred traditions, keeping in mind our highest duty as Indian people: to preserve the purity of our precious traditions for our future generations, so that our children and our children's children will survive and prosper in the sacred manner intended for each of our respective peoples by our Creator.

Wilmer Stampede Mesteth (Oglala Lakota), traditional spiritual leader and Lakota culture instructor, Oglala Lakota College, Pine Ridge, South Dakota

Darrell Standing Elk (Sicangu Lakota), President, Center for the SPIRIT, San Francisco, California, and Pine Ridge, South Dakota

Phyllis Swift Hawk (Kul Wicasa Lakota), Tiospaye Wounspe Waokiye, Wanblee, South Dakota

SUGGESTED READING

Arden, Harvey, ed. *Noble Red Man: Lakota Wisdomkeeper Matthew King.* Hillsboro, Ore.: Beyond Words Publishing, 1994.

————. *Wisdomkeepers: Meetings with Native American Spiritual Elders.* (Photographs by Steve Wall.) Hillsboro Ore.: Beyond Words Publishing, 1990.

Bettelyoun, Susan. *With My Own Eyes: A Lakota Woman Tells Her People's History.* Lincoln: University of Nebraska Press, 1998.

Black Elk, Wallace, and William Lyon. *Black Elk: The Sacred Ways of a Lakota.* San Francisco: Harper and Row, 1990.

Bleeker, Sonia. *The Sioux Indians: Hunters and Warriors of the Plains.* New York: William Morrow & Company, 1962.

Bopp, Judie, Michael Bopp, Lee Brown, and Phil Lane. *The Sacred Tree.* Twin Lakes, Wisc.: Lotus Light, 1990.

Boyd, Doug. *Mystics, Magicians and Medicine People: Tales of a Wanderer.* New York: Paragon House, 1989.

————. *Rolling Thunder: A Personal Exploration into the Secret Healing Powers of an American Indian Medicine Man.* New York: Random House, 1974.

Brave Bird, Mary, and Richard Erdoes. *Ohitika Woman.* New York: Grove Press, 1993.

Brown, Dee. *Bury My Heart at Wounded Knee.* New York: Henry Holt, 1991.

Brown, Joseph E. *Animals of the Soul: A Native American Bestiary.* Rockport, Mass: Element, 1991.

————. *Animals of the Soul: Sacred Animals of the Oglala Sioux.* Rockport, Mass.: Element, 1997.

Bucko, Raymond. *The Lakota Ritual of the Sweat Lodge*. Ph.D diss., University of Chicago, 1992. Microfilm.

Catches, Pete. *Oceti Wakan: Sacred Fireplace*. Pine Ridge, S. Dak.: Oceti Wakan, 1997.

Churchill, Ward. *Indians Are Us: Culture and Genocide in Native America*. Monroe, Maine: Common Courage Press, 1994.

Clark, Robert A. *The Killing of Chief Crazy Horse: Three Eyewitness Views*. Lincoln: University of Nebraska Press, 1988.

Crow Dog, Mary, and Richard Erdoes. *Lakota Woman*. New York: Grove Weidenfeld, 1990.

Crummett, Michael. *Sun Dance: The 50th Anniversary Crow Indian Sun Dance*. Helena, Mont.: Falcon Press, 1993.

Curtis, Natalie. *The Indian's Book: Authentic Native American Legends, Lore and Music*. New York: Bonanza Books, 1987.

Dakota Textbook. New York: American Tract Society, 1872.

Deloria, Vine, Jr. *Custer Died for Your Sins: An Indian Manifesto*. Norman: University of Oklahoma Press, 1988.

Deloria, Vine, Jr., and Clifford M. Lytle. *American Indians, American Justice*. Austin: University of Texas, 1983.

Densmore, Frances. *Teton Sioux Music and Culture*. Lincoln: University of Nebraska Press, 1992.

Enochs, Ross. *The Jesuit Mission to the Lakota Sioux*. N.p.: Sheed & Ward, 1996.

Erdoes, Richard. *American Indian Myths and Legends*. New York: Pantheon Books, 1984.

———. *Crying for a Dream: The World Through Native American Eyes*. Santa Fe: Bear & Co., 1990.

———. *Lame Deer: Seeker of Visions*. New York: Simon and Schuster, 1972.

———. *The Sun Dance People: The Plains Indians, Their Past and Present*. New York: Random House, 1972.

Feraca, Stephen E. *Wakinyan: Lakota Religion in the Twentieth Century*. Lincoln: University of Nebraska Press, 1998.

Fitzgerald, Michael, and Thomas Yellowtail. *Yellowtail: Crow Medicine Man and Sun Dance Chief—An Autobiography*. Norman: University of Oklahoma Press, 1992.

The Grammar of Lakota: The Language of the Teton Sioux Indians. St. Louis: John S. Swift & Co., 1939.

Hamilton, Henry W., and Jean T. Hamilton. *Sioux of the Rosebud: A History in Pictures*. Norman: University of Oklahoma Press, 1971.

Hammerschlag, Carl A. *The Dancing Healers: A Doctor's Journey of Healing with Native Americans*. San Francisco: Harper & Row, 1988.

Hausman, Gerald (ed). *Prayer to the Great Mystery: The Uncollected Writings and Photography of Edward S. Curtis*. New York: St. Martin's Press, 1995.

Hill, Ruth. *Hanta Yo*. New York: Warner Books, 1981.

Hutchens, Alma A. *Indian Herbalogy of North America*. Boston: Shambhala, 1991.

Lame Deer, Archie Fire, and Richard Erdoes. *Gift of Power: The Life and Teachings of a Lakota Medicine Man.* Santa Fe: Bear & Co., 1992.

Lame Deer, Archie Fire, and Helene Sarkis. *The Lakota Sweat Lodge Cards: Spiritual Teachings of the Sioux.* Rochester, Vt.: Destiny Books, 1994.

Lapointe, James. *Legends of the Lakota.* N.p.: The Indian Historian Press, 1975.

Lazarus, Edward. *Black Hills, White Justice: The Sioux Nation versus the United States, 1775 to the Present.* New York: Harper Collins, 1991.

Lewis, Thomas. *The Medicine Men: Oglala Sioux Ceremony and Healing.* Lincoln: University of Nebraska Press, 1990.

Mails, Thomas. *Dog Soldiers: Bear Men and Buffalo Women of the Plains Indians.* New York: Bonanza, 1985.

———. *Fools Crow.* Lincoln: University of Nebraska Press, 1990.

———. *Fools Crow: Wisdom and Power.* Tulsa, Okla.: Council Oak Books, 1991.

———. *Peoples of the Plains.* Tulsa, Okla.: Council Oak Books, 1997.

———. *Spirits of the Plains.* Tulsa, Okla.: Council Oak Books, 1997.

———. *Sun Dancing at Pine Ridge.* Sioux Falls, S. Dak.: Center for Western Studies, 1978.

Marshall, Joe. *Dance House: Stories from Rosebud.* Santa Fe: Red Crane Books, 1998.

Matthiessen, Peter. *In the Spirit of Crazy Horse.* New York: Penguin Books, 1992.

McLaughlin, Marie. *Myths and Legends of the Sioux.* Lincoln: University of Nebraska Press, 1990.

Medicine Eagle, Brooke. *Buffalo Woman Comes Singing: The Spirit Song of a Rainbow Medicine Woman.* New York: Ballantine, 1991.

Neihardt, John. *Black Elk Speaks: Being the Life Story of a Holy Man of the Oglala Sioux.* New York: Time Life Books, 1993.

———. *The Sixth Grandfather: Black Elk's Teachings.* Lincoln: University of Nebraska Press, 1984.

Parlow, Anita. *Cry, Sacred Ground: Big Mountain USA.* Washington, D.C.: Christic Institute, 1988.

Powers, Marla. *Oglala Women: Myth, Ritual and Reality.* Chicago: University of Chicago Press, 1986.

Powers, William. *Oglala Religion.* Lincoln: University of Nebraska Press, 1977.

———. *Sacred Language: The Nature of Supernatural Discourse in Lakota.* Norman: University of Oklahoma Press, 1986.

Rockwell, David. *Giving Voice to Bear.* Niwot, Colo.: Roberts Rinehart Publishers, 1991.

Sams, Jamie. *Dancing the Dream.* New York: HarperCollins, 1999.

Sams, Jamie, and David Carson. *Medicine Cards: The Discovery of Power Through the Ways of Animals.* New York: St. Martins, 1999.

Sams, Jamie, and Twylah Nitsch. *Other Council Fires Were Here Before Ours.* San Fransisco: HarperSanFrancisco, 1991.

Scout Cloud, Lee. *The Circle Is Sacred: A Medicine Book for Women.* Tulsa, Okla.: Council Oak Books, 1995.

Silko, Leslie Marmon. *Ceremony.* New York: Penguin Books, 1986.

Standing Bear, Luther. *Land of the Spotted Eagle.* Lincoln: University of Nebraska Press, 1978.

Starita, Joe. *The Dull Knives of Pine Ridge: A Lakota Odyssey.* New York: G.P. Putnam's Sons, 1995.

Stars, Ivan, Peter Iron Shell, and Eugene Buechel. *Lakota Tales and Text: Wisdom Stories, Customs, Lives and Instruction of the Dakota Peoples.* Pine Ridge, S. Dak.: Red Cloud Lakota Language and Cultural Center, 1978.

Steinmetz, Paul B. *Pipe, Bible and Peyote among the Oglala Lakota: A Study in Religious Identity.* Syracuse, N.Y.: Syracuse University Press, 1998.

Steltenkamp, Michael. *Black Elk: Holy Man of the Oglala.* Norman: University of Oklahoma Press, 1993.

Stolzman, William. *The Pipe and Christ.* N.p.: Tipi Press, 1992.

St. Pierre, Mark, and Tilda Long Soldier. *Madonna Swan: A Lakota Woman's Story.* Norman: University of Oklahoma Press, 1995.

———. *Walking in the Sacred Manner: Healers, Dreamers and Pipe Carriers—Medicine Women of the Plains Indians.* New York: Simon and Schuster, 1957.

Sun Bear. *The Book of the Vision Quest: Personal Transformation in the Wilderness.* New York: Prentice Hall Press, 1987.

———. *The Medicine Wheel: Earth Astrology.* New York: Fireside Book, 1992.

———. *The Path of Power.* New York: Prentice Hall Press, 1988.

Thunder, Mary Elizabeth. *Thunder's Grace: Walking the Road of Visions with My Lakota Grandmother.* Barrytown, N.Y.: Station Hill Press, 1995.

Twofeathers, Manny. *The Road to the Sundance: My Journey into Native Spirituality.* New York: Hyperion, 1996.

Votget, Fred W. *The Shoshoni-Crow Sun Dance.* Norman: University of Oklahoma Press, 1984.

Walker, James. *Lakota Belief and Ritual.* Lincoln: University of Nebraska Press, 1991.

———. *Lakota Myth.* Lincoln: University of Nebraska Press, 1983.

———. *Lakota Society.* Lincoln: University of Nebraska Press, 1982.

White Hat, Albert Sr. *Reading and Writing the Lakota Language.* Salt Lake City: University of Utah Press, 1999.

Young Bear, Severt, and R.D. Theisz. *Standing in the Light: A Lakota Way of Seeing.* Lincoln: University of Nebraska Press, 1994.

Zimmerman, Bill. *Airlift to Wounded Knee.* Chicago: Swallow Press, 1976.